Preface

It's about TI:ME!

The creative force behind this guide is the Technology Institute for Music Educators (or TI:ME), a non-profit organization whose goals and objectives include the development of in-service teacher training and certification in the area of music technology. TI:ME is devoted to helping music teachers learn how to integrate the tools of technology into the music curriculum to improve teaching and learning in music. In addition to fostering the effective use of technology in a number of core competency areas (each represented by a chapter of this book), TI:ME materials support the National Standards for Arts Education as adopted by the Music Educators National Conference (MENC) as well as the National Educational Technology Standards (NETS) of the International Society for Technology in Education (ISTE).

The History of TI:ME

In the summer of 1995, TI:ME was formed to address several issues. First, there was a need to codify technology into a cohesive set of standards. Next, a certification process was explored to recognize the achievement of in-service music teachers in music technology. Finally, it became clear that there was a need for a new organization, national in scope and focused on the subject of teacher training in music technology. A national advisory board was established and met in October of 1996 setting in motion the tasks that led to the creation of a World Wide Web site, the publication of a book of strategies, a newsletter, the criteria for membership, and the development of a comprehensive curriculum for in-service teacher training in music technology.

TI:ME Officers

The leadership of TI:ME includes John Dunphy, Executive Director; Thomas Rudolph, President; Michael Moniz, Vice President/Secretary; and Lee Whitmore, Treasurer. There is also an 18-member board of directors and a large National Advisory board, all noted for their expertise and practical experience with the use of technology in music education.

More about TI:ME

To learn more about TI:ME, point your Web browser to www.ti-me.org to discover the many ways this organization is working to help music educators employ the teaching tools of our day effectively and with confidence.

Acknowledgments

Many thanks are due many persons for their energy and input in producing this guide!

All of the authors spent far more hours than they bargained for in researching and writing their chapters. I hold them all in the highest regard and appreciate the excellent standard they set for their work on this project. The authors have performed a great service to their profession in creating this valuable resource for music educators interested in using technology in their teaching.

The Technology Institute for Music Education (TI:ME), its officers, and especially President, Tom Rudolph, and Executive Director, John Dunphy, have been behind this book all the way. All the members of TI:ME's Publications Committee (Mike Lawson, Sandi MacLeod, Joe Perry, Floyd Richmond, Tom Rudolph, Ken Simpson, and Scott Watson) have given hours of their time in discussions and deliberations and helped move this book from idea to reality.

Several folks from Primedia (publishers of *Electronic Musician* and *Music Education Technology* magazines)—Editor Steve Oppenheimer and Associate Publisher Joe Perry—have cheered us on as we developed this idea, even graciously lending us advice and technical data.

Mike Lawson of Thomson Course Technology PTR saw the benefits of our guide and fought hard to bring it to life.

I received invaluable aid from Christine Nass in preparing the summary tables that conclude each chapter. Christine's excellence with Excel and sensitivity to our mission helped greatly.

It would be an oversight to neglect to make some acknowledgments of a more personal nature here as well. I'll always appreciate Temple University composition professor and composer, Maurice Wright, for first exposing me to music technology when he showed me sequencing and notation applications (as well as a host of more arcane tools) when I studied there in the 1980s. I applaud the progressiveness of my administrators and colleagues in the Parkland School District (Allentown, PA) who have always given me the encouragement and support to try technological solutions that benefit our students.

Finally I must express my love and appreciation to my wife, Kim, and kids, Ben and Abby, for sacrificing many hours this summer that we might have been together so that I could work on this project.

Scott Watson
Coplay, Pennsylvania
August 2005

Contributors

List of Contributing Authors

Scott D. Lipscomb, Northwestern University

Sandi MacLeod, University of Vermont

Keith Mason, Belmont University

Dennis Mauricio, Hilltop High School

Michael Moniz, Schoolhouse Music Services/MIDI Schoolhouse, Berklee College of Music

Don Muro, performer, composer, lecturer and educator

Rocky J. Reuter, Capital University Conservatory of Music

Floyd Richmond, Valley Forge Christian College

Thomas E. Rudolph, Haverford School District

Kimberly C. Walls, Auburn University

Scott Watson, Parkland School District

Lee Whitmore, SoundTree

About the Editor

Scott Watson, D.M.A., has taught instrumental and classroom music in the Parkland School District (Allentown, Pennsylvania) for nearly 20 years. Dr. Watson regularly leads courses in music education technology for the Villanova Summer Music Studies Program and Temple University, where he has also been full-time Assistant Professor of Music Theory and Technology. Watson has presented numerous clinics and workshops at state and national music teacher conferences, is a regular contributing author for *Music Education Technology* magazine, and serves on the Board of Advisors for the Technology Institute for Music Educators (TI:ME) as chair of its Publications Committee.

An award-winning composer as well, Watson's music for band is published by Alfred Publishing, C.L. Barnhouse, and Shawnee Press (Concert Works Unlimited).

Contents

Introduction

Why This Guide? Why Now?

The idea for this book, *Technology Guide for Music Educators*, has been germinating for years and is the response to requests for such a resource from many quarters. For some time, music educators have been asking if there was a resource to which they could turn for listings of software and other technology products to best accomplish their curricular goals.

Our authors regularly deliver professional development training and present workshops at state and national conferences for music educators. They also encounter pre-service and in-service teachers interested in technology in the university courses they lead during the academic year and over the summer. Often participants in one of these settings, ready to move forward with whatever technology they've just encountered, will ask for a recommendation: "What's a good software sequencer I can use with my Windows computer?", "Can you suggest a good entry-level synth keyboard for the technology lab I'm proposing to my district?", or "What's a good software title for teaching composition to my 3rd through 5th grade general music students?" The implementation of technology in the schools is on the rise, and a guide such as this to answer all these questions and more is an idea whose time has come!

Description

This *Technology Guide for Music Educators* presents, in a clear and accessible fashion and according to the six competency areas described below, those technology products used and valued most by music educators. In addition to descriptions of product features, you'll also find other information valuable to educators, such as grade level appropriateness and ideas for integrating the technologies covered into the music curriculum. Each chapter includes a summary table of the products presented, including information such as system requirements and manufacturer Web sites, and a list of resources, such as pertinent articles or books for the reader who wants to go further.

The guides currently available to music educators are commercial in nature, for the most part, and promote specific brands or retailers. The strength of the *Technology Guide for Music Educators* is that it is *by* music educators, *for* music educators. Each chapter deals with one of the technology competencies identified by the Technology Institute for Music Educators (TI:ME), the largest organization for K-12 music education technology. In its seminal publication, *Technology Strategies for Music Education* (now in its 2nd edition), TI:ME outlined for music educators six areas they are likely to encounter as they teach music in the twenty-first century and for which they may want to acquire a basic competency. The chapters of this guide are devoted to explaining these six areas, as well as reviewing exemplary products in that area.

Chapter 1, **"Electronic Musical Instruments,"** deals with keyboard synths, digital pianos, and a host of other gear that is more and more likely to appear in music rooms and on stage in our schools. As you will read, not all keyboards are created equal—or even for the same purpose! And some instruments exist virtually, as software synths.

Chapter 2, "**Music Production**," is much more than just recording! It encompasses the software and hardware used to bring a student's or teacher's arrangements and compositions to life. Multitrack audio and sequencing software, from professional digital audio workstations to entry-level loop-based sequencers, make up the heart of this area. Nonetheless, we've covered all the other details you'll want to know about, including waveform audio editors, microphones, audio and MIDI interfaces, and mastering (burning) software.

Chapter 3, "**Music Notation Software**," presents today's music educators with the best options for typesetting music—from beginner level to professional-quality—and suggests ways that both teachers and students in class and ensembles can benefit greatly.

Chapter 4, "**Technology-Assisted Learning**," covers the software and Internet resources used most by music educators to teach, reinforce, and review various parts of their curriculum. This roundup of Web sites and programs is bound to have something for everybody.

Chapter 5, "**Multimedia**," brings together content generated via many modes into a product that benefits from the unique contributions of its parts. This area includes the software and supporting tools for creating slideshow presentations, movies and DVDs, and Web pages. Music educators are becoming increasingly involved in multimedia creation as programs become easier to use, the cost of memory storage devices becomes more accessible, and educators realize its benefits.

Chapter 6, "**Productivity Tools, Classroom and Lab Management**," gathers under its umbrella some of the most ubiquitous as well as the most specialized software and hardware employed by educators today to administer, organize, and manage the details of their teaching. This area includes applications many of us couldn't do without, such as text editors, spreadsheet and grading programs, as well as lab management systems that coordinate the audio streams of teacher and student computers and synthesizer keyboards to make easy the job of working with technology in a group setting.

Throughout this guide, our authors commend numerous software and hardware products for various music education applications. These products were selected because we have found them to be useful either in our own teaching or in the teaching of educators with whom we have worked or observed. Because technology evolves quickly, and new products are being introduced all the time, it is practically impossible to include every worthy product in this guide. On the other hand, you can take confidence in the fact that the software and gear highlighted in these pages are products that have been field-tested and used with success in the trenches. The authors, however, have taken a concept-oriented rather than a product-specific approach in describing the usefulness in music education of products in their chapters, allowing for the carry-over of their suggestions to similar products you may find or already use.

Some teacher tools didn't fit as nicely into our six chapter categories as we'd have liked, but because of their usefulness we found a way to include them for you. Take the *iPod*, for instance. When I first requisitioned one for use in my teaching, my principal—being the careful steward of resources that the tax-payers expect her to be—asked me how I would use it. I replied that I was surprised I was the first music teacher in the district to request one considering all it can do! You can read all about that in Chapter 2, "Music Production," where we've grouped it with *iTunes*. Then there's the *SpectraScope* direct-to-CD recorder. You may have seen it if you've visited the vendor's exhibits at your state's music teacher convention in the last few years. It's used more in rehearsals and concerts than in recording studio scenarios, but you can read about it in Chapter 2 as well. Another great tool that doesn't quite fit our book's template is *Amazing Slow Downer*. It allows you to slow down audio without lowering its pitch. You can imagine the benefits for students working with accompaniment tracks; and you can read about it in Chapter 4, "Technology-Assisted Learning." One area that we haven't tackled in our guide is drill design software. There are a handful of products out there, with *Pyware's 3D* used perhaps most widely, but it's pretty specialized software that appeals to a select group (marching band directors, who in many cases hire out the task of drill design to professionals).

Meet the Authors

We have assembled a team of nationally and internationally known educator-experts for each chapter of this guide. These contributors are highly regarded music education technology generalists, but each has earned a reputation for his or her special knowledge in the area of their chapter.

ELECTRONIC MUSICAL INSTRUMENTS

Don Muro is a performer, composer, lecturer, and educator specializing in music and technology. He has written five books and more than 80 articles and has presented solo synthesizer concerts throughout the United States, Europe, and Asia. He is a member of the TI:ME Board of Directors, a regular columnist for *Music Education Technology* magazine, and has lent his expertise to organizations such as the New York State Education Department, New York State School Music Association, and MENC.

Rocky J. Reuter, D.M.A., is Professor of Music at the Capital University Conservatory of Music, where he heads the music technology and composition areas; he is also Director of the Recording/Electronic Music Studio, and Founder/Director of the Capital University MIDI Band. Dr. Reuter is the Vice President of the Association for Technology in Music Instruction (ATMI) and a TI:ME board member, serving as chair of its Conference Committee. In addition to making numerous music technology presentations at ATMI and TI:ME national conferences, he is a composer whose acoustic and electronic works have been performed and broadcast nationally and internationally.

MUSIC PRODUCTION

Michael Moniz is the founder of Schoolhouse Music Services and the MIDI Schoolhouse, which provides music technology consulting services, professional development programs, music technology training, and artist-in-residence programs.

An associate professor at Berklee College of Music and adjunct professor for Salem State and Fitchburg State Colleges, Moniz also serves as the Technology Chairperson for the Massachusetts Music Educators Association and as Vice President of TI:ME. A former music educator and music administrator, he has trained over 1000 teachers in the last decade at his Summer Music Technology Institute and employed music production technology with teachers and students in his creativity/composition artist-in-residence program, Komposing Kids.

Keith Mason is the Coordinator of Music Technology at Belmont University in Nashville, Tennessee, where he teaches courses in arranging and music technology. He has more than 20 years of experience in that city's music industry as a composer, arranger, and producer for several music labels and television jingles.

MUSIC NOTATION SOFTWARE

Thomas E.Rudolph, Ed. D., is President of TI:ME and teaches music in the Haverford School District, Pennsylvania. He is an adjunct assistant professor at the University of the Arts in Philadelphia and—as one of the most highly regarded music education technology experts in the nation—has published seven books in music technology, including *Finale: An Easy Guide for Music Notation and Teaching Music with Technology* (Berklee Press) and *Teaching Music with Technology* (GIA).

Sandi MacLeod, Ed. D., is a faculty member at the University of Vermont. As coordinator of the Vermont MIDI Project (www.vtmidi.org) since 1996, she has led the community of educators, students, professional composers, and musicians as they promote music composition with the integration of technology as an essential element of the curriculum. Dr. MacLeod's research interests and numerous presentations examine music composition in the classroom, critique and reflection, and learner-centered education with the integration of technology.

TECHNOLOGY-ASSISTED LEARNING

Floyd Richmond, D. A., teaches music education at Valley Forge Christian College and teaches TI:ME courses around the country, including Ball State University, Kent State University, and Villanova University. As a music technology specialist, he is frequently called upon for school in-service days, as well as local, state, and national conferences. He is the author and editor of numerous articles, chapters, and books on music technology and is chair of TI:ME's education and curriculum committee.

MULTIMEDIA

Scott D. Lipscomb, D.M.A., is Associate Professor of Music Education and Music Technology at Northwestern University. His research interests, published in scholarly journals and presented at numerous conferences, include film music perception, technology integration in the music classroom, tonality judgment in elementary school children, and the development of interactive instructional media to enhance music learning. Dr. Lipscomb is President of ATMI and a member of the TI:ME Advisory Board, serving as chair of its Research Committee.

Kimberly C. Walls, Ed. D., is Professor of Music Education at Auburn University. She is a contributing author for several Silver Burdett elementary series including *Making Music*, and *Making Music with Technology* and has published numerous articles related to music education technology in professional journals. Dr. Walls co-founded the *Journal of Technology in Music Learning* and the National Symposium for Music Instructional Technology, and is also a TI:ME board member.

PRODUCTIVITY TOOLS, CLASSROOM AND LAB MANAGEMENT
Lee Whitmore, Ed.D., is Founder and Managing Director of SoundTree, the educational division of Korg USA, Inc. Dr. Whitmore has been a leading advocate for the integration of technology in music education for 15 years, authoring course materials and several books on the use of MIDI and electronic musical instruments in the classroom and presenting hundreds of hours of instruction using synthesizers and keyboards in education. Whitmore previously served as an adjunct instructor at Columbia University Teachers College and is currently the Treasurer of TI:ME.

Dennis Mauricio teaches music technology at Hilltop High School in Chula Vista, California. He is co-author of *Fundamentals of Music Technology* (Consultant Help Software), an innovative music technology curriculum for secondary students, and composer of music for technology ensembles published by Ogilvy Music. Mauricio is also active as a technology clinician at state and regional music education conferences.

The Folks Behind the Guide
Besides their shared enthusiasm for and expertise with technology, each author plays a vital role as a member of TI:ME. If you are an educator interested in using technology in your teaching, whether you are just starting out or have been at it for years, you should consider joining TI:ME. TI:ME membership holds many benefits, including a two-tiered certification program, annual regional and national conferences, a quarterly newsletter and free subscriptions to prominent music technology magazines, and a Web site packed with members-only content, including a database of lesson plans that incorporate technology (searchable by competency, content, and MENC National Standard). Each summer, institutions of learning across the country and even internationally, offer hundreds of music education technology courses using TI:ME materials and curriculum. This *Technology Guide for Music Educators*, along with other resources, is an example of the work that TI:ME is doing to help music teachers become competent and comfortable using the teaching tools of our day. If you'd like to put today's technology to work for you and your students, but you're not sure where to start, turn to TI:ME. You can discover the world of TI:ME by visiting www.ti-me.org.

A very helpful partner in the creation of this guide was Primedia, publisher of *Electronic Musician* and *Music Education Technology* magazines, who has shared data from their *2005 Computer Music Product Guide* to help with our chapter summary tables. There is no better general-purpose music technology monthly than *EM* and no better magazine for music educators interested in technology than *MET*. I urge you to visit www.metmagazine.com and sign up for the free subscription you are entitled to as a music educator. Another partner in the conception of this guide was the Association for Technology in Music Instruction (ATMI). Many of our authors are active members of this organization geared toward higher education. ATMI, through its annual conferences and Web site (atmi.music.org), continues to champion research and methods that will improve music learning through the use of technology.

Let Us Help

Many music educators ask themselves, "Must I use technology to do my job well?" If you are early or mid-career, this question really misses the point, since it is inevitable that you will encounter technology in the course of your tenure. If your district has strategically implemented its use and provided adequate in-service training, then chances are you'll be pleased at what the latest educational tools can do for you and your students. As we proceed into the still young twenty-first century, it is impossible for me to imagine a school district music position in which at least some of the technology discussed in the pages of this guide—a word processing program, an electronic grade book, a synth keyboard, a few well-chosen instructional software titles, perhaps a unit for recording directly to CD—would not be used. Others may find that they desire to transform their positions more aggressively with the use of technology, establishing keyboard or music tech labs and creating new units or even entire courses, and will come to rely heavily on the software presented in the chapters on music production, music notation software, lab and classroom management, or even multimedia.

The *Technology Guide for Music Educators* is here to help educators in these scenarios and everywhere in between! By culling through the myriad products on the market and cross-referencing these with the practical experience of successful educators, the guide presents technology-based tools and techniques that can enhance both the experience of teaching your students and your student's experience of learning and performing music.

Scott Watson

CHAPTER 1

Electronic Musical Instruments

By Don Muro and Rocky J. Reuter

The current generation of electronic instruments contains sounds and performance features that make it possible to create music that is expressive, dynamic, and aesthetically pleasing. These instruments are also the most powerful teaching tools available to educators. Music technology labs equipped with keyboards or other controllers can be used to teach students topics such as performance skills (solo and ensemble), sound design, theory, composition/arranging techniques, music recording techniques, and listening skills.

This chapter is divided into five sections. Section 1 covers the different types of electronic keyboards available. Section 2 covers various alternate (non-keyboard) controllers. Section 3 covers software instruments, and Section 4 covers electronic instrument performance. Section 5 is a list of resources. With the exception of Section 5, each section includes explanations of concepts, definitions of terms, and recommended models.

Section 1: Electronic Keyboards

The most basic definition of the term "electronic keyboard" is simply any keyboard instrument that requires electricity to produce sound. There are dozens of electronic keyboard models available in different sizes, with different features, and in a wide price range.

1

Before examining the types of electronic keyboards available, it will be useful to list the most common features of these instruments.

Electronic Keyboard Features

The features on electronic keyboards can be divided into two groups: sound production features and control features.

Sound production features affect the sonic capabilities of the instrument.

SOUND PRODUCTION FEATURE #1—SONIC PALATE

The sonic palate refers to both the variety and the quality of sounds available on an instrument. Unless you are teaching only group piano classes in a lab, any keyboard with internal sounds you are considering should be General MIDI (GM) compatible. The GM specification is an industry standard that defines specific play-back features and capabilities for instruments. GM sounds are a standardized set of 128 sounds that are compatible with any GM instrument made by any manufacturer.

Although the original GM specification remains the industry standard, manufacturers have developed extensions of this speci-fication. These extensions include General MIDI Level 2 (GM2, developed by the MIDI Manufacturers Association), GS (developed by Roland), and XG (developed by Yamaha). These extensions increase both the number of available sounds and the amount of control available for sound editing and musical performance. All three extensions are compatible with the original GM specification.

Any GM compatible instrument will also be multitimbral and will be able to play back up to 16 different sounds or timbres simul-taneously.

SOUND PRODUCTION FEATURE #2—POLYPHONY

Polyphony in this context means the number of voices (or indi-vidual pitches) that an instrument can play at the same time. For example, a six-string acoustic guitar is a six-voice instrument—it can play up to six pitches at once. An acoustic piano is an 88-voice instrument. Most instruments manufactured today have at least 32 voices; 32-voice polyphony will be adequate if you are using a key-board primarily for live playing and basic song arranging. If you are planning to create elaborate orchestrations, however, you should select an instrument with at least 64-voice polyphony.

SOUND PRODUCTION FEATURE #3—KEYBOARD PERFORMANCE MODES

If you plan to teach performance techniques, these three performance modes can dramatically enhance the sound of an instrument.

▶ *Split*—This mode allows you to split the keyboard into separate areas or zones. You can then assign different sounds to each zone. For example, you can assign a bass sound to the lower two octaves and assign a piano sound to the remaining octaves. Some keyboards allow you to create many split points across the keyboard.

▶ *Layer*—This mode allows you to create thicker textures by stacking or layering sounds on top of each other. For example, if you layer a piano sound with a string section sound, you will hear both sounds simultaneously when you play the keyboard.

▶ *Velocity switch*—This mode allows you to activate specific sounds by varying the speed with which you strike a key. For example, you could play a string orchestra sound that would add timpani and brass only when you played with greater velocity. For contemporary music you could use the switch feature to add brass "stabs" to an electric piano sound.

SOUND PRODUCTION FEATURE #4—EFFECTS PROCESSOR

An effects processor is a device that changes or enhances a sound, usually by adding ambient effects such as delay (echo) or reverberation. Effects processors can greatly improve the sounds in an instrument. Most keyboards have at least one effects processor.

SOUND PRODUCTION FEATURE #5—AUDIO/OUTPUT CAPABILITIES

There are three choices when it comes to hearing any electronic instrument:

▶ *Audio outputs*—An instrument with at least two outputs (Left and Right for stereo) is recommended. These outputs are used to connect the instrument to lab controllers, to an external amplifier, or to a sound system.

▶ *Internal speakers*—Some keyboard instruments have internal speakers. This feature makes it easy for students to hear themselves when performing as an ensemble.

▶ *Headphone output*—This output gives students the option to practice silently. If you are using a lab controller, however, a headphone output is not necessary.

Control features include various ways that an instrument can be controlled in live performance and in use with computers.

CONTROL FEATURE #1—KEYBOARD SPAN (THE NUMBER OF KEYS)

Instruments are available with keyboard spans ranging from two octaves (25 keys) to more than seven octaves (88 keys—the range of an acoustic piano). A span of at least four octaves is recommended for labs, so that two students sitting at one keyboard can each have a playable range of two octaves.

CONTROL FEATURE #2—KEY WEIGHT

Electronic keyboards are available with three types of key weights.

▶ *Non-weighted*—This keyboard action offers no resistance and is similar to most organ keyboards. This is the most practical and cost-effective choice for most labs.

▶ *Semi-weighted*—This action offers substantially more resistance than a non-weighted keyboard, but is not as heavy as a full-weighted action.

▶ *Full-weighted*—This action tries to duplicate the feel and response of an acoustic piano. On some instruments the keys in the lower registers have a heavier touch that gradually becomes lighter as you play higher notes on the keyboard. This is sometimes referred to as a "graded hammer action."

CONTROL FEATURE #3—VELOCITY SENSITIVITY/AFTERTOUCH

Most electronic keyboards are velocity sensitive. In other words, the instrument can respond differently to the various speeds with which you strike a key. High velocities most often produce a louder and brighter sound.

If you plan to teach advanced performance techniques, you may want to consider an instrument that also has *aftertouch*. Aftertouch is a feature that allows you to change a sound by applying pressure to any key which is being held. Aftertouch is most often used to increase the brightness of a sound or to add vibrato to a sound.

CONTROL FEATURE #4—PITCH BENDER

A pitch bender is a controller that allows the performer to slide or "bend" a note's pitch up or down. The pitch bender is located on the left side of the keyboard and is usually configured as either a wheel or a joystick. (A joystick is a controller with two axes: the left-right axis controls one parameter of sound, and the up-down axis controls a different parameter.) This feature is important when using instrumental sounds such as guitars, trombones, and saxophones.

CONTROL FEATURE #5—MODULATION CONTROLLER

A modulation controller allows you to change or "modulate" a parameter of a sound such as vibrato or brightness. This is an important feature because it enables you to add expression to your playing. The modulation controller is usually a wheel or a joystick located on the left side of the keyboard. (Most X/Y joysticks have pitch bend assigned to the left-right axis and modulation assigned to the up-down axis.)

CONTROL FEATURE #6—SLIDERS/KNOBS

Simply put, sliders and knobs enable you to control various parameters of a sound. Sliders enable you to "slide" up and down through a range of settings; knobs enable you to dial through a range of settings. For example, if you are using a string section sound, you could use sliders and/or knobs to vary the sound's articulation and brightness. In general, the more sliders and knobs on an instrument, the greater control you can have over the sound and over the expressive potential of the instrument. Many instruments feature "assignable" sliders and knobs, which means that their functions can be user defined to control a variety of functions.

CONTROL FEATURE #7—INPUTS FOR FOOT SWITCHES/FOOT PEDALS

A foot switch is similar to a light switch—it switches between only two values—"on" or "off." Most keyboards have at least one foot switch input for a sustain footswitch, which is important when using piano sounds.

A foot pedal is similar to a dimmer or a rotary light controller; it allows you to change values or amounts gradually in small increments. Foot pedal inputs are usually assigned to control volume. A volume (or expression) foot pedal will allow you to control volume while keeping both hands on the keyboard. Some instruments also include assignable foot pedal inputs.

CONTROL FEATURE #8—MIDI CAPABILITY

MIDI is an acronym for *Musical Instrument Digital Interface*, and virtually every electronic keyboard manufactured today is MIDI capable. MIDI is a standardized protocol for communication between electronic music devices as well as between those devices and computers.

MIDI was developed in 1983 by a consortium of hardware and software manufacturers responding to a proposal by Dave Smith of Sequential Circuits. The communications protocol became known as the MIDI Specification 1.0 and included the basis of the language and its implementation. In 1984, the MIDI Manufacturers Association (www.midi.org) was formed to oversee the standardization and development of the MIDI Protocol. This protocol assures users that the basic functions of MIDI will be consistent from one manufacturer to another. The protocol also allows for the implementation of special features by individual manufacturers.

In general, any action performed on an electronic instrument generates a digital code that is sent as a MIDI instruction. For example, when a key is pressed on an electronic keyboard, three codes are transmitted: Note On, Note Number, and Velocity Number. These record the exact time a note was played, the key pressed, and its relative loudness. Three codes are also required when the key is released. If the pitch bender or modulation controller is used, a continuous series of codes track the exact position of the joy stick or wheel as it is moved. If the sustain pedal is pressed or released another specific code is generated.

These codes serve the same function as the paper roll on a player piano. While they do not themselves represent audio signals, they represent all of the information required to recreate what has been played. This capability allows a performer on one keyboard to control the sound on a second keyboard. It also makes it possible for a computer application to store the performance information and to replay a performance on one or more MIDI keyboards.

MIDI Ports
MIDI Ports are generally found on all electronic instruments and come in three varieties: OUT, IN, and THRU (**Fig. 1**).

FIG. 1: The three MIDI ports

Two or more synthesizers can be connected to each other without the use of a MIDI Interface. In this case, a standard MIDI cable with a 5-pin DIN connector is used to connect the ports.

The MIDI OUT port allows performance data generated on the keyboard to leave the instrument and be sent through a MIDI cable to another instrument or a computer. In **Fig. 2**, a MIDI cable is used to connect the OUT port of Keyboard 1 to the IN port of Keyboard 2, which will execute the performance data generated on Keyboard 1.

FIG. 2: A basic MIDI connection between two keyboards (master on bottom; slave on top).

MIDI IN allows performance data from another keyboard or a computer to enter the keyboard and control its internal playback capabilities. In other words, performing on the master keyboard will result in playback on the slave keyboard.

The MIDI THRU port allows all data entering the MIDI IN port to be passed through the keyboard unaltered to a second keyboard or tone generator. In other words, it is like a Y-cable that simply splits (copies) the signal for additional keyboards to use. In **Fig. 3**, both Keyboard 2 and Keyboard 3 will execute the performance data generated on Keyboard 1.

FIG. 3: MIDI cable configuration for controlling two slave keyboards with one master keyboard (master on bottom; slave 1 in the middle; slave 2 on top getting data from slave 1's THRU port).

New electronic instruments often use USB ports to transmit and receive MIDI data. USB (Universal Serial Bus) is a standard interface port on computers. USB supports the connection of up to 127 devices simultaneously, any of which may be plugged into or unplugged from the USB bus at any time. The USB port offers a convenient way to connect MIDI instruments and equipment using one USB cable instead of two MIDI cables. In addition, Yamaha has introduced another high-speed interface called mLAN. This interface is based on the FireWire interface originally developed by Apple Computer in the 1990s. FireWire can carry several types of data simultaneously. These data types include MIDI data, audio data, video data, control data and computer files. At this point mLAN is just beginning to appear on a few products, but it may play an important part in the future of music technology.

MIDI Interface

These devices are covered in Chapter 2, "Music Production," but are mentioned briefly here as they pertain to polyphony on a MIDI keyboard. MIDI interfaces are required only when a computer is involved. The interface is literally a translator between the codes required for a MIDI keyboard and those required for a computer. The MIDI protocol allows for 16 discrete channels of data to flow through a MIDI cable. Therefore, each MIDI keyboard or tone generator—with its single MIDI OUT jack—may only produce 16 different timbres, sometimes called "patches" or "programs," at a time (one per channel). Simple MIDI Interfaces with one IN and one OUT port are limited to transmitting 16 independent MIDI channels, but are adequate for a basic school lab MIDI workstation. If you'd like your computer software to trigger sounds from two MIDI instruments (i.e. a keyboard and a tone generator), allowing for up to 16 timbres on each, then a MIDI interface with two MIDI OUT ports is necessary (**Fig. 4**).

FIG. 4: Mark of the Unicorn's FastLane USB MIDI Interface, with two OUT ports allowing for 32 independent channels

Expanded interfaces have up to 8 or more independent IN and OUT ports capable of transmitting 16 independent MIDI Channels on each OUT port (**Fig. 5**).

FIG. 5: Mark of the Unicorn's MIDI Express, with 8 OUT ports allowing for 128 independent channels

Originally, interfaces were connected to a computer via a dedicated serial port, such as that used for a gaming joystick. Modern interfaces, however, connect to the computer's USB or FireWire ports and may include both MIDI and audio capabilities.

USB Connection
Some MIDI keyboards can be directly connected to a computer's USB port without requiring a MIDI Interface.

9

Types of Electronic Keyboards

Electronic keyboards can be classified into the following categories: low-cost electronic keyboards, keyboard controllers, digital pianos, synthesizers, and workstations.

LOW-COST ELECTRONIC KEYBOARDS

Definition: Electronic keyboards aimed primarily at the home market and are self-contained, introductory instruments with limited professional capabilities.

These instruments are sometimes referred to as "romplers"— instruments that specialize in the playback of samples stored in ROM chips. The advantages of these instruments include their low cost, small size, and integrated speakers. In addition, most instruments include pre-programmed accompaniment patterns as well as complete songs. The disadvantages include lower quality sounds, limitations in editing pre-programmed sounds and, in most cases, the lack of a pitch bender and modulation controller. More expensive instruments in this class usually include integrated sequencers as well as additional sounds and accompaniment patterns. In general, these keyboards are most suitable for younger students.

An example of a low-cost electronic keyboard is the Casio *CTK900 Portable Keyboard* (**Fig. 6**). This instrument features 61 keys, 32-voice polyphony, GM sounds, split/layer functions, an assignable foot pedal input, and integrated speakers. $299 (Note: prices shown are retail.)

FIG. 6: Casio CTK900 Portable Keyboard

Additional recommended models in this category include

▶ Casio *WK3200* (similar to the CTK900 with additional features including 76 keys and a pitch bend/mod wheel). $449

▶ Yamaha *PSR* series *E203* (GM sounds, standard MIDI interface). $159

▶ Yamaha *273* (GM and XGlite sounds, standard MIDI interface). $279

▶ Yamaha *293* (GM and XGlite sounds, USB MIDI IN/OUT). $369

▶ Yamaha *450* (GM and XGlite sounds, standard MIDI interface, internal 3.5-inch floppy drive for storing/loading songs*)*. $699

▶ Roland *EXR-5* (64-voice polyphony, USB MID IN/OUT GM2/ GS/XG compatible, internal 3.5-inch floppy drive). $795

Of the models listed, the Casio *CTK900* is the least expensive. The Yamaha *PSR 450* strikes a balance between price and features with its combination of more than 600 sounds (including a very good piano sound for this price range), a pitch bend wheel, and a large LCD display. The Roland *EXR-5* is at the high end of this group but features high-quality sounds and both pitch bend and modulation controllers.

KEYBOARD CONTROLLERS
Definition: A keyboard controller is a keyboard with no internal sound generating capability. It simply sends control signals to an external sound generator or software synthesizer.

Keyboard controllers vary in size (the size of the keys), range (the number of keys), and action (non-weighted, semi-weighted, full-weighted) and are used to control software instruments or tone generators (see below). The advantages of keyboard controllers include low cost and compact size. For this reason, many new school lab installations are employing keyboard controllers rather than keyboard synthesizers. A keyboard controller combined with a laptop computer is also a great solution for a portable music workstation. In either scenario the sounds are produced by software driven by a computer's processor; therefore, a faster, modern computer is necessary. The primary disadvantage of a keyboard controller is portability—in order to perform with a controller keyboard anywhere outside the lab, you must also bring a computer or a tone generator plus an amplifier or a sound system. Higher priced entries in this class usually include larger displays, more assignable controllers, and sturdier construction.

Compact Keyboard Controllers (up to 49 Keys)

25-key Controllers. The primary justification for 25-key controllers in an educational setting is space limitation. Although these keyboards can be used for sequencing, notation, and sound design, the limited note range prohibits the development of all but the most rudimentary keyboard skills. Additionally, the small size limits their use to one student at a time. (Note: All models listed below feature velocity sensitivity and one footswitch input.)

The Alesis *Photon 25* (**Fig.7**) is an example of a 25-key controller. It features a 25-key keyboard, twelve assignable controllers with three assignment layers per knob, a pitch bend/modulation joystick, an octave transpose switch (+/- five octaves), a foot pedal input, a USB computer interface, MIDI IN/OUT, USB/AC/battery power. $249.00.

FIG. 7: Alesis Photon 25

Additional recommended 25-key controllers

▶ E-MU *X-Board 25* (includes aftertouch, 16 assignable controllers, pitch bend and mod wheels). $199

▶ Edirol *PCR-M1* (27 controllers, pitch bend and mod controls, and a foot pedal connection). $249

▶ M-Audio *O2* (18 controllers, pitch bend and mod controls). $179

▶ M-Audio *MK-425C* (21 assignable controllers including pitch bend and mod wheels). $189

▶ Novation *ReMOTE LE 25* (semi-weighted keyboard with aftertouch, a pitch bend/mod joystick, a pressure sensitive X-Y touchpad, a foot pedal input, 48 controllers.) $399

Of the models listed, the M-Audio *MK-425C* represents a good value with its simple interface using a keypad and LCD.

Note: Edirol also manufactures two 32-key controllers: the PCR-M30 (with a high quality keyboard), and the PCR-A30 (with an integrated audio interface with mic/instrument input).

49-key Controllers. Keyboard controllers with 49 keys are well-suited for lab use. As mentioned previously, two students sitting at one keyboard can each have a playable range of two octaves.

The Edirol *PCR-M50*. (**Fig. 8**) features a 49-key, velocity sensitive keyboard, 8 assignable knobs, 8 assignable sliders, 9 assignable switches, sustain and expression pedal inputs, octave switch and transpose buttons, a pitch bend/modulation joystick, a USB computer interface, MIDI IN/OUT, USB/AC power. $285

FIG. 8: Edirol PCR-M50

Additional recommended 49-key controllers

▶ Alesis *Photon X49* (an expanded version of the *Photon 25* with full sized pitch and mod wheels and an integrated audio interface). $499

▶ E-MU *X-Board X49* (an expanded version of the *X-Board 25*). $229

▶ Korg *Kontrol 49* (16 assignable controllers, 16 trigger pads for drumming, and a foot pedal input). $499

▶ M-Audio *Keystation 49e* (pitch bend and mod wheels). $129

▶ M-Audio *Radium 49* (16 assignable controllers, pitch bend and mod wheels). $199

▶ Novation *ReMOTE 49* (a larger version of the *ReMote 25*). $499

▶ Studiologic *TMK 49* (pitch bend and mod wheels). $219

▶ Studiologic *VMK-149* (weighted action and aftertouch, 25 assignable controllers and a foot pedal inputs). $999

Of the models listed, the M-Audio *Keystation 49e* is the least expensive; however, the lack of any assignable controllers on this controller as well as on the Studiologic *TMK 49* is a drawback for most lab applications, especially with older students. The Korg *Kontrol 49* is the only controller with trigger pads, which are always attractive to younger students. The M-Audio *Radium 49* represents a solid combination of affordability and features.

61-key and 88-key Controllers. The primary advantage of these keyboards is the immediate access to a wide key span. The features are essentially the same as those found on 49-key controllers. Since most K-12 labs are used by students with minimal or no keyboard skills, an 88-key controller may seem extravagant, especially when considering the additional space needed at each station.

DIGITAL PIANOS

Definition: A digital piano is a keyboard instrument designed primarily to emulate the sound and, in most cases, the feel of an acoustic piano. Manufacturers usually provide only non-editable keyboard-oriented sounds.

Digital pianos are available in two different configurations: portable/tabletop models, and console/furniture models that include integrated stands and speaker systems. The primary justification for a digital piano lab is the teaching of traditional piano skills. Almost all models offer some type of weighted action. The integrated sound systems on console models facilitate classroom ensemble performance. However, the lack of GM sounds on most models requires the use of a software GM instrument for most software applications. In addition, performance options are often limited by the omission of pitch bend, modulation and foot pedal controllers.

Portable/Tabletop Models

The Roland *RD-300SX* (**Fig. 9**) is an example of a portable digital piano. It includes the following features: progressive hammer action, 128 voice polyphony, GM2 sounds, pitch bend/modulation joystick (a rare feature on digital pianos), damper and control pedal jacks, USB computer interface, MIDI IN/OUT.

FIG. 9: Roland RD-300SX
Portable Digital Piano

Additional recommended portable/tabletop models

▶ Casio *Privia PX100* (32-note polyphony, internal speakers). $699

▶ Korg *SP200* (60-note polyphony, 30 sounds, supports half-pedaling pedal). $1100

▶ M-Audio *ProKeys 88* (126-note polyphony, 14 sounds, pitch bend and mod wheels, sustain, sostenuto and expression pedal inputs). $749

▶ Roland FP-2 (64-note polyphony, GM2 sounds, damper, soft, and sostenuto pedal inputs, internal speakers). $1495

▶ Yamaha *P60* (32-note polyphony, 10 sounds, internal speakers). $899

▶ Yamaha*P120* (64-note polyphony, 14 sounds, internal speakers). $1495

Of the models listed, the M-Audio *ProKeys 88* represents the best combination of digital piano features and affordability.

Console/Furniture Models
Note: All console/furniture models contain internal speakers.

FIG. 10: Yamaha YDP113
Console Digital Piano

The Yamaha *YDP113* Console Digital Piano features 32-note polyphony, 10 sounds, and dual headphone jacks. $1295.00. (**Fig. 10**).

Additional console models

▶ Casio *AP38* (64-note polyphony, 16 sounds, dual headphone jacks). $1499

▶ Korg *EC-150* (60-note polyphony, 30 sounds, dual headphone jacks). $1449

▶ Roland *F-50* (64-note polyphony, 20 sounds). $1395

▶ Roland *FP-2C* (64-note polyphony, GM2 sounds). $1695

Of the models listed, the Yamaha *YDP113* is the least expensive and offers good value. The Roland *FP-2C* offers greater polyphony as well as GM2 sounds.

SYNTHESIZERS

Definition: Synthesizers, unlike the previous categories, are unique because they allow users to modify internal sounds and to create entirely new sounds. Synthesizers are available in two categories: hardware synthesizers (described here) and software synthesizers (see Section 3).

Synthesizers usually have a greater number of high quality sounds than low-cost electronic keyboards. Most synthesizers are optimized for live performance and include controllers such as pitch benders, modulation controllers, aftertouch, and inputs for foot switches and assignable foot pedals. The sound editing/creation features on a synthesizer are important in labs where sound synthesis and sound design will be taught.

Often, several variations of the same model keyboard are produced with 61, 76, and/or 88 keys. In general, the more keys, the higher the price. If you're only using the synthesizer in a lab setting, a 61-key model will work well. If a synthesizer is primarily for keyboard performance, you may want to consider a 76-key model. Some synthesizer keyboards have expansion cards slots which allow additional banks of sounds to be purchased (relatively inexpensively) and installed later.

Note: All models have 61-key velocity sensitive keyboards, 64-voice polyphony, headphone jacks, and pitch bend and mod wheels.

The Alesis *QS 6.2* synthesizer (**Fig. 11**) features: a keyboard with release velocity and aftertouch, expansion capabilities for adding additional samples and programs, four edit/control sliders, two assignable pedal inputs, and a foot switch input. $899 (The QS 8.2 is an 88-note version with a full-weighted keyboard action. $1499 Note: Neither of these instruments comes with GM sounds.

FIG. 11: Alesis QS 6.2 Synthesizer

Additional models

▶ Korg *X5D* (64-voice polyphony, high-quality sounds with GM compatibility). $900

▶ Roland *Juno-D* (64-voice polyphony, GM2 compatible, Mac/PC editing software). $749

▶ Yamaha *S03* (64-voice polyphony, GM and XG compatibility, Mac/PC editing software.) $629

All of these instruments are recommended, but the lack of GM sounds on the Alesis QS 6.2 should be considered.

WORKSTATIONS

Definition: A workstation is a keyboard synthesizer with the capability to record, edit, and play back multi-part arrangements.

Keyboard workstations provide an all-in-one solution for performing and recording. Workstations feature the highest quality and greatest number of sounds, a variety of sound synthesis engines, sampling, powerful effects processing and routing, and versatile real-time controls. All workstation models have integrated MIDI sequencers; a few models also include digital audio recording capabilities. Some workstations have floppy disc or Flash media drives that allow users to save and load MIDI sequencer files. Although most labs have computers with sequencing software, the workstation sequencer makes it possible to play back sequences and digital audio files without a computer.

The Korg *Triton LE 61* Workstation (**Fig. 12**) features aftertouch, 512 programs/384 combinations, 16 track 200,000 note sequencer with 200 songs, 89 different effects, 2 assignable switches, 4 assignable knobs. $1,600.00.

FIG. 12: Korg Triton LE 61 Workstation

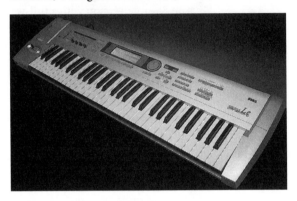

Additional recommended models

▶ Alesis *Fusion 6HD* $2,399

▶ Korg *Triton Extreme 61* $2,800

▶ Roland *Fantom X-a* $1,699

▶ Yamaha *Motif 6* $2,250

Section 2: Alternate Controllers and Sound Modules

While the most common controllers, keyboard emulators, are widely found in music rooms, many music programs have not yet begun to explore the added educational value and practical application of alternate controllers, such as drum and mallet emulators, woodwind and brass emulators, and guitar and string emulators. Like keyboard emulators, alternate controllers bring a great deal of flexibility to both the performers and the ensembles in which they are used. That is, they enhance the possibilities afforded by their acoustic and non-MIDI electronic counterparts, and they help musicians to learn important skills and techniques appropriate to the popular music styles of the late 20th and 21st centuries.

Although some alternate controllers include an integrated sound generator, many rely on an external sound module (also known as a *tone module* or *tone generator*). These controllers began as independent rack-mountable synthesizers that consisted of one or more sound engines, but which lacked the keys. Thus they provided additional sounds and MIDI channels, but were less expensive to produce and purchase and were easy to transport.

In a studio setting, any number of modules can be triggered by single keyboard, alternate controller, or a sequencer, resulting in an efficient use of space while providing a much larger collection of sounds. In a lab setting consisting of keyboard controllers and sound modules, only the modules need to be replaced in order to benefit from newer technology.

Today, sound modules come in many varieties and sizes, each with a particular application in mind. Generally, they include MIDI IN, OUT, and THRU ports, a variety of audio out jacks, and integrated sound effects and other production features.

Compact stand-alone sound modules have been designed specifically for transportability. These instruments allow users to sequence simple melodies or completely orchestrated compositions quickly using input buttons on the face of the sound module. Playback can be heard via headphones, integrated speakers, and/or external speakers. While their diminutive size makes it possible to easily carry several units into a classroom or carry one in your pocket, their features and capabilities are comparable to many full-sized sound modules.

The *Yamaha MU-15* sound module (**Fig. 13**) features 676 XG/GM instrument sounds and 21 Drum Kits, 16 independent channels, 32-note polyphony, three independent effects units, comprehensive editing functions, headphone jack, and is extremely portable as it is the size of a VHS tape. $300

Slightly larger sound modules are generally designed to provide expanded sound sets for an existing keyboard or as a robust hardware playback engine for a software sequencer. They tend to be 2 standard rack units high and half the rack width and may require special adaptors to be mounted in a rack.

FIG. 13: *Yamaha MU-15 sound module*

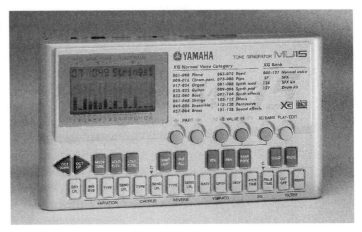

The Edirol *Sound Canvas SD-80* (**Fig. 14**) features 1,050 sounds that are GM2/GS/XGlite compatible, including 30 drum sets; 32-part, 128-voice polyphony; and many connectivity options, including MIDI, USB, Coax S/P DIF, Optical S/P DIF and headphone/audio out jacks.

FIG. 14: *Edirol Sound Canvas SD-80*

Finally, full-sized sound modules (four or more rack units high and full rack width) include all of the components of their synthesizer counterparts except the keyboard, thus providing the user with all of the sounds and production features of the original unit at a substantially lower cost. For example, the Korg *Triton-Rack* sound module (**Fig. 15**) essentially consists of the internal components of the Triton Studio keyboard series. While the *Triton Rack* lists at $2,500, the 61-key *Triton Studio* lists at $3,400.

In many instances, sound modules are specifically designed to match a particular type of alternate controller. In the examples that follow, alternate controllers are paired with appropriate sound modules.

FIG. 15: Korg Triton-Rack

Percussion Controllers (Drum and Mallet)

Percussion controllers were among the first alternate controllers to be introduced. They generally emulate various types of drums and mallet instruments and include uniquely arranged pads either played with sticks, the hands, or mallets.

Drum controllers come in various sizes, from small practice pads to complete drum sets. Practice Pad controllers can be used by beginners as well as professionals. They generally provide "silent" practice via headphones or amplification via integrated speakers. In addition, they often include an integrated metronome and sound enhancement effects.

For example, the *Roland RMP-5 Advanced Rhythm Trainer* (**Fig. 16**) includes a tunable mesh drumhead, over 40 onboard sounds, a multiple function *Rhythm Coach* that helps develop performance techniques (Time Check, Stroke Balance, Auto Up/Down), a performance assessment mode, audio input jacks (to play with CDs) and an audio output jack for headphones or external speakers. $279

FIG. 16: Roland RMP-5 Advanced Rhythm Trainer

Larger units with multiple triggers allow the performer to assign given sounds to particular pads, providing a compact percussion set up or an extremely compact drum set. Instruments such as the Yamaha *DD5 7-Pad GM Digital Drum System* (**Fig. 17**) can be used in either practice or performance settings. It features seven touch-sensitive pads, tempo control, 174 GM-compatible percussion voices, 100 integrated rhythm accompaniment styles, 50 programmed drum kits, reverb and chorus effects, MIDI IN/OUT ports, a headphone jack, integrated stereo speakers, and an audio out jack for headphones or external amplification. This type of unit would be particularly effective at home, in small practice spaces, or to add percussive effects in a jazz band or young tech ensemble setting.

FIG. 17: Yamaha DD5 7-Pad GM Digital Drum System

This concept has been expanded to include more complex and extremely expressive hand-percussion emulators, such as the Roland *HDP-15 HandSonic* (**Fig. 18**). The *HandSonic* features over 600 assignable sounds; 15 trigger pads that can each be assigned a different sound or multiple tunings of a single sound, including the ability to play chromatic scales (e.g., pan drums); two ribbon controllers and a D-beam (invisible light beams that trigger a sound when broken); three knobs for real-time control over several selectable parameters; and audio out jacks. $1,295

FIG. 18: Roland HDP-15 HandSonic

This type of controller can be used to emulate drums that may be too expensive for the average music program (such as a set of congas), is applicable to any performance setting at any level where hand percussion sounds are desired, and is playable by any level of performer.

FIG. 19: Yamaha DTXPL Digital Drum Set ($1,059)

Electronic drum sets are available with either flat polymer-based trigger pads (**Fig. 19**) or flexible mesh drum heads over shells (**Fig. 20**). It is important to test these different styles of drum set pads prior to purchase as they each have a unique feel. While many drummers report that the mesh pads feel more like acoustic drum heads, some prefer the feel of the polymer pads. Note that the cymbal pads are also extremely different on these two examples. Each pad is independent and is connected to a specialized percussion sound module (see left corner of each set) that assigns a particular sound to each signal. In many cases, pads have multiple trigger points that can provide variations of the triggered sounds or even entirely different sounds.

The sound modules (sometimes called "brains") include large banks of sounds that are extremely realistic, ranging from band/orchestral percussion to a variety of sampled acoustic drums to synthetic sounds and effects. In addition, the modules provides banks of predetermined setups that allow the performer to quickly change from one type of drum set to another, to a set of timpani, or to electronic-oriented sounds at the touch of a button. Finally, most modules incorporate basic sequencers so that rhythm loops or even chord progressions can be programmed for playback. A MIDI OUT port is often included so that the drum triggers can control other MIDI devices. Add the fact that an electronic drum set can be played by anyone who can play an acoustic drum set, and you have an extremely cost effective and virtually unlimited performance instrument appropriate to many performance settings at a cost far less than its acoustic counterparts.

FIG. 20: Roland V-Drums Pro-Series TD-20S-WT ($6,699)

Mallet Controllers

Mallet controllers generally emulate the techniques used to play a vibraphone or marimba. The *MalletKat Pro 5.0*, by Alternate Mode, features neoprene rubber pads covering force-sensing resistors that respond when a mallet hits the pad. When hit, the resistor creates a signal that is sent to either an integrated sound module or via MIDI to any external sound module.

Other manufacturers have built specialized analog-to-MIDI converters that are attached to acoustic mallet percussion instruments. Wernick Musical Instrument's *Mark V Xylosynth* (**Fig. 21**) is one such example. Because the *Xylosynth* is, in fact, an acoustic instrument, they feel no different to the performer than the standard instrument. Yet, it is capable of triggering any sound from its integrated sound module or, via MIDI, any external sound module or synthesizer.

FIG. 21: Mark V Xylosynth ($3,200)

Photo by Scott Gilbert

Wind Controllers

Wind controllers are available as either woodwind or brass emulators. They are based on the wind controller technology that was incorporated into a few of the early keyboard synthesizers, such as the *Yamaha DX-7*. Although wind controllers can be used to trigger any MIDI device, specialized sound modules (**Fig. 22**) are specifically designed to react to the needs of a wind controller.

FIG. 22: Yamaha VL70-m Tone Generator (top, $799.95) and Roland XV-2020 Tone Generator (bottom, $695).

(Photographic image of Yamaha instrument(s) is used with the permission of Yamaha Corporation of America.)

A woodwind emulator is typically referred to as an EWI (Electronic Wind Instrument, **Fig. 23**) and can be configured to use either traditional saxophone or flute fingerings, with the exception that the fingerings are the same in all octaves. Although there is a plastic reed-like mouthpiece, the reed does not vibrate as it would on the saxophone or clarinet. Rather, it is used to control pitch bend or vibrato. Inside the mouthpiece there is a tube, which

25

looks like a small metal oboe reed, used to measure the velocity of the wind stream and therefore controls the volume of the sound module. On the back of the EWI are a pitch bend wheel and octave buttons that quickly shift the pitch by as many as five octaves. Additional buttons allow the performer to automatically change to different timbres on the sound module or to sustain one note while playing others.

FIG. 23: *Yamaha WX-5 Wind Controller ($749.95)*

(Photographic image of Yamaha instrument(s) is used with the permission of Yamaha Corporation of America.)

A brass emulator is typically referred to as an EVI (Electronic Valve Instrument). The Steiner *MIDI EVI* (**Fig. 24**), which is still available, was one of the first EVIs designed. Like an EWI, the EVI does not require the performer to play in the normal manner—the brass player's lips do not buzz when playing the EVI. Instead, the player simply blows into a reed-like "mouthpiece" and controls the pitch by pressing on Steiner's three valve-like buttons. Scalar passages on the Steiner are played using a combination of the "valves" and the large round cylinder at the "bell" end of the EVI, which is used to change half octaves).

FIG. 24: *The Steiner MIDI EVI*

The most recent EVI to be released is the *Morrison Digital Trumpet* (**Fig. 25**). Presenting a dramatic improvement to the design of the EVI, the *MDT* is actually shaped like and held similarly to an acoustic trumpet. It has actual trumpet valves that move exactly like those on a trumpet. However, instead of diverting air through tubes as they do on an acoustic trumpet, the valves interrupt light beams that cause digital signals to be produced within the *MDT*'s circuitry.

FIG. 25: The Morrison MDT

Unlike their acoustic counterparts, a wind emulator will instantly produce wonderful tones regardless of who is playing the controller because the instruments themselves do not make sounds. Rather, they produce data that is used to control the patches of any MIDI synthesizer or sound module. Therefore, the EVI can sound like a trumpet, a drum set, a laser gun, or any imaginable sound.

However, wind controllers—unlike the other alternate controllers discussed in this section—do require performers to develop some new and unique performance techniques. For example, the three valves of the *MDT* (like those of an acoustic trumpet) only cover one half of an octave. While the acoustic trumpeter must then shift his or her embouchure to play the rest of the octave, the MIDI trumpeter must press a particular button with the left hand. Fortunately, as with any instrument, specific techniques such as these can be learned relatively easily by any performer willing to spend a short time practicing the instrument.

String Controllers

String controllers consist primarily of traditional string instruments (guitar, banjo, violin, viola, and so on), which have been specially fitted with analog-to-MIDI converters that sense the vibrations of the string and convert them to digital codes that control a synthesizer or sound module.

Guitar Controllers

Guitar controllers consist of two types. For the first, a special pickup, such as the Roland *GK3 MIDI Guitar Pickup* ($195 + the cost of the guitar), is simply attached to the body of any hollow or solid body electric guitar using supplied double-sided tape. Unfortunately, the tape does not hold up over time and can create problems during use. The second type consists of an integrated pickup and MIDI jacks, such as the Godin *SynthAccess* guitar (**Fig. 26**, $2,195 depending on finish). This method provides much greater security and the guitar an integrated sound module and mixer. The Godin is an instrument of very high quality.

FIG. 26: Godin LGX-SA guitar

A special multi-pin cable connects a MIDI guitar to a sound module, such as the Roland *GR-33* (**Fig. 27**). The specialized pickups send a signal for each string so that each can be independently tracked. While it is unusual to do so, this means each string can potentially be assigned a different timbre to create a very unique sound. The sound module converts the signals to digital code that is sent to the MIDI OUT port so that other MIDI devices can be controlled. The *GR-33* features over 350 sounds, 25 multi-effects, an assignable expression pedal, and an onboard arpeggiator. $695

FIG. 27: Roland GR-33 guitar synthesizer (sound module)

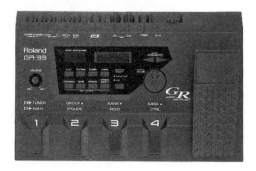

Regardless of the controller type, the guitar can be played with or without invoking the MIDI sounds and the sound of the guitar and the sound module can be mixed as desired.

Orchestral Controllers

Orchestral controllers, like guitar controllers, function best when specialized pickups are built directly into the body of the instrument. In the case of the Zeta MIDI instruments shown in **Figs. 28-30**, the bridge of each instrument has integrated pickups that allow the strings to simply be amplified. When attached via a proprietary cable to a Zeta *Synthony II MIDI Controller* $2,495 (**Fig. 30**), the signals are converted to digital code. Like the *GR-33*, the *Synthony* tracks each string independently to trigger its integrated sounds or other MIDI devices connected to its MIDI OUT port. The Zeta *5-String Fusion* ($3,595, **Fig. 28**) is a combined viola and violin with a solid body. Likewise, the Zeta *Strados Fusion* Cello ($3,095, **Fig. 29**) has a solid body.

FIG. 28: Zeta 5-String Jazz Fusion violin

FIG. 29: Zeta Strados Fusion cello

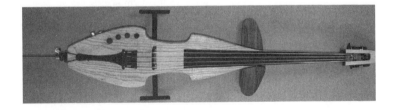

FIG. 30: Zeta Synthony II MIDI Controller (sound module)

Similar to its guitar pickup, Roland offers its *GK-3B* MIDI bass pickup. Because the application is the same, it is worth considering the Zeta's *Upright Bass* (for traditional technique) or the Zeta *Crossover Bass* (for electric bass technique), both capable of either simple amplification or MIDI control. It should also be noted that Zeta has a wide range of orchestral string in a variety of price ranges fitted with pickups for both amplification and MIDI compatibility.

Like percussion controllers, string controllers require virtually no new playing techniques since the instruments are acoustic instruments merely modified by adding circuitry that carries electronic signals to MIDI sound modules.

Unique Controllers

Unique controllers, like electronic instruments in general, have been designed in many shapes and varieties over the years. Unlike the alternate controllers discussed previously, instruments such as the *Zendrum*, the *MIDI Glove*, and Don Buchla's *Lightning* (designed specifically based on human hands) require performers to learn entirely new techniques to negotiate these unique controllers. It is likely that this fact alone has led to the relative obscurity of such instruments. Imaginative inventor/composers such as Tod Machover, however, are designing more and more unique controllers that can be used by performers of any age to create an array of interesting sounds and effects. As alternate controllers become more widely used, they will no doubt continue to develop to meet the needs of future musicians and perhaps appear in more K-12 music education scenarios.

Section 3: Software Instruments

A software instrument (also called a *virtual instrument*) is software that uses a computer to produce sounds. Macs and Windows PCs both include software instruments as part of their operating systems—Macs are shipped with *QuickTime*, and Windows PCs are shipped with Microsoft's *GS Wavetable SW Synthesizer*. Both of these software instruments include the General MIDI sound set for playing MIDI files. As described in Chapter 3 ("Music Notation Software"), both Finale and Sibelius music notation programs now include software instruments for optional use as well.

Many third-party software companies produce different types of software instruments for both Macs and Windows PCs. Because software instruments use the computer's memory and CPU to produce sound, they are generally less expensive than electronic keyboards. Software instruments can be used in a lab to give students a variety of high quality sounds in categories ranging from ethnic to electronic to symphonic. In labs where sound synthesis and sound design are taught, software instruments can be used to demonstrate virtually every type of synthesis and sampling technique. In labs where performance techniques are taught, software instruments can be used to create sophisticated sound combinations and layers.

Educators considering using software instruments and keyboard controllers instead of electronic keyboards with integrated sounds should be aware that software instruments can sometimes be CPU intensive and require a lot of the computer's power, especially when several software instruments are being used simultaneously. In addition, some software instruments come with huge libraries of sampled sounds on CDs or DVDs and may exceed the capacity of the lab computers' hard disks. Finally, in order to use the keyboard outside of the lab, you will need to bring both the keyboard controller and the computer.

Software Instrument Formats

Software instruments are designed to run as a plug-in, a standalone program, or both. "Plug-in" means that a software instrument runs as an application inside a host program such as a sequencer. "Standalone" means that the instrument can operate by itself without the need for a host program.

In order for a software instrument to function correctly as a plug-in, it must use a plug-in format compatible with the host program. Here are the most common formats:

▶ *VSTi (Virtual Studio Technology instrument)*—Developed by Steinberg. VSTi2 and VST are extensions to the original VSTi format. This format runs on both Macs and PCs.

▶ *DXi (Direct X instrument)*—Developed by Cakewalk (based on Microsoft's DirectX multimedia plug-in engine for Windows). This format runs only on PCs.

▶ *AU (Audio Units)*—Developed by Apple for Mac OS 10.x.

▶ *RTAS (Real Time Audio Suite)*—Developed by Digidesign for *Pro Tools LE*. RTAS plug-ins will not work in other sequencers.

▶ *MAS (MOTU Audio System)*—Developed by Mark of the Unicorn for their Digital Performer software (Mac only).

There are two types of software instruments—software synthesizers (softsynths) and software samplers. Some softsynths imitate hardware synthesizers by using specific synthesis techniques to generate waveforms in real time. Other softsynths use sample playback techniques to imitate hardware synthesizers as well as acoustic instruments. A sample playback softsynth uses a closed architecture that lets you select sounds from a pre-defined number of audio files and assign them to a MIDI keyboard or controller. You cannot import additional audio files.

Here is a listing of representative software synthesizers. The abbreviation "M" stands for Mac; "W" stands for Windows PC; "S" stands for standalone. Prices shown are retail.

▶ Edirol *VSC-MP1 Virtual Sound Canvas* (M/W; S; VST, DXi)—16 parts; up to 128-voice polyphony; 902 sounds plus 26 drum sets; reverb, chorus, and delay effects. The least expensive third-party GM softsynth on the market. $50

▶ Edirol *HQ HyperCanvas* (M/W; S; VST, DXi)—16 parts, up to 128-voice polyphony, GM2 (General MIDI Level 2) compatible. $205

▶ Arturia *Minimoog V* (M/W; S; VST, DXi, AU, RTAS)—A softsynth with over 300 presets emulating the classic *Minimoog* analog synthesizer (**Fig. 31**). $199

▶ Native Instruments *Xpress Keyboards* (M/W; S; VST, AU)—Software emulating three classic keyboards: the Hammond *B3*, the Sequential Circuits *Prophet 5*, and the Yamaha *DX7*. $119

▶ M-Audio *Drum & Bass Rig* (M/W; S; VST, RTAS, AU)—Sampled drums and percussion sounds as well as electric bass samples. Includes a loop creator as well as a monophonic bass synthesizer. $129

▶ Steinberg *Virtual Guitarist* (M/W; VST)—A guitar accompaniment plug-in combining more than 1.5 GB of acoustic and electric guitar samples including with variations in tone and phrasing for strums, mutes, and finger picking. $249

▶ EastWest *Bosendorfer 290* (M/W; S; VST, AU, RTAS)—An emulation of the Bosendorfer grand piano. $199

▶ Garritan *Personal Orchestra* (M/W; S; VST, AU, RTAS)—*Personal Orchestra* contains samples of all the major instruments in a symphony orchestra-strings, brass, woodwinds, and percussion—as well as instruments not found in other orchestral libraries—a Steinway concert grand piano, a Stradivarius violin, Guarneri Violin, Gagliano Violin, Wurlitzer and Venus concert harps, Haynes flutes, Heckel bassoons, a Mustel celeste, a Rudolf von Beckerath concert pipe organ, a harpsichord, and many other instruments. $279

FIG. 31: The Arturia Minimoog

A software sampler uses an open architecture and allows you to import and assign *any* audio file on your computer to a MIDI keyboard or controller. The term "sampler" is actually a misnomer, since most soft samplers do not actually allow you to sample new sounds. However, on most soft samplers you can assign any audio file to any key (or keys) on a MIDI keyboard at any pitch. In many cases you can also use the soft sampler's editing functions to change the sound of each audio file in a setup.

Soft Sampler Libraries and Sample Formats

Several software companies bundle soft samplers with libraries of sounds. These libraries can vary greatly in quality and size, with the EastWest Quantum Leap Symphonic Orchestra Platinum Edition requiring a huge 68 GB of hard disk space. There are several proprietary sample formats that can be read by most soft samplers. These formats include AKAI, E-MU, Roland, Kurzweil,

GIGA, Kontakt, EXS24, SF2, LM4, LM4 MkII, REX, WAV, Acidized WAV, AIF, and SD II (Mac only). When selecting sounds, be sure that the sample format can be played by your soft sampler. Here is a list of popular soft samplers.

▶ MOTU *MachFive* (M/W;VST, DXi, AU, RTAS)—*MachFive* is promoted as a universal soft sampler. Although it does not include a bundled library, it includes support for virtually all sample formats, unlimited polyphony, built-in effects, and much more. $395

▶ Steinberg *HALion Player* (M/W; VST, DXi, AU)—*HALion Player* provides a low-cost yet high-quality way of playing any of the hundreds of commercially available *HALion* libraries as well as Wav, AIFF, Rex, Rex2, Zgr, and LM4 instrument files. It includes over 160 instruments featuring high-quality programs and samples such as drums, strings, pianos, guitar, bass, or synth sounds (**Fig. 32**). $129

FIG. 32: The HALion Player

Native Instruments *Kontakt 2* (M/W;VST, DXi, AU, RTAS): *Kontakt 2* imports virtually every sample format available. In addition, it is bundled with a 15GB sound library of orchestral instruments, pianos, drum kits, and loops. $579

Section 4: Performance with Electronic Instruments

What's been happening over the last several decades is that music is becoming, more and more, something that producers do by themselves for listeners who listen by themselves. Before electronics, music was always something that was done by musicians and listeners being together and interacting. I think that kind of interaction is the most important aspect of music—*culturally.*

—Bob Moog in the Hans Fjellestad documentary film, *Moog*

As Moog suggests, if our technology-based culture is to reach its pinnacle, it will require us to meaningfully incorporate electronic instruments into the performance of live music. Therefore, we, as music educators, must begin to teach electronic instrument performance techniques and develop live performance opportunities for our students.

Solo Performance

Certainly, it is possible for a single performer to perform on any of the instruments discussed in the previous sections. This is obvious in regard to electronic keyboards, where students could create electronic versions of previously composed composition as did Wendy Carlos (e.g., *Switched on Bach*). Similarly, electronic versions of Bach's solo string compositions could be performed on MIDI violin or cello. However, modern performers should not be limited to performing new versions of previously composed compositions. As performers become accomplished on the various alternate controllers, composers will begin to write music specifically for such instruments, and should be encouraged to do so.

Through the means of technology, entire digital band can be sequenced and used as an accompaniment for the soloist (much like the *Music Minus One* recordings of the past). While this sort of "solo" performance is acceptable, it is potentially far less productive than live ensemble performance.

Ensemble Performance

The time of the electronic music ensemble as an important educational ensemble has come. If one looks to the past, the single most important pre-20th century instrumental ensemble would probably be the orchestra, in both the professional and educational musical worlds. During the first half of the 20th century, bands became the primary instrumental educational ensembles. Just as the music education curriculum incorporated jazz ensembles during the latter part of the 20th century, it must now embrace the music technology ensemble at the beginning of the 21st century.

Performance is the keystone to any music program. In the end, it *is* what we do as musicians. While all music programs hope to instill a love of music and an understanding of the musical arts through its history, literature, and theoretical applications, it is the performance of music that the students remember the most.

CREATING A TECHNOLOGY ENSEMBLE

Why take the time, energy, and resources to start a technology ensemble in your school? Let's begin with the middle school or high school. In addition to providing a valuable and rewarding performance experience for the current music students, a tech ensemble can attract to the school music program a variety of talented students that don't currently perform in the traditional band, jazz band, or choir. The tech ensemble could be of interest to any student who has studied piano or who has a synthesizer at home (a common reality due to the relative low cost when compared to that of an acoustic piano).

You might be surprised to find out how many members of the student body have played on a synthesizer, but who have not been interested in participating in the traditional music ensembles. In most cases, you will have enough interested students by just announcing that you'd like to form such a group. The truth is, if done well, it won't take long for a technology ensemble to become one of your most popular offerings.

At the elementary level, a keyboard-only ensemble is probably most appropriate. At the middle school level, an ensemble that includes synthesizers, a MIDI guitar, MIDI drums and an alternate percussion controller would provide a minimum orchestration. High school programs should incorporate as many types of MIDI controllers as possible. Universities should consider two levels of tech ensembles: one that serves as a lab experience for music education students and one that is a high-end performance ensemble.

Convincing the Administration

You may find yourself in the position of convincing an administrator that this is the way to go. There are several ways you can approach the subject.

▶ The National Committee for Standards in the Arts has defined seven competencies for music technology, including Electronic Musical Instruments.

▶ Inform the administration that a technology ensemble can reach into the potentially under-served talent pool of students not currently participating in the traditional school music program.

▶ Show the administration that there is community support by seeking the help of technology related businesses in your district. Most schools are striving to make major advancements in technology related areas—don't let your program be left out.

Budgetary Considerations

What does it cost to create a technology ensemble? Although equipping a mature technology ensemble requires considerable funding, beginning a tech ensemble does not require a radical change in your current budget.

INSTRUMENTS

Buy only what you absolutely need. To help limit the funding needed, begin by seeking out students who already own a synthesizer or alternate controller. In doing this, you won't have to fund the purchase of all of the necessary equipment in the first few years since the student equipment will bolster that which already exists in or can be purchased by the music department. The number of students who own and would be willing to use their own instruments in such an ensemble will probably surprise you. With regard to drums, you can always start with the drum set patches built into nearly every synthesizer or a drum machine controlled by a sequencer. There are also pitch-to-MIDI converters that can be attached to traditional acoustic instruments or used with a microphone.

Remember, whatever instruments and equipment you purchase with school funding will be useable for many years to come. As with any other school purchase, make sure the instrument is a quality product. You should also be sure that you like a majority of the sounds it creates—you'll be living with them for a long time—and that you have the ability to either download or create new sounds for that instrument. Although this guide lists keyboards, etc. we feel are worthy of your attention, there is no substitute for playing and hearing an instrument yourself. Start with whatever you can pull together, then add one or two new pieces of equipment each year.

AMPLIFICATION

Keyboards with integrated speakers, in most cases, will not be sufficient for ensemble performance. In fact, performance-quality keyboards and most alternate controllers do not have integrated speakers. There are two options available to solve this problem.

(1) Each instrument can be connected to an amplifier that is specifically designed for that particular type of instrument

(e.g., a keyboard amp, guitar amp, or bass amp). Some amps include multiple input channels. Again, students who own instruments without integrated speakers will probably own some sort of amplifier.

(2) All of the instruments can be connected to a PA system, which may take up less room than individual amplifiers and which will allow you or a student sound engineer to easily balance the individual instruments as needed. Small ensembles can get by with relatively compact and inexpensive PA systems, such as the Fender *PD-250* (**Fig. 33**), which features a central mixer/amplifier onto which the speakers attach for convenient portability. Fender also has both smaller and larger systems. These are truly compact and extremely easy to set up and run. Unlike most competing systems, the Fender systems come complete with two microphones and XLR cables, which conveniently fit into an integrated storage compartment, and speaker stands.

FIG. 33: Fender 6-Channel Passport PD-250 Portable Sound System

More mature tech ensembles will require a larger system, including a mixing board, large house speakers with either cross-over speakers (which include circuitry that directs various frequency bands to the appropriate high-, mid- and low-range speakers) or independent high/mid-range speakers and sub-woofers, and outboard sound effects units, such as compressors and reverb.

Mackie makes modular components that can be combined to meet the specific needs of a given ensemble. For example, Mackie's *VLZ-Pro Analog Mixer* (**Fig. 34**) provides 16 studio-grade mic preamps, 16 balanced 1/4 inch line inputs, 16 channel inserts, 3-band active EQ with sweepable midrange, RCA tape outputs (for recording directly from the mixer), and a rugged steel main chassis with an integrated power supply. $1,100

FIG. 34: Mackie 1604 VLZ-Pro Analog Mixer with SA 1232Z Active 3-Way Speakers

When combined with Mackie's *SA 1232Z Active Speakers* (**Fig. 34**), which have integrated amplifiers and cross-over circuitry (thus providing quiker setup and fewer cables), this system will provide a mid-sized ensemble with a sound system that will fill most auditoriums or gymnasiums with ample sound. $1,999

The addition of effects units (approximately $150–$300 each), such as reverb units and compressors will allow a sound technician to shape the quality of the sound to provide the audience with an optimal aural experience.

In some performance situations, stage monitors will be helpful to the performers. However, in most cases, simply putting the house speakers behind the ensemble will solve most hearing issues. If this is done, care must be taken to avoid feedback if microphones are used.

Finally, components such as direct boxes (which boost the signal of guitars and basses to the mixer's required input level) are not needed with either keyboards or sound modules, whose output is appropriate for mixers.

The eMusic Library

One of the biggest challenges you will face is finding appropriate music for a technology ensemble. Although you will rarely open a music catalog and immediately find a list of pieces for a tech ensemble or pick up ready-made arrangements at your local music store, there are a lot of options when it comes to literature.

    (1) Some publishers and Web sites sell works specifically arranged for technology ensembles—most often keyboard

ensembles, but often capable of being used by a more diverse ensemble (see "Sheet Music Resources" in Section 5; also, typing "electronic keyboard ensemble" into a Web search engine will result in several interesting hits). Hal Leonard Publishing provides two series called *Artist Transcriptions* and *Transcribed Scores* (including music by electronically oriented artists and groups such as Manheim Steamroller, Enya, Shadowfax, Chic Corea Elektric Band, and the Yellowjackets) that can be used for more mature ensembles.

(2) You can make your own transcriptions by taking traditional keyboard or chamber ensemble works and assigning a "part" to each performer. This is similar to creating an ensemble version of Wendy Carlos' *Switched on Bach* recordings of the 1970s. Since a MIDI instrument can be easily transposed any transposing instrument part can be read as-is by a student and still sound the correct pitches. For example, if the student is reading a transposed French horn part, simply transpose the keyboard down a perfect fifth (7 half steps) so that the correct concert pitches are sounded.

(3) You should encourage the creation of new music by ensemble members, and might even require each member to arrange a piece or to write one original work for the group as part of the ensemble grade. In doing so, you create a library to which you can return in future years.

(4) Develop a habit of improvising regularly—not necessarily only "jazz" improvisation, but unrestricted improvisation that explores the unique sounds and textures of the available MIDI instruments. Each performance can also include one or more improvisations based on previously rehearsed concepts.

(5) Finally, network with other educators who have established electronic ensembles in their schools. You will find that they have the same issues you have and, in most cases, they will be willing to trade unpublished materials with you or recommend good resources for electronic ensemble literature.

Rehearsing a Technology Ensemble
Rehearsals for the tech ensemble may seem a little different than the acoustic ensemble rehearsal, primarily because both the students and the director must get used to the fact that each

instrument can make an amazing variety of sounds. In fact, it sometimes takes longer for the director to understand what is happening than it does for the students—especially during improvisations.

IMPROVISING

Extremely useful at the beginning of the academic year, improvisational exercises can provide an efficient and fun way to get the students to know the sounds available on the various instruments. A good exercise is to use only "sound effect" patches in an improvisational setting. You can also set up "story lines," specific moods, or forms that you want the performers to evoke musically. In many instances, improvisations can lead to the creation of a composition. Improvisations of these types can also be featured during live performances. Continuing to improvise throughout the year will provide an extremely powerful musical experience for the entire ensemble.

ORCHESTRATION

A great deal of rehearsal time will be used orchestrating the music. This is why it is so important for the students to know the sounds available on the instruments. Regardless of the repertoire you select for performance, don't just use your electronic instruments to imitate acoustic instruments. Find unique electronic sounds (voices/patches/programs) that bring a new or unique approach to the music. Orchestration is often one of the most time-consuming activities during the tech ensemble rehearsal. Performers must know the available sounds on the instrument they play so that orchestrating a composition will be accomplished efficiently.

SPACE AND SETUP

Even a mature tech ensemble can be set up in a relatively small space (e.g., 8' x 8'). While it would be most convenient to leave the ensemble set up permanently, you may not have enough room, or you may not feel comfortable leaving the equipment set up on a daily basis for security reasons. If this is the case, assign each performer specific tasks to make the setup process as efficient as possible. If the ensemble's rehearsal time doesn't fit into the regular daily schedule, try to rehearse after school one day and before school the next to avoid the need to set up and tear down the equipment between rehearsals.

Conclusion

Much like the jazz bands and swing choirs introduced in the '70s, the tech ensemble will grow into a self-sustaining ensemble that is respected in the music program for providing options to the more traditional elements of the music program. It provides students with another small ensemble experience that can be an extremely creative musical adventure.

The mature tech ensemble will consist of some of your most talented students because of its popularity. It can include several performers on a variety of MIDI controllers, one or two sound technicians who run the sound system and effects units, and one or more vocalists who can be featured with the ensemble.

Although a tech ensemble is an equipment-intensive undertaking and one that requires time to generate a library of music, it is also a fulfilling musical experience that will become a favorite of both the students and the audience alike.

Finally, a live electronic ensemble brings technology into the music curriculum in an extremely practical way, provides a wonderfully expanded education to music students, and gives them additional tools to move into the musical world of the 21st century.

Section 5: Reference Materials

Books

Aikin, Jim. *Software Synthesizers: The Definitive Guide to Virtual Music Instruments*. San Francisco, CA: Backbeat Books, 2003.

Alexander, Peter Lawrence. *How MIDI Works*. Milwaukee, WI: Hal Leonard Corporation, 2001.

Ballora, Marc. *Essentials of Music Technology*. Upper Saddle River, NJ: Prentice Hall, 2002.

Battier, Marc. *Aesthetics of Live Electronic Music* (includes CD). Langhorne, PA: Harwood Academic Publications, 2000.

Huber, David Miles. *The MIDI Manual, Second Edition*. Boston, MA: Focal Press, 1999.

Rudolph, Thomas E. *Teaching Music with Technology (Second Edition)*. Chicago, IL: GIA Publications, 2004.

Snyder, Michael. *All About Electronic Percussion*. Milwaukee, WI: Hal Leonard Corporation, available Fall 2005.

Weinberg, Norm. *The Electronic Drummer*. Cedar Grove, NJ: Modern Drummer Publications, 1989

Williams, David and Peter Webster. *Experiencing Music Technology*. Belmont, CA: Wadsworth Publishing, 2005.

Articles

Muro, Don. "The Play's the Thing." *TI:ME Newsletter*, Sept. 2004. (www.ti-me.org/imho/muro2004-09.html)

_____. "Classroom Performance." *Music Education Technology*, Nov. 2004. (http://metmagazine.com/mag/classroom_performance/)

Reuter, Rocky J. "MIDI Basics for Music Educators: Let's Not Make This Difficult!" *Lentine's Music Website*, Articles, (www.lentine.com/articles/backup/mbasics.htm)

_____. "The MIDI Ensemble." *Lentine's Music Website*, Articles, (www.lentine.com/articles/backup/the%20MIDI%20ensemble.htm)

DVDs

Fjellstad, Hans. *Moog: A Documentary Film*. Plexifilm.

Venderosa, Tony. *Live Electronic Music*. AMD/Yamaha.

Videos

Muro, Don. *An Overview of Electronic Instruments*. J.D. Wall Publishing.

Sheet Music Resources

Carden, Joy. *Carden Keyboard Ensemble Library* and *Carden Keyboard Series*—An expansive collection of arrangements and original compositions specifically for electronic keyboard ensembles of varying sizes.

Hal Leonard Publications. *Artist Transcriptions* and *Transcribed Scores*—Transcriptions of songs and/or entire CDs by groups that incorporate electronic instruments.

Muro, Don. *Four Easy Quartets for Synthesizers.* J. D. Wall Publishing.

Muro, Don. *Three Easy Trios for Synthesizers.* J. D. Wall Publishing.

Ogilvy, Susan. Ogilvy Music (www.sospace.com)—Over 150 keyboard ensemble compositions and arrangements (4–8 electronic keyboards) rated for elementary, intermediate, and advanced players.

Purse, Lynn. Ensemble Set 1 and Ensemble Set 2; Celebration of Bells, Deck the Halls, and Greensleeves; and Dance of the Dawn Children — all for electronic keyboard ensemble.

Warner Brothers Publishers. *Play Together Series*—A series of arrangements of previously composed compositions (e.g., *Also Sprach Zarathustra*, Amazing *Grace*, *Moonlight Sonata*, etc.) arranged for up to eight electronic keyboards.

Internet Resources

Arturia (www.arturia.com/en/default.php)
Alesis (www.alesis.com)
Alternate Mode (www.alternatemode.com)
Casio (www.casio.com)
Clavia (www.clavia.se)
E-Mu (www.emu.com)
Edirol (www.edirol.com)
Fender (www.fender.com/home.php)
Garritan (www.garritan.com)
Godin (www.godinguitars.com)
Korg (www.korg.com)
Kurzweil (www.kurzweilmusicsystems.com)
M-Audio (www.m-audio.com)

Morrison Digital Trumpet (www.patchmanmusic.com/mdt.html)
Mackie (www.mackie.com)
Mark of the Unicorn (www.motu.com)
Moog Music (www.moogmusic.com)
Native Instruments (www.nativeinstruments.de/index.
php?id=home_us)
Novation (www.novationmusic.com)
Pintech (www.pintechworld.com)
Roland (www.rolandus.com)
Steinberg (www.steinberg.de/Steinberg/defaultb0e4.html)
Steiner (www.patchmanmusic.com/NyleMIDIEVI.html)
Studiologic (www.studiologic.net)
Wernick (www.wernick.net)
Yamaha (www.yamaha.com)
Zeta (www.zetamusic.com)

Electronic Musical Instruments*
ELECTRONIC KEYBOARDS
LOW COST

Manufacturer	Product	Web Site	Number of Keys	Type of Action	Aftertouch	Number of Splits	Computer Interface	Displays	Independent MIDI Ins/Outs	Foot Pedals	Foot Switches	Polyphony	Dimensions (WxHxD)	Weight (lbs.)	Special Features	List Price
Casio	CTK900	www.casio.com	61	Non-weighted	No	N/A	MIDI	Backlit LCD	1/1	1		32	N/A	N/A	GM compatible	$229
Casio	WK3200	www.casio.com	76	Non-weighted	No	N/A	MIDI	Backlit LCD	1/1	1		32	N/A	N/A	GM compatible, pitch bend wheel, modulation switch	$349
Roland	EXR-5	www.rolandus.com	61	Non-weighted	No	N/A	USB	Backlit LCD	1/1		1	64	N/A	N/A	GM2/GS/XG compatible, integrated 16-track sequencer, floppy drive	$795
Yamaha	PSRE203	www.yamaha.com	61	Non-weighted	No	1	MIDI	Backlit LCD	1/1		1	32	37 1/4 x 4/1/3 x 13 2/3"	9 lbs. 11ozs.	GM compatible; includes Yamaha Education Suite	$159
Yamaha	PSR273	www.yamaha.com	61	Non-weighted	No	1	MIDI	Backlit LCD	1/1		1		36.3 x 5.2 x 14.8"	11.66 lbs.	GM/XGlite compatible; includes Yamaha Education Suite	$279
Yamaha	PSR293	www.yamaha.com	61	Non-weighted	No	1	USB	Backlit LCD	1/1		1	32	37.5 x 5.75 x 15.25"	15 lbs. 7 oz.	GM/XGlite compatible; includes Yamaha Education Suite	$369
Yamaha	PSR450	www.yamaha.com	61	Non-weighted	No	1	MIDI	Backlit LCD	1/1		1	32	37 1/2 x 6 2/3 x 15 1/4"	18 lbs. 12 oz.	GM/XGlite compatible, pitch bend wheel, 6-track sequencer, floppy drive	$699

KEYBOARD CONTROLLERS

Manufacturer	Product	Web Site	Number of Keys	Type of Action	Aftertouch	Computer Interface	Displays	Independent MIDI Ins/Outs	Foot Pedals	Foot Switches	Programmable Controllers
Alesis	Photon 25	www.alesis.com	25	Semi-weighted	No	USB, MIDI	4-character LED	1/2	1	1	10 knobs, 10 buttons
Alesis	Photon X49	www.alesis.com	49	Non-weighted	No	USB, MIDI	2x16 line LCD	1/1	1	1	10 knobs, 10 buttons, 9 faders
Edirol	PCR-A30	www.edirol.com	32	Non-weighted	No	USB, MIDI	3-digit LED	1/1	1	1	8 sliders, 8 knobs, 9 buttons
Edirol	PCR-M1	www.edirol.com	25	Non-weighted	No	USB, MIDI	3-digit LED	1/1	1	1	8 knobs, 6 buttons
Edirol	PCR-M50	www.edirol.com	49	Non-weighted	No	USB, MIDI	3-digit LED	1/1	1	1	8 faders, 8 knobs, 9 buttons
E-MU Systems	X-Board 25	www.emu.com	25	Non-weighted	Yes	USB, MIDI	3-digit LED	0/1	0	1	16 knobs
E-MU Systems	X-Board X49	www.emu.com	49	Non-weighted	Yes	USB, MIDI	3-digit LED	0/1	0	1	16 knobs
Korg USA	Kontrol 49	www.korg.com	49	Non-weighted	No	USB	Backlit LCD	0/0	1	1	8 knobs, 8 sliders, 16 trigger pads, vector joystick
M-Audio	Keystation 49e	www.m-audio.com	49	Non-weighted	No	USB, MIDI	None	0/1	0	1	None
M-Audio	O2	www.m-audio.com	25	Non-weighted	No	USB, MIDI	3-digit LED	0/1	0	1	8 knobs, 8 buttons
Novation	ReMOTE 49	www.novationmusic.com	49	Semi-weighted	Yes	USB, MIDI	LCD	1/2	1	1	8 knobs, 8 sliders, 8 encoders, X/Y touchpad
Novation	ReMOTE LE 25	www.novationmusic.com	25	Semi-weighted	No	USB, MIDI	LCD	0/1	0	1	9 knobs, 9 buttons
Studiologic	TMK 49	www.studiologic.net	49	Non-weighted	No	MIDI	None	0/1	0	1	None
Studiologic	VMK-149	www.studiologic.net	49	Full-weighted	Yes	MIDI	LCD	0/2	1-3	1-3	8 knobs, 8 buttons, 8 sliders

Real-Time Controls	Dimensions (WxHxD)	Weight (lbs.)	Special Features	List Price
Octave +/- buttons, AXYZ Dome on/off, configuration buttons, value/enter encoder, knob layer button, audio input/output levels	18" x 3.5 x 9.5"	4.0 lbs.		$249
Octave +/- buttons, AXYZ Dome on/off, configuration buttons, value/enter encoder, knob layer button, dedicated transport controls for remote control of software/hardware	N/A	N/A	Bundled with Steinberg Cubase LE software	$499
Octave Shift buttons, Transpose button	25 5/8 x 3 7/16 x 9 3/16"	5 lbs 12 0z.	Built-in 24-bit/96kHz audio interface, USB powered	$395
Octave Shift buttons, Transpose button	18 x 1 x 9"	2.7	Ultra-Slim design	$249
Octave Shift buttons, Transpose button	32 13/16 x 3 7/16 x 9 3/16"	7 lbs 5 oz.		$285
Octave Shift buttons	N/A	N/A	Includes Proteus X LE software (PC only)	$199
Octave Shift buttons	N/A	N/A	Includes Proteus X LE software (PC only)	$229
	28.74 x 3.39 x 12.56"	10.8 lbs.	separate LCD for each knob/slider pair	$499
Octave Shift buttons	32 x 8.5 x 3"	6.6 lbs.		$129
Octave Shift buttons	17.5 x 1.5 x 8.5"	3 lbs.		$179
Octave Shift buttons, dedicated transport controls	N/A	N/A		$499
Octave Shift buttons, dedicated transport controls	N/A	N/A		$249
Octave Shift buttons	32 x 2.5 x 7"	5.5 lbs.		$159
Dedicated transport controls	30.8 x 4.75 x 13.75"	24.5 lbs.	Includes MIDI/USB converter	$999

PORTABLE/TABLETOP DIGITAL PIANOS

Manufacturer	Product	Web Site	Type of Action	Number of Splits	Computer Interface	Displays	Independent MIDI Ins/Outs	Foot Pedals	Foot Switches
Casio	Privia PX100	www.casio.com		1	MIDI	None	1/1		Damper pedal, soft/sostenuto pedal
Korg	SP200	www.korg.com		N/A	MIDI	None	1/1		Damper pedal
M-Audio	ProKeys 88	www.m-audio.com		1	USB, MIDI	3-digit LED	1/1	1	Sustain and sustenuto
Roland	FP-5	www.rolandus.com		1	USB	LCD	0/0		Damper, sustenuto, soft
Roland	RD-300SX	www.rolandus.com		N/A	USB, MIDI	LCD	1/1		N/A
Yamaha	P120	www.yamaha.com		1	MIDI	3-digit LED	1/1	1	Sustain and soft/sostenuto
Yamaha	P60	www.yamaha.com		0	MIDI	None	1/1	0	1

CONSOLE DIGITAL PIANOS

Manufacturer	Product	Web Site	Type of Action	Number of Splits	Computer Interface	Displays	Independent MIDI Ins/Outs	Foot Pedals	Foot Switches
Casio	AP38	www.casio.com		1	MIDI	None	1/1	0	Damper, soft, sostenuto
Korg	EC-150	www.korg.com		0	MIDI	None	1/1		Damper, soft, sostenuto
Roland	F-50	www.rolandus.com		1	MIDI	None	1/1		Damper
Roland	FP-2C	www.rolandus.com		1	USB, MIDI	LED	1/1		Damper
Yamaha	YDP113	www.yamaha.com							

SYNTHESIZERS

Manufacturer	Product	Web Site	Number of Keys	Type of Action	Aftertouch	Number of Splits	Computer Interface	Displays	Independent MIDI Ins/Outs	Foot Pedals	Foot Switches
Alesis	QS 6.2	www.alesis.com	61	Non-weighted	Yes	16	MIDI	LED	1/1	2	1
Korg USA	X5D	www.korg.com	61	Non-weighted	No	8	MIDI	LCD	1/1	1	1
Roland	Juno-D	www.rolandus.com	61	Non-weighted	No	8	MIDI	LCD	1/1	1	1
Yamaha	S03	www.yamaha.com	61	Non-weighted	No	16	Serial, MIDI	LCD	1/1	1	1

WORKSTATIONS

Manufacturer	Product	Web Site	Number of Keys	Type of Action	Aftertouch	Number of Splits	Computer Interface	Displays	Independent MIDI Ins/Outs	Foot Pedals	Foot Switches
Alesis	Fusion 6HD	www.alesis.com	61	Semi-weighted	Yes	16	USB, MIDI	LCD	1/1	1	2
Korg USA	Triton Extreme 61	www.korg.com	61	Non-weighted	Yes	16	USB, MIDI	TouchView graphical interface	1/1	1	2
Korg USA	Triton LE 61	www.korg.com	61	Non-weighted	Yes	16	MIDI	LCD	1/1	1	2
Roland	Fantom X-a	www.rolandus.com	61	Non-weighted	Yes	16	USB, MIDI	LCD	1/1	1	2
Yamaha	Motif ES6	www.yamaha.com	61	Non-weighted	Yes	16	USB, MIDI	LCD	1/1	2	2

Programmable Controllers	Real-Time Controls	Polyphony	Dimensions (WxHxD)	Weight (lbs.)	Special Features	List Price
		32	N/A	27.6 lbs.	10 sounds, 20 rhythms, 1 song sequencer (2 tracks, 5200 notes), 2 headphone jacks	$649
		60	52.3 x 4.8 x 11.2"	40.7 lbs.	30 sounds	$1,100
	Dedicated remote MIDI controller buttons	126	13" x 5.9" x 57"	48 lbs.	14 sounds, pitch and modulation wheels	$749
		64	N/A	N/A		$1,799
		128	N/A	35 lbs.	GM2 sounds	$1,599
		64	53 5/16 x 5 5/16 x 13 5/32"	40.8 lbs.	14 sounds, 3 song sequencer (2 tracks, 10,000 notes)	$1,495
		32	52 13/16 x 5 7/16 x 13 15/16"	35.3 lbs.	10 sounds	$899

Programmable Controllers	Real-Time Controls	Polyphony	Dimensions (WxHxD)	Weight (lbs.)	Special Features	List Price
		64	N/A	N/A	16 sounds, 1 song sequencer (2 tracks, 8,000 notes), 2 headphone jacks	$1,499
		60	53.93 x 17.20 x 32.56"	94.8 lbs.	30 sounds, 2 headphone jacks	$1,449
		64	N/A	N/A	20 sounds, sequencer	$1,395
		64	N/A	N/A	GM2 sounds, backing accompaniments	$1,695
			52 15/16 x 32 1/2 x 16 _"	79 lbs 6 oz.	10 sounds, 2 headphone jacks	$1,295

Programmable Controllers	Real-Time Controls	Polyphony	Dimensions (WxHxD)	Weight (lbs.)	Special Features	List Price
		64	3.5" x 36" x 11.25	18.5	GM sounds	$899
		64	N/A	N/A	GM sounds	$900
		64		11 lbs 1 oz.	GM2 sounds, D beam controller	$749
		64	37 7/8 x 3 7/16 x 11 1/4"	13.23 lbs.	GM/XG sounds	$629

Programmable Controllers	Real-Time Controls	Polyphony	Dimensions (WxHxD)	Weight (lbs.)	Special Features	List Price
		N/A	35.5 x 4 x 14"	30.4 lbs.	4 synthesis types, 8-track hard disk recording, 32-track MIDI sequencer	$2,399
		60	43.64 x 4.61 x 14.17"	31.75 lbs.	16-track digital audio/MIDI sequencer, assignable controllers	$2,800
		62	41.15 x 3.75 x 11.91" x 3.75	17.2 lbs.	16-track sequencer	$1,600
		128	N/A	N/A	Digital audio/MIDI sequencer, assignable controllers	$1,699
		128	41 1/4 x 5 3/8 x 15 1/2"	34.2 lbs.	Digital audio/MIDI sequencer, assignable controllers	$2,399

TONE GENERATORS

Manufacturer	Product	Web Site	Earliest Recommended User‡	Format	Sounds	Special Features	List Price
Edirol	Sound Canvas SD-80	www.edirol.com	MS	1u half-rack	660 GM2/GS/XGlite, 23 drum sets	USB, S/PDIF	$850
Korg	Triton Rack	www.korgus.com	MS	2u full-rack	Up to 2,057, incl. GM2	Sampler, 13 types of synthesis, FireWire, headphone	$2,500
Roland	GR-33 Guitar Synthesizer	www.rolandus.com	MS	Floor pedals	350+	Expression pedal	$695
Roland	XV-2020	www.rolandus.com	MS	1u half-rack	768		$695
Yamaha	MU-15	www.yamaha.com	E	Handheld	676 XG/GM, 21 Drum kits	Stereo/headphone	$300
Yamaha	VL70-m	www.yamaha.com	MS	1u half-rack	256	Physical modeling	$800
Zeta	Synthony II	www.zetamusic.com	MS	2u full-rack	128		$2,495

ALTERNATE CONTROLLERS
PERCUSSION

Manufacturer	Product	Web Site	Earliest Recommended User	Dimensions (WxHxD)	Weight (lbs.)	Pads	Sounds	Presets	Outputs	MIDI Ports	Special Features	List Price
Roland	HDP-15 HandSonic	www.rolandus.com	E	16 x 16 x 3"	4	21 rubber, 2 ribbon	654	160 + 80 user	Stereo, headphone	In, Out	1 piece design, 17 reverb/delay settings, 85 multi effects, D Beam, onboard sequencer	$1,295
Roland	RMP-5 Advanced Rhythm Trainer	www.rolandus.com	E	10 x 14 x 3"	3	1 tunable mesh	48	N/A	Stereo/headphone	None	1 piece design, variable metronome, rhythm coach	$279
Roland	V-Drums Pro-Series TD-20S-WT	www.rolandus.com	MS	7 x 5 x 4"	35	10 multi-zone mesh	500+		8-ch. mixer, headphone		Stand with cable control, onboard sequencer	$6,699
Yamaha	DD5 Digital Drum System	www.yamaha.com	E	22 x 14 x 7"	11	7 polymer	174, GM	50	Stereo speakers with bass port, headphone	In, Out	1 piece design, Tap Start tempo control, hand or stick play, 100 accomp. rhythm styles	$300
Yamaha	DTXPL Digital Drum Set	www.yamaha.com	MS	4 x 4 x 4"	25	8 polymer pads	214	32 + 10 user	Stereo out, headphone	Out		$1,059

MALLET

Manufacturer	Product	Web Site	Earliest Recommended User	Octaves	Type of Action	Dimensions (WxHxD)	Weight (lbs.)	Special Features	List Price
Alternate Mode, Inc.	malletKAT 5.0	www.alternatemode.com	MS	3, expandable	Touch Sensitive	47 x 11 x 2.5"	28	Optional integrated sounds, latch modes per pad, keyboard acts as multiple CC# controller	$2,863
Wernick Musical Instruments	Xylosynth	www.wernick.net	MS	3 (4 available)	Touch Sensitive	48 x 10 x 4"	Undefined	Integrated sounds	Custom built (contact manufacturer)

WIND

Manufacturer	Product	Web Site	Earliest Recommended User	List Price
Morrison	MDT	www.patchmanmusic.com	MS	$2,495
Steiner	EVI	www.patchmanmusic.com/NyleMIDIEVI.html	HS	$750
Yamaha	WX-5 Wind Controller	www.yamaha.com	MS	$750

GUITAR/BASS

Manufacturer	Product	Web Site	Earliest Recommended User	List Price
Godin	LGX-SA Guitar	www.godinguitars.com	MS	$2,195
Roland	GK MIDI Guitar pickup	www.rolandus.com	MS	$195
Roland	GR-33 Guitar Synthesizer	www.rolandus.com	MS	$695
Roland	GK-3B MIDI Bass pickup	www.rolandus.com	MS	$199

ORCHESTRAL

Manufacturer	Product	Web Site	Earliest Recommended User	List Price
ZETA Music Products	4-String Jazz Standard Cello	www.zetamusic.com	MS	$3,295+
ZETA Music Products	5-String Jazz Fusion Violin	www.zetamusic.com	MS	$3,295+
ZETA Music Products	5-String Standard Upright Bass	www.zetamusic.com	MS	$3,295+
ZETA Music Products	5-String Strados Crossover Bass	www.zetamusic.com	MS	$2,295+

SOFTWARE INSTRUMENTS
SOFTWARE SYNTHESIZER

Manufacturer	Product	Web Site	Version	Minimum System Requirements	Format	Multitimbral (# of Parts) per Instance	Synthesis Methods	Special Features	List Price
Arturia	Minimoog V	www.arturia.com	1.1	Windows 98SE/2000/ XP or Mac OS 9.2/10.2 or higher, 256 MB RAM, 1 GHz	Standalone, DXi, VSTi, RTAS/HTDM, MAS, AU	1	Subtractive, analog model	PWM, chorus, delay, modulation matrix	$199
EastWest	Bosendorfer 290	www.soundsonline.com/		Windows XP/ME/98, Pentium III/Athlon 500 Mhz, 256 MB RAM; Mac OS 9.2, OS 10.2.6 or higher, G3 500 Mhz, 256 MB RAM; 2 GB free hard disk space, DVD drive	Standalone, VST, DXi, AU, RTAS	1	Sample playback	Uses Kontakt audio engine	$199
Edirol	HQ HyperCanvas	http://edirol.com/	1.5	Windows 98/ME/SE/ 2000/XP, 128 MB RAM; Mac OS 8.6, 9.x, 192 MB RAM	Standalone, VST, DXi	16	Sample playback	Software synth for General MIDI 2 sounds	$205
Edirol	Virtual Sound Canvas	http://edirol.com/	3.23	Windows 98/ME/SE/ 2000/XP, 64 MB RAM; Mac OS 8.6, 9.x, 128 MB RAM	Standalone, VST, DXi	16	Sample playback	GM2/GS compatible, MIDI to WAV/AIFF file conversion, 100 royalty-free MIDI files included	$50
Garritan	Personal Orchestra	http://garritan.com/		Windows XP, Pentium 4/Athlon 2.0 GHz; Mac OS X or higher, G4 1.25 MHz; 2 GB of free hard disk space	Standalone, VST, DXi, AU, RTAS	N/A	Sample playback	Uses Kontakt audio engine	$279
M-Audio	Drum & Bass Rig	www.m-audio.com							
Native Instruments	Xpress Keyboards	www.nativeinstruments.com		Windows XP, Pentium III/Athlon 500 MHz, 256 MB RAM; Mac OS 10.2.6, G4 500 MHz, 512 MB RAM	Standalone, VST, AU	1	Sample playback		$119
Steinberg	Virtual Guitarist	www.steinberg.net	N/A	Windows 98/ME/2000/XP Pentium II/ AMD 400, 256 MB RAM; Mac OS 9/X G3 500, 256 MB RAM	VST	8	Sample playback	27 different acoustic/electric guitar "players" sync to song tempo, effects	$249

SAMPLER LIBRARY/SAMPLE FORMAT

Manufacturer	Product	Web Site	Earliest Recommended User	Special Features	List Price
MOTU	MachFive				
Native Instruments	Kontakt 2				
Steinberg	HALion Player				

MISCELLANEOUS

Manufacturer	Product	Web Site	Earliest Recommended User	Special Features	List Price
Fender	Passport 250 Portable Sound System	www.fender.com	MS	6 channels, 2 mics and cables, integrated storage	$1,000
Mackie	1604 VLZ-Pro Analog Mixer	www.mackie.com	HS	16 channels, 3-band active EQ with sweepable midrange, RCA tape outputs, integrated power supply	$1,100
Mackie	SA 1232 Active 3-Way Speakers	www.mackie.com	N/A	136 dB output, 1 horn, 1 high/mid, 2 12" woofers	$1,999
MOTU	FastLane USB MIDI Interface	www.motu.com	N/A	USB, 2 MIDI In/Out, status lights, multiple colors	$79
MOTU	MIDI Express	www.motu.com	N/A	USB, 8 MIDI In/Out, expandable	$249

*Much of the data in these tables was previously published in *Electronic Musician's Computer Music Product Guide*, a product of Primedia, and is reprinted with the permission of the publisher.
‡ E=Elementary, MS=Middle School, HS=High School, N/A=Not Applicable
NOTE: For detailed specifications and updates, please visit the manufacturers' Web sites.

CHAPTER 2

Music Production

By Michael J. Moniz and Keith V. Mason

"Technology has forever changed the way music is produced, recorded, and distributed. An understanding of new music production techniques is essential for today's music teacher."

Section 1: Overview of Music Production

Music production encompasses that area of music technology related to the manipulation and editing of sound, music creation through loop-based music production software, and the capturing of music performances through either MIDI sequencing (recording) and/or live audio. The scope of software programs and hardware based systems available for use by music educators has become more affordable and accessible to those at many skill levels. This chapter will focus on commonly used applications for both students and teachers in a multitude of settings in the music classroom, rehearsal, or concert hall.

Some of the earliest methods employed by music educators in recording and editing live performance were accomplished on reel-to-reel tape, four-track recorders, and cassettes. In the earliest days of MIDI, capturing performances was limited to hardware-based MIDI sequencing. The visual representation of sound through the use of computers and software has made sequencing and editing of both MIDI and digital audio more accessible to the masses.

The choice of a Windows or Macintosh operating system computer for music making is clearly a user preference dictated by cost, comfort level, software availability, and/or technical and local support. Both platforms have similar capabilities and many programs offer versions for both platforms. While there are some platform specific programs, like Apple Macintosh-based *Digital Performer* and *GarageBand* or Windows-based *ACID* and *Sonar*, you can usually find a comparable piece of software that will accomplish the same results using a different visual interface but similar tools and skills.

One of the most exciting developments in recent years is the ability to work with digital audio on a personal computer. Macintosh and Windows computers purchased today, even at the low end of the price range, are capable of professional quality results only limited by the experience and skill level of the user. And while recording and editing digital audio can be a complex process whose results are clearly affected by skill and knowledge, music educators desiring to record classroom music activities, lessons, or performances for analysis and evaluation can achieve more than satisfactory results. Technology clearly empowers musicians at all levels to capture their art and create, edit, and produce music in their own unique voice.

Software

The variety of software used in music production may be listed in catalogs, and on music seller Web sites, as sequencing, digital audio recording, editing, burning, software synthesis, software instruments, and samplers. Decide what you want the software to help you accomplish (recording, editing, burning, etc.) and look for a program that best fits your need and skill level. Music retailers that specialize in sales to educators will often list software as entry, intermediate, or advanced by indicating a suggested grade level. Be advised that one person's idea of entry level may be advanced for another person. Programs used by professionals in recording studio environments offer the greatest capability and require advanced skills. It is usually a good idea to locate the company website for software you are considering and see if there is a "demo" version that will provide you with the opportunity to take the software for a "test drive" before purchase. And while the price of a piece of software will sometimes suggest the complexity and capability of the software, there are "lite" versions of many programs. These still have enough of the powerful features and capabilities of the full versions to be adequate for the music educator, but are significantly less expensive.

Hardware

The availability of powerful hardware-based systems as portable as hand-held digital recorders (DAT, minidisk, etc.) or large digital audio workstations (DAW) provide a wealth of choices to fit a variety of budgets for recording and editing both MIDI and audio. Some systems can store the performance data onto digital tape, while others will write to either mini disc, direct-to-CD, or to a large hard drive. In addition to these recording devices, you'll need cables and stands for microphones, an audio interface for recording to computer, and a digital mixer for recording and controlling all aspects of line inputs and effects. There is no more important piece of equipment needed than quality microphones. A good condenser and/or dynamic mic with XLR connectors are a must for those in need of the highest quality capture of a live performance.

Benefits for Teachers

Music teachers can use recording and editing software to record music for use in the classroom and rehearsal and to create a wide variety of other materials to enhance student learning. In the book, *Technology Strategies for Music Education*, the authors systematically catalog dozens of such ways, including

▶ Creating guided listening examples

▶ Creating accompaniments for classroom, choral, or instrumental practice

▶ Immediate feedback for evaluation of rehearsal / performances

▶ Authentic assessment

▶ Publishing mp3 files on the Internet for home practice and listening assignments

▶ Teaching musical concepts including pitch, timbre, volume, style and form

Benefits to Students

Students can use music production software in the classroom, practice room, and on their computers at home for a variety of creativity, appreciation, and performance activities. Some of these applications, highlighted in *Technology Strategies for Music Education*, include

▶ Composing and arranging music

▶ Enhancing critical listening skills

▶ Portfolio assessment / document progress over time

▶ Creating audition CDs for festivals or college entrance

▶ Use for practice and performance

▶ Creating music for other art forms such as ballet, video, and poetry

This passage from "Sequence-stration," which describes the usefulness of software sequencers in music education, drives home the point:

Many educators *sequence* (the verb for creating a sequencer file) accompaniments for use with their students in class, rehearsals and performances. It's like having a virtual accompanist at your disposal! You don't even need to be a proficient keyboard player to do it. Playing notes from your MIDI keyboard or other controller, you can record the music for each track in as slow a tempo as you like and then have it all play back at full speed. You can even enter one note at a time using a MIDI controller or computer keyboard and mouse, which is called "step recording" or "step entry."

If you make a mistake, or just want to try something different, making edits is a breeze. Notes can be altered individually or in groups in a variety of graphic and text-based modes, at least one of which will seem intuitive to you....

Good pianists may want to record accompaniments in real time so they can use them in class or in rehearsals. Freed from the piano, they can give their full attention to conducting, attend to classroom-management issues, or assist students in other ways.

Sequencing software also allows you to alter parameters that you don't normally get to fiddle with when using CD-based accompaniment tracks. For instance, you can slow the tempo without lowering the pitch—useful when first teaching a song. You can mute all but one track to help strengthen that part for a *Music-Minus-One* effect. You can even post your sequences to the Web for students to access and work with at home. (*Music Education Technology*, Fall 2003)

Today's educators, increasingly busy and distracted by non-instructional chores, may be apprehensive about investing even a few hours into learning new skills, such as those required to work with music production software. Nonetheless, there are great advantages and—as we will share—many of the programs presented in this chapter are easy to learn, with intuitive interfaces, allowing you to begin projects with them upon your first encounter.

Selecting Music Production Tools

Selecting the right tool for you and your students' needs is essential for success. A listing of software programs and hardware commonly used by music educators is included in the charts for each category and in the summary table at the conclusion of this chapter.

What to Consider when Buying Audio Editing and Mastering Software

▶ *Burning support*—Almost all audio editing and mastering programs support some form of CD burning. If you don't have another program for burning CDs or DVDs, is the built in one good enough? Do you need DVD audio support?

▶ *File types*—Most editors will accept many of the major sound file formats such as WAV, MP3, AIF, SND, AU, RAW, and so on. This may also include opening one file type and saving as another. Be sure the software you buy will work with all the file types you regularly use.

▶ *Built-in features*—Standard tools usually include editing commands such as cut, copy, and paste, and digital signal processing (DSP) operations such as amplify (gain and/or normalize), basic reverbs, equalization (EQ), and various filters. Do you need to time- or pitch-stretch? If so, will the built in features be enough, or will you require a stand-alone program or plug-in.

▶ *Plug-ins*—Plug-ins are programs that run within a host application, greatly expanding its functionality. Plug-ins come in various formats to enable it to communicate with the host program (see the discussion of these formats in Section 3 "Software Instruments" in Chapter 1). Does the program support the plug-in format you will want to use?

▶ *Support*—Does the program have a good built-in help file? Are there books, videos, Web sites that can provide additional technical support?

What to Consider when Buying Sequencing and Multi-track Recording Software

▶ *Audio or MIDI?* Does the program allow the format you need to record? How many tracks?

▶ *Views*—There are many different ways of viewing and editing your data. In addition to the regular notation window, look for a piano roll (graphical view), event list (MIDI data), arranger/ overview (move large chunks of music at once) and event controllers (graphically adjust MIDI data such as volume and pan).

▶ *Effects*—Does the program offer the MIDI and audio effects you will require? For example, can you shift the pitch of your singing, or add reverb to your recordings?

▶ *Plug-in support*—Will you want to add on effects such as pitch correction and auto-tune, surround sound or stereo expanders? If so, make sure that the software supports third-party plug-ins formats such as DirectX or VST.

▶ *Support*—Does the program have a good built-in help file? Are there books, videos, Web sites that can provide additional support? Are there local people available to help?

Section 2: List and Description of Software Options

There are a variety of software programs from which to select. This section will focus on exemplary programs more commonly used by music educators. A more extensive listing in this chapter's summary table clearly demonstrates that there are many other programs available that can achieve similar results. For more specific information about other titles, consult the Web sites listed.

Digital Audio/Waveform Editing

STEREO (2 CHANNEL)

Peak / Peak LE (Mac)
BIAS *Peak/Peak LE* are two of the most popular stereo audio editing, processing, and mastering programs for Mac OS. *Peak* is a powerful and flexible program that gives the user a large selection of digital-audio editing and processing options.

Peak can be used for numerous audio-editing/processing projects. Students could learn to import or record various types of audio files directly into *Peak*. Once these files have been captured, students will see the waveform editing screen and hear how various processors (EQ, reverb, compression, etc.) effect and alter the original audio file.

Students can digitize analog sources such as old vinyl records or cassette recordings directly into *Peak* by recording playback (in real time) via the computer's line input. Typically you would connect the analog source to the computer with a cable with 2 RCA jacks (stereo left and right) on one end and a single, 1/8" stereo phone jack on the other end. Be sure your computer's System Preferences are configured so that sound input is from the "Line In" port (rather than the internal microphone). Once these audio recordings are in *Peak*, students can then learn to use various editing tools and processors to clean up the signal by eliminating the noise ("pops" and "clicks") from the original recordings. Using the same program, students could then learn the techniques used in the mastering process of a recording project, and "burn" a final CD of the newly created master recording.

Peak is also capable of importing and playing back *QuickTime* movies and digital video (DV). Students could use *Peak* to edit the audio for various video projects, such as movies created with digital video applications (that is, *iMovie*).

Sound Studio (Mac)

Sound Studio is a very affordable Mac OS X application that allows you to record and edit two-channel audio. *Sound Studio* enables you to digitize vinyl records and analog tapes, record live audio, create customized mixes with various cross-fades, apply EQ with various digital effects, and save mastered audio files in several different digital audio file formats (**Fig. 1**).

FIG. 1: Applying a Fade In to a sound file with Sound Studio

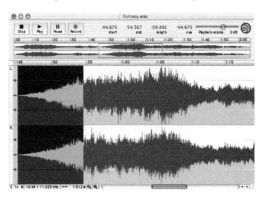

Sound Studio is compatible with several different third party audio interfaces. The program is capable of recording audio up to 24-bit / 96 kHz sample rate. In conjunction with Mac OS X's CoreAudio, the program features low-latency monitoring. *Sound Studio* can also automate recording and stopping based on using timers or audio levels.

Students can use *Sound Studio* for various types of audio editing projects. The program could also be used as a compositional or sound designing tool. Have students record simple acoustical sounds in *Sound Studio*. Afterwards, student can use various editing features to tweak and alter the original sound into something uniquely their own. The newly created sound can then be saved in one of several different audio formats, imported into a DAW program or a sampler and then become a unique part of the student's sequence or live performance.

Sound Forge/Sound Forge Audio Studio (Windows)

Perhaps the most complete and easy-to-use applications for Windows users are Sony's *Sound Forge* and *Sound Forge Audio*

Studio. Formerly Sonic Foundry products, these are now part of the Sony Media Software family.

Sound Forge 8 (Windows)

Sound Forge is a professional stereo audio editor with a massive feature list that includes a powerful set of audio processes and tools for recording, editing, effects processing, and creating streaming media. Like *Peak*, *Sound Forge* has all of the advanced features necessary for post-production with nondestructive editing, over 40 real-time effects and processes, and more than 200 presets that make manipulating audio both quick and effective.

The complete list of features is overwhelming, but includes normalization, cross-fading audio tracks, pan, time stretch, fixing uneven sound levels, trimming unwanted sections, synchronizing audio with video, support for MOV, AVI, WMA, MPEG-1, and MPEG-2 formats. VU meters make monitoring recording and playback easy. Using its Audio Restoration tools you can eliminate clicks, pops, and other noise from files and vinyl recordings. *Sound Forge* can save audio in many popular formats including WAV, MP3, Windows Media, *QuickTime*, and *RealMedia*.

The ability to create your own music loops and samples to use with the ACID family of software programs is a valuable feature for music composition. Extracting audio from a CD and built-in "track at once" CD burning makes it an excellent tool for creating short listening examples.

Sound Forge Audio Studio (Windows)

Audio Studio is a lite version of the more powerful *Sound Forge* stereo audio recording and editing program, but still includes more than 30 built-in effects and compatibility with more than a dozen popular audio and video formats. Many of the basic features of *Sound Forge 8* are available including CD audio extracting and built-in "track at once" CD burning. This program has more than enough power for use in most school applications and is a good choice for students to learn about and explore digital audio editing since it uses the same interface as *Sound Forge 8*, making the transition to the more powerful program a smooth process.

MULTI-TRACK

Audacity (Mac/Windows)

Audacity is *free* software! It was developed by a group of volunteers and distributed under the GNU General Public License published by the Free Software Foundation. It is a cross-platform program available for Windows 98, ME, 2000, & XP, Mac OS 9 and X, Linux, and UNIX.

While it started as a simple sound editor, it has evolved into a powerful editor that supports multi-track recording. Something not even *Peak* or *Sound Forge* allow. *Audacity*'s user interface is simple and the program includes many high-quality built-in effects, including Echo, Change Tempo, Reverb, Amplify, Echo, Fade In/Out, Reverse, Phaser, Bass Boost, Noise Removal, and also supports VST plug-ins.

Audacity's full feature set allows the user to record multiple tracks of live audio; convert tapes and records into digital recordings; import sound files, edit them, and combine them with other files or new recordings; export recordings in several common file formats; cut, copy, paste (with unlimited undo), splice, and mix sounds together; and change the speed or pitch of a recording. *Audacity* supports uncompressed audio standards such as WAV and AIFF in addition to OGG and MP3 files. A free MP3 encoder, *LAME*, is available for download on their website.

Although it can import and display MIDI files, they cannot be played or edited as of the current version. Another limitation of *Audacity* is that it does not offer the ability to extract audio from a CD or to burn a CD. These features commonly found in commercial products must be accomplished with third party software.

If your production is complex, *Audacity* might be impractical; but for simple recording, editing, and mixing of a few tracks, it is more than adequate. Whether you plug in an inexpensive microphone with a 1/8" stereo jack into your computer's mic input or use a digital mixer / interface and expensive condenser mic, you can easily record CD quality audio. The *Audacity* manual, a separate download, is very helpful and provides simple, non-technical information on the use of the program's features. This is an excellent program for teachers and students to start in the area of editing and recording audio with minimal financial investment.

Recording

MIDI SEQUENCING/DIGITAL AUDIO/LOOPING

Software in this category emulates a multi-track recording environment. One important distinction, however, is between MIDI tracks and audio tracks. Recording into audio tracks works basically like a digital tape recorder, where you are actually capturing an audio signal. However here you can record into multiple tracks and you get a lot of editing options after you record. MIDI tracks, on the other hand, are more similar to information on old-fashioned player piano rolls. MIDI data is not an audio signal, but rather instructions (data) describing the performance. Like a player piano roll, a MIDI track needs an instrument (such as a synth keyboard or tone module) to perform the stored data. A *sequence* is that string of data.

MIDI sequencing programs provide several methods of recording musical data onto one or more tracks. The most common method for entering data is real-time recording using a MIDI keyboard: A musician record-enables a track, sets a record tempo, and performs to a metronome click. A method available to the non-keyboardist is *step recording* (sometimes called *step entering*): the notes (which key, what duration) are entered one at a time by typing them into an event window or clicking them in with an insertion tool into either a piano roll or notation window. This method is a particularly valuable feature for use by students and teachers with limited keyboard skills, and of course whether music has been played in real or step time, it can be played back at any tempo you set. If your keyboard skills are weak, or your non-keyboardist students will be sequencing, you should definitely investigate how step recording is implemented in the software you are considering.

For many years now, those music educators familiar with software sequencers have tapped their potential for instructional chores. Using sequences of concert music in vocal and instrumental sectional rehearsals helps teachers (especially those not able to accompany at the keyboard) drill parts at various tempi. Muting and soloing tracks gives the instructor many options for reinforcing a student's part or seeing if they can stand on their own. Since a sequence can be started and stopped by the touch of a key anywhere in the song, many teachers appreciate the freedom they gain during playback to circulate around the room, demonstrate choreography, or even attend to an instrument repair! There are many,

many more ways a sequencer can help teach vocal, instrumental, and classroom music.

Software in this section can also give a great amount of creative power to students. Ideas for projects include recording spoken word with sound effects, arranging or orchestrating an existing file, arranging or composing a 12-bar blues, improvising and recording a percussion duet with a partner, or scoring a brief video clip. Again, only your imagination limits the number of captivating ideas to engage your students.

ENTRY LEVEL

GarageBand (Mac)

GarageBand is a fully self-contained music production application that combines several different features within a single program (**Fig. 2**). *GarageBand* may be categorized as a SSW (Soft Synth Workstation). It contains several different software-based synthesizer and sampler devices that can be programmed by its own internal MIDI sequencing. On the other hand, *GarageBand* cannot incorporate sounds from an external synth keyboard or tone generator. Of course, a synth keyboard may be used as a controller to input note data. There are additional software instruments that can be purchased through Apple to increase the number of software-based instruments. Since *GarageBand* is also capable of employing AU (Audio Units) instruments, there are numerous companies creating third party virtual instruments that can be implemented within *GarageBand*.

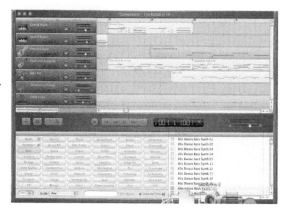

FIG. 2: *GarageBand's main window showing software instruments used (upper left), audio and MIDI track data (upper right), and loop browser (bottom).*

GarageBand has the ability of incorporating audio *loops* within the program. Loops are brief—generally 4 to 16 beats in length—

pattern-oriented recordings, such as drum beats, bass lines, guitar licks, or keyboard accompaniment patterns. These loops easily recognize user-defined tempos and keys from the sequencer settings. The loops will automatically adjust themselves to match tempos and keys. This aspect of the program would enable younger students to quickly create simple song ideas as they learn to create loop-based songs.

With the use of an audio interface, *GarageBand* is also capable of recording live audio. Though the Audio editing features are somewhat limited to basic features, the overall result of the recorded audio is of very good quality. This is yet another excellent tool which students could use to create their own musical productions. *GarageBand* can only use loops that are created specifically for *GarageBand*.

Students could learn to combine all the features of *GarageBand* (software based instruments, MIDI sequencing, audio loops, live recording) to create an entire musical production without ever leaving the one program. Students can then create a final master by exporting their song directly to *iTunes*. From there, students could then burn a master CD of their final recording without ever leaving the computer.

GarageBand2, released in spring 2005, includes some major improvements. Foremost among these is a traditional notation view and the ability to import standard MIDI files (SMFs) into a project. Although you still can't export *GarageBand* MIDI tracks as SMFs, these additions improve what is already an extremely useful and popular program for educators.

INTERMEDIATE LEVEL

Home Studio Version 2 (Windows)
The Cakewalk programs have long been favorite choices for both professionals and non-professionals using a Windows-based computer. *Home Studio* provides everything you need to turn your computer into a powerful multi-track recording studio. With support for real-time effects, software synths, MIDI effect plug-ins and ACID formatted audio loop technology, *Home Studio* has many of the advanced features of its big brother, *SONAR*, at a lower cost.

Some key features of *Home Studio* include 64 audio tracks and unlimited MIDI tracks; a graphic mixer with real-time audio and

MIDI effects; Plug-and-play DXi soft synths; loop creation; save in ACID-format, MP3, WAV, WMA and MIDI files; *ReWire* support to integrate *Home Studio Version 2* with *Project5, Kinetic, Reason*, and other *ReWire* synths; simultaneous multiple tracks recording with support for multi-channel audio cards; recording at up to 24-bit resolution and 96 kHz sampling rate; click and drag to paint drum tracks with new pattern brush and Drum Editing Grid; support for VST effects & instruments through Cakewalk VST Adapter (included); burning music directly to CD with the free *Pyro Express* CD maker and WAV ripper; and support for all Windows compatible audio.

Home Studio also provides a fast and effective way to create, edit, and dub soundtracks for digital video files. You can import Windows AVI or MPEG video into *Home Studio*, then make and edit music and sound effect soundtracks for classroom projects.

Logic Express (Mac)

Logic Express is a very comprehensive DAW (Digital Audio Workstation) program. Despite its "lite" status, this program boasts the MIDI and audio recording features of most high-end DAW programs. *Logic Express* is very capable of extensive MIDI/audio recording, playback, editing, and manipulations. The program also comes with a nice compliment of audio effect plug-ins, enabling the user to apply reverb, delay, EQ, etc. to any audio track. This program also comes bundled with a set of virtual instruments and a full-featured software-based sampler. *Logic Express* is also capable of utilizing Apple Loops for use in *GarageBand*. Spanning three music production categories, this program is a multi-track audio/MIDI recorder and editor, soft-synth workstation, and a Loop program. *Logic Express* is the underling to Apple's *Logic Pro*. The main difference between the two lies in the slightly limited number of virtual instruments and the number of DSP plug-ins that are provided in the *Express* version as compared to the *Pro* package.

This program is very attractive to educators due to its features, functions, and pricing. A variety of musical projects are possible with this program. Students can learn about MIDI programming, how to recording live audio, the use of virtual instruments, and combining all the different features in the creation of a musical production.

ADVANCED USE

SONAR 4 (Windows)

SONAR has been one of the most widely used music production programs on the Windows platform. Powerful recording, editing, composing and navigation tools in version 4 combined with surround sound and AV capability provides a powerful tool for use in the secondary classroom.

Some of the many features include recording, editing, arranging, and mixing unlimited tracks of audio and MIDI; support for any sampling rate (44.1, 48, 88.2, 96, 192, 384 kHz); loop-based composition, construction, and editing tools with ACID loop and MIDI clip support; support for DirectX and VST audio effects; 3 DXi soft synths; unlimited undo/redo with edit history; multiple views (arrange, drum editor, event list); loop construction; lyrics; markers; multi-track piano roll; staff notation; play list; soft synths; tempo list/graph, and video. *SONAR* has extensive, context-sensitive online help as well as a printed manual.

As with almost all sequencing programs that record MIDI, *SONAR* has some notation capabilities, but these are limited in scope. The use of a dedicated notation program, like those listed in Chapter 3 ("Music Notation Software") is highly recommended to achieve the best results for printed music.

Digital Performer (Mac)

Digital Performer (*DP*) has been one of the most popular Mac OS audio/MIDI sequencing programs for many years. It is recognized for its numerous features, powerful MIDI and audio editing functions, flexibility, and ease of use. *DP* is a professional level DAW program that is capable of managing and producing virtually any project. In addition to its audio and MIDI strengths, *DP* makes it easy to import QuickTime video into a project, allowing students to use it to create their own film score.

High-end DAW programs tend to be more challenging then their entry-level counterparts. However, *DP* utilizes a graphic user interface (GUI) that is very intuitive and clear. Most junior high aged students, and older, would find *DP* manageable with little effort needed in navigating the basic features of recording, editing, and playback of both MIDI and audio. Its Track Overview window resembles a multi-track recording studio (**Fig. 3**), its Transport

Controls those of a conventional cassette deck, and its graphic mixer emulates the real thing. Users can work any of several views: a Graphic Editor (bars on a grid representing musical events), a QuickScribe Editor (traditional staff notation), or an Event List (lines of code describing musical events). *DP* handles all major audio functions such waveform editing, digital signal processing, support for virtual instruments (it doesn't come bundled with its own software instruments, but many may be purchased and easily used as plug-ins), and importing loops.

FIG. 3: Digital Performer's Track Overview window emulates a multi-track recording environment.

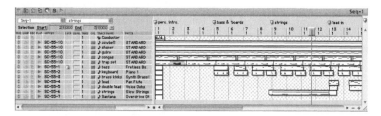

So much good can be said about this program! Teachers using *DP*, however, would tell you that the Track Overview window (which can't be enlarged) is a little hard on the eyes, and that *DP*'s Step-Record function is a little clumsy.

Programs such as *DP* offer the music educator the most options for music production projects ranging from basic composition to elaborate audio recordings and sound designing.

Cubase SE (Mac/Windows)

Steinberg provides a suite of full-featured sequencing programs the entry level *Cubase SE* to its programs for advanced users, such as *Cubase SX3* and *SL3*.

Cubase SE is a hybrid program that offers all of the key functions for recording and editing with up to 48 audio tracks, unlimited MIDI tracks, 24-bit/96 kHz audio resolution, support for up to 16 VST instruments, a complete set of audio and MIDI effects plug-ins, a video thumbnail track for arranging music for video and ReWire support. It is based on the same technology as *Cubase SX* and *SL,* and its affordable pricing makes it an excellent cross-platform program for educational settings with mixed platform labs or Mac OS labs in school with students using Windows at home.

Live 4 (Windows/Mac)

Live is a software package from Ableton that allows you to compose, record, remix, improvise and edit live performance. Beginning as an *ACID*-like program for the Mac, with the ability to automatically match loop tempos of different samples in real time, it has evolved in version 4 to incorporate MIDI sequencing and the use of virtual instruments, making it a more complete package.

Like many professional quality programs, it has an extensive feature list that includes on-the-fly editing; record unlimited takes on unlimited tracks; clip envelopes that allow complete control of volume, pitch, timing and effects for segments or notes within audio file; audition audio from a disk; cross fading; and built-in effects complete with automation.

Ableton includes a CD full of royalty-free loops in various styles. The entire collection is organized by instrument and category. Available for both the PC and Mac, it is a logical step up for *GarageBand* users and is a versatile DAW program with its MIDI sequencing, loop-based production, virtual instruments and built-in effects.

ProTools LE (Windows/Mac)

Pro Tools is probably the multi-track recording program most used in professional recording studios. *Pro Tools* was one of the first programs designed for the home-based computer. Although *Pro Tools LE* is capable of both audio and MIDI recording and editing, the program tends to be used primarily as a multi-track audio program. *Pro Tools LE* can record and play back up to 32 audio tracks at a sample rate of up to 96kHz. The program does enable the user to set the bit rate and sample resolution as desired.

Pro Tools LE is packaged with one of the following hardware interfaces: *M-Box*, *Digi 002* Rack, or *Digi 002* control surface/interface. The *M-Box* connects to the computer via USB while the other two utilize FireWire. *Pro Tools LE* comes bundled with several audio effect plug-ins. The *Digi 002* interfaces come with a few more plug-ins than does the *M-Box* package. There are numerous audio plug-ins available for the *Pro Tools* format that can be purchased from various developers.

Educators will find *Pro Tools LE* to be an excellent program for recording their ensembles. *Pro Tools* software, combined with Digidesign hardware, enables music directors and students to produce multi-track recordings of any-sized ensemble. Once an ensemble has been recorded, the program provides numerous features for mixing, editing, processing, and mastering a professional sounding recording.

Loop-Based Music Production

THE ACID FAMILY OF PROGRAMS

The *ACID* product family offers two levels of loop-based music production tools—*ACID Pro 5*, and *ACID Music Studio* software. Additionally, there is also a free program, *ACID Xpress,* and the low cost *SuperDuper MusicLooper* program for use by elementary students. These were formerly Sonic Foundry products that are now part of the Sony Media Software family. The *ACID* products allow you to select audio loops from an explorer window, drag them onto the program's track view, and arrange them into multiple-track projects, automatically matching the tempo and key of each loop.

ACID Xpress (Windows)

ACID XPress is a free program based on *ACID Pro.* Like other loop-based programs you can make your own original music by selecting pre-recorded loops and using your mouse to paint them in the desired track and measure.

You can download sample songs from http://mediasoftware. sonypictures.com, or use any of the Sony *Sound Series* libraries. A limitation of this version is that you can only create 10 full tracks. While you can save an unlimited number of songs in *ACID* format, you are limited to exporting up to 20 files to MP3 format. This is a great program to introduce students to loop-based music creation. Because it is free, students can download it at home and continue to explore making music and publish their songs for others to hear at www.acidplanet.com.

Super Duper MusicLooper (Windows)

This low cost program designed for young students, once installed, accesses over 700 varied audio loops located on the installation CD. A very student friendly interface offers a paint brush to draw loops and an eraser to edit. The creation of unlimited tracks; volume, key, and tempo controls; live audio recording with a microphone; and the ability to export songs as WAV and WMA files make this a powerful choice for introducing students to contemporary music making with technology. Students can also e-mail their compositions as MP3 files from directly within the program.

ACID Music Studio (Windows)

ACID Music Studio is a powerful intermediate-level, loop-based music creation program. Although excellent for creating music using loops, it has limited MIDI sequencing capabilities. *Music Studio* comes with more than 1,700 studio-quality, royalty free loops but live vocals, guitar, keyboard, or other sounds can be added to the pre-recorded loops by plugging in a microphone or instrument into your computer interface and clicking record.

This is a lite version of *ACID Pro,* but still allows you to create unlimited tracks and a large number of studio-quality effects are included. Many of the basic features of *ACID Pro* are included in this version making it a good choice for those on a limited budget.

Loop-based music creation is fun and easy to learn. Students can quickly create musical compositions in a wide range of genres and learn about form using the large library of high quality loops provided free with the program. Classical, country, jazz, blues, rock, rap, hip hop, and electronic are just a few of the many genre choices included in the program.

ACID Pro (Windows)

First introduced in 1998, *ACID Pro* created a totally new way to create music using loop technology which has become the industry standard. This is a professional level, loop-based composition program that makes it possible to produce music with an unlimited number of pre-recorded and live audio, as well as MIDI, tracks.

The feature list is rather large but includes support for VST effects, multiple VST instruments and *ReWire*, and 5.1 surround sound audio mixes. *ACID Pro* facilitates scoring your own videos and creating music for web sites and Flash animations. Its Media Manager technology provides ways to tag, organize, and search collection of loops quickly. *ACID Pro* can import and *beat map* (adapt tempo to project) complete songs imported from a CD and can save to a variety of formats including WAV, WMA, RM, AVI, and MP3.

Included with *ACID Pro* are more than 1,000 loops from the Sony *Sound Series* collection, an extensive loop library spanning a variety of musical styles—country, middle eastern, jungle, trance, hip-hop, rock, classical, ambient, reggae, and salsa.

FLStudio (Windows)

FL Studio, formerly known as *FruityLoops*, is a pattern-based sequencer (see **Fig. 4**) that uses more of a programming feel for music making as you create both drum and audio loops. As a software synthesizer and sequencer, this program is easy enough for beginners to learn, but you'll find tools meant for more serious music creation.

FIG. 4: FLStudio interface showing tracks and pattern blocks

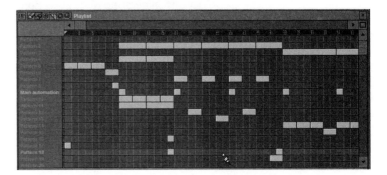

With *FL Studio* you create your songs in pieces (patterns) using the Step Sequencer and the Piano Roll view and then connect the loops together as a song in a Playlist window. Once the song is complete you can add a wide range of digital effects to your instruments including reverb, phaser, flanger, and so on.

FL Studio utilizes MIDI and DirectSound (internal mixing), with 16-bit, 44.1kHz stereo output. You'll also get support for VST plug-ins; individual panning, volume, pitch, mix, resonance, and cutoff on each note; digital effects such as fading, reverb, time stretching, audio envelopes, a new pad controller plug-in, and a *VideoPlayer* plug-in. The program allows for unlimited tracks of unlimited length. It is available in multiple versions from professional to consumer: *XXL*, *Producer Edition*, *FruityLoops Edition*, and *Express*.

This is a unique tool for students with limited keyboard skills to create music and provides a teacher with an opportunity to reach and teach students about music patterns, form, and sound in a contemporary environment.

MIDI ARRANGER

Band-in-a-Box (Windows/Mac)
Band-in-a-Box is considered an algorithmic program designed to help you quickly generate a MIDI accompaniment by typing in chord patterns and selecting one of hundreds of pre-set musical styles. It can be a good starting place for original compositions, generating rhythm section parts in unfamiliar styles, or to put together accompaniment parts for melodic song creation. Accompaniments created in *BIAB* can be saved as standard MIDI files (SMFs) and imported into most notation and sequencing programs for additional part creation. The Pro version provides all of the features of the program and over 135 styles of music. The MegaPak version provides all of the available styles numbering over a thousand.

You can record a melody using MIDI keyboard or a single audio track if you are using a Windows-based computer. Your recording can be enhanced using digital signal processing plug-ins such as reverb and compression and the program can also render the completed song as a stereo 16-bit, 44.1kHz WAV file and then burn it to a CD from within the program.

In the music classroom this program can be an excellent option when a pianist is not available or when you want to get out from behind the piano to walk around and assist students with posture and breathing. Choir and band directors can setup looping of chord patterns for students to practice improvisation or use it as a music-minus-one practice tool for piano, guitar, bass and drummers.

As a composition tool, *BIAB* provides opportunities to explore various chord patterns, learn about song form and style in the pop genre and using the Melodist feature, you can let the program generate an entire song with melody and chords. You can set the computer to make all of the choices for you, or you can have it generate a chord pattern for a melody that you import.

Sound Synthesis

SOUND DESIGN

Reason (Windows/Mac)
Reason falls into the category of a Soft Synth Workstation (SSW).

These SSW applications are an all inclusive software-based music system. These programs come with a full complement of software-based synthesizers, samplers, loop players, mixers, a MIDI-based sequencer, and various audio effect processors. All components can be integrated together for a very complete ready-to-go music system. These SSW programs are infinitely expandable within themselves and work efficiently with other DAW programs (via the *ReWire* technology). For the most part, these programs are only limited by the processor capacity of the host computer.

The educational implementations of SSW programs are vast. Various musical and technical projects can be employed by these applications. The study of synthesis and synthesis techniques are possible by the various virtual instruments used within the program. Some instruments emulate analog-based synthesizer topologies while others may range from FM synthesis to granular synthesis to digital sampling. All the instruments can be modified via real-time knob and slider controls.

Theses SSW programs also make excellent compositional tools. Having so many synthesizers and samplers within one program, along with a graphical-based sequencer, students can easily combine and record different instruments all within one program. No external sound module is needed. All that is needed to play and record the virtual instruments is a MIDI Controller and a MIDI interface.

DSP (Digital Signal Processing)

The use of DSP can provide ways to enhance an audio signal by adding echo, reverb, or equalization. More extreme application of DSP plug-ins can drastically alter a signal. Just as we might adjust the equalizer on our CD players to boost the bass or thin out the middle range to get a better quality of sound, most of the programs mentioned in this chapter have the ability to add other digital effects such as chorus, reverb, phaser, flange, and more. Electronic hardware such as digital mixers, digital audio workstations, and keyboard synthesizers also possess many of these same capabilities.

A better understanding of digital signal processing effects and their appropriate use can help students to understand sound, foster their critical listening skills, and even unlock their creativity. In his article, "A Return to Modernism," Scott Watson relates how students might learn to compose electronic art music in the tradition of mid-twentieth century pioneers like Vladimir Ussachevsky and

Otto Leuning using today's recording technology: Digital Signal Processing effects, with their ability to transform simple sounds into sonically rich and complex events, figures largely in such an undertaking.

Virtual Instruments

Virtual instruments include software synthesizers and samplers and allow sounds to be realized by programs residing on your computer, without the need for conventional synth keyboards or tone generators. For samplers, a brief sampled of a professional musician's sound is recorded and digitized; for synthesizers, various synthesis methods are emulated in the digital realm. When these virtual instruments function within another program (such as a software sequencer) they are called *plug-ins,* and the sounds must be converted to a format that the software can access. Virtual instruments that can perform on their own, without a host application, are called *standalone.*

The faster processors and larger storage capabilities of computers in recent years have made the use of software synthesis and sampling applications practical in home studio and school settings. The process demands a fast computer processor, lots of RAM, and a large storage capacity for the audio files. The minimum computer requirement can be as much as the following: Windows—2 gigabytes (GB) of free hard disc space, Windows XP, Pentium 4/Athlon 1.8GHz or better; Macintosh—OSX, G4 733MHz or better. This increased functionality has led to the appearance of more and more virtual instruments that are reasonably priced and available with General MIDI as well as more specific sound sets.

Readers interested in virtual instruments should consult the "Software Instruments" section of Chapter 1 ("Electronic Musical Instruments") for a thorough explanation and many recommendations for both plug-in and standalone applications. One of the most popular software instrument libraries in use in education, however, is the *Garriton Personal Orchestra.*

Garritan Personal Orchestra (Mac/Windows)

Garritan Personal Orchestra contains samples of all the major instruments in a symphony orchestra—strings, brass, woodwinds, and percussion, as well as a Steinway concert grand piano, a Stradivarius violin, Wurlitzer and Venus concert harps, Haynes flutes, Heckel bassoons, a Mustel celeste, a Rudolf von Beckerath concert pipe organ, a harpsichord, and many other exquisite instruments.

This library can be used with notation programs like *Finale* and *Sibelius* and music production programs to create a realistic sounding reproduction of any music score. This opens a new world to the critical listening skills we want our students to develop. The MIDI synthesized sounds of most soundcards and *QuickTime* produce inferior sound qualities. Virtual instruments now provide the quality of sound we have long needed.

MASTERING/BURNING (CD PRODUCTION)

The final step in the music production process is mastering and finally burning the finished product to CD. In today's digital world many of our students do this sort of thing on a regular basis, creating audio CDs selected from the MP3 collection on their *iPod* or other personal music player. Using *iTunes* or Windows *Media Player* on their computer they create a playlist of their favorite tunes to be burned. Prior to the actual burn they have the opportunity to add/change the EQ settings, normalize, cross-fade tracks and place a two second gap between tracks. It is a brave new world!

iTunes (Mac/Windows)

iTunes is a free computer program from Apple computer for both Mac OS X and Windows XP and 2000 computers that helps you to organize your CD collection (**Fig. 5**). With *iTunes* you can rip (extract) the audio from a CD and store it on your computer as either uncompressed AIFF, WAV, or Apple Lossless files or compressed formats like MP3 and AAC (Advanced Audio Coding). Using AAC or MP3, you can store more than 100 songs in the same amount of space as a single CD. Using the new Apple Lossless format you'll get the full quality of uncompressed CD audio using about half the storage space. You can listen to songs encoded in AAC or Apple Lossless formats in *iTunes* and on *iPods* that come with a dock connector, but if you plan to listen to your music using a different program or MP3 player, choose MP3.

FIG. 5: iTunes interface showing the source pane (left), music organization pane (top) and library pane (bottom).

iTunes will automatically import artist, album, and song information from the online CDDB online database. Once on your computer you can organize your music into playlists. You can buy music files by track or entire album from the online *iTunes Music Store*.

The *iPod* is a portable music player. The fidelity coming from this palm-sized player will astound you, whether connected to headphones for personal listening or to powered speakers (via a 1/8" stereo phone cable). When connected to your computer, it automatically updates your *iTunes* library with any new songs you've added. With *iTunes* you can also convert MIDI and WAV files to MP3 format.

For today's music educator, *iTunes* and *iPod* can be extremely useful. A playlist may contain CD tracks that go with instructional units from a text, or that accompany an ensemble's concert music. Transferred to an *iPod*, an entire CD library can be held in your hand!

Roxio Toast 6 (Mac) and Easy Media Creator 7.5 (Windows)
Roxio's *Toast* and *Easy Media Creator* are full-featured programs that have powerful tools to record to CD and DVD. You can burn or copy data, audio, photo, video CDs, and DVDs. Other features include converting LPs and cassettes to CD and removing any pops, clicks, and hiss present. You can also rip audio CDs to MP3, WMA, Ogg Vorbis (a new audio compression format), and WAV files, and

automatically import artist, album, and song information from the CDDB Web site.

These programs also provide many tools to edit audio CD tracks that include applying custom sound effects and normalizing the volume of multiple audio tracks taken from different sources before you burn your CD. (Normalizing is useful if a track was recorded at too low a level; the process raises the level of the highest peak to 0 dB and then adjusts the rest of the signal proportionally.) You also have the ability to adjust the volume, fade-in/fade-out, and stereo pan of any point in a track.

To complete your project, these programs will help you create personalized disc labels, DVD case inserts, and booklets from dozens of professionally designed templates; or, you can create your own with full-featured text editing and design tools. You can import photos from a hard drive, scanner or digital camera and place the text within the available label space. You can even print labels directly on disc with supported printers and burners.

Section 3: List and Description of Hardware Options

Depending upon your setup and the scope of your projects, you may also need hardware to complete your workstation. The choice of hardware depends upon your music production goals and may include an interface, cables, mixer, microphones, and/or hard disk recorders.

Interfaces

The physical connection of a MIDI keyboard to a many computers that have a USB port is accomplished by means of a USB MIDI interface. Most people have a simple setup requiring one MIDI in and one MIDI OUT connection. The MIDISport *UNO* (see **Fig. 6**) is a good choice for this setup because it incorporates the interface, USB cable, and MIDI cables into one unit. With other MIDI interfaces listed you would need to purchase two MIDI cables to complete the connections. The USB cable comes standard with the purchase of the interface. A reliable 2-IN and 2-OUT MIDI USB MIDI interface is the *FreeStyle USB* by Mark of the Unicorn (MOTU).

FIG. 6: MIDISport Uno MIDI interface

If recording audio is your prime goal then one of the audio interfaces would be your choice. If you want the ability to record both MIDI and audio, one of the hybrid audio/MIDI interfaces is necessary unless you are willing to settle for the your quality of sound recorded via your computer's built-in or external microphone. For more information regarding the implementation of MIDI on keyboards, including the use of MIDI interfaces, consult the "Electronic Keyboard Features" section of Chapter 1, "Electronic Musical Instruments."

Portable/Direct-to-Disk Recorders

If you need to record your ensembles "in the field" or move room to room in your school then portability and a quick easy setup is going to be important. You may want to consider a portable recorder like the Edirol *R-1* (**Fig. 7**) or SuperScope *CDR300*.

FIG. 7: Edirol R-1

The Edirol records to a 64MB memory card, has built-in effect processors and allows for data transfer to a computer for post-production editing. The SuperScope (and a similar device by Marantz, the *Pro CDR300*) unit records direct to CD-R or CD-RW in real time and has XLR and phone jack connectors for high-quality microphones.

Many ensemble directors use the *SuperScope* for rehearsal and concert recording and report their pleasure with its performance. The *SuperScope PSD300* dual drive CD recorder has some extra features such as allowing the user to adjust playback tempo (without changing the pitch) and two trays for copying CDs.

Digital Audio Workstations (DAW)

Digital audio workstations are powerful, self-contained units with many of the features and capabilities discussed in the software programs. The Korg *D1600mk11* and Roland *VS-2000CD* (see **Fig. 8**) record to large 40GB hard drives and can mix, master, and burn a final project to CD all within the unit itself.

FIG. 8: Roland VS2000CD

Microphones

High-quality microphones with XLR connectors from established companies like Shure, Sennheiser, AKG, and Blue will complete your recording studio setup. Two common types of microphones are dynamic and condenser.

Dynamic microphones are the easiest to use, the least expensive, and are often used by professionals in both live and studio environments to pick-up individual instruments and vocals. The Shure *SM57* and *SM58* are two excellent choices.

Condenser microphones are the best available and the most expensive. Unlike dynamic microphones, condenser microphones require a power source to run. Power is either drawn from a battery within the microphone or by phantom power. Phantom power comes through the mic cable to the mic from a source like a mixer or hard disk recorder. Consider condenser microphones for concert recording for ensembles.

Mixers

The heart of any studio is the mixer, which can take two or more audio signals (like multiple microphones or line inputs) and mix them for balance, set recording levels, add digital effects, EQ, and assign pan position, etc. A mixer as simple as the Behringer *UB802* would be a good choice for a limited two-microphone input setup. More advanced setups requiring inputs for four to 16 microphones would require something like the Mackie *1604-VLZ Pro* (**Fig. 9**).

FIG. 9: Mackie 1604-VLZ Pro mixing board

Section 4: Using Music Production Tools with Students

The use of music production tools with students is an excellent way to address composition, arranging, physics of sound, and development of critical listening skills. It takes time to learn and gain confidence with higher-end applications. There is no substitute for experience and learned skills using these tools. Here are a few thoughts and resources to help you get started.

Begin Slow and Small

Find out which of your students are tech-savvy, and ask them if they are involved in recording at home. Use their experience as resource assistants in troubleshooting issues. You may be amazed at how knowledgeable and skilled they are with the technology. Check to see if there are any parents in your school involved in recording, and see if they would offer to work with you and your students.

Take one of the TI:ME courses involving the use of music production tools, such as *Basic Skills: Electronic Instruments, MIDI Sequencing, and Notation* (1A); 2A—*Advanced Sequencing* (2A); or *Digital Audio* (2B). Also visit www.berkleemsuic.com and look into taking one of their many online courses such as *Desktop Music Production* or *Producing Music With Pro Tools*.

Book Resources

Two book resources that can provide practical teaching applications of technology are the *Strategies for Teaching Technology* edited by Sam Reese, Kim McCord, and Kim Walls (published by MENC) and *Technology Strategies for Music Education, 2nd edition* (published by TI:ME, distributed by Hal Leonard).

Strategies for Teaching Technology includes a number of music production lesson plans organized by the MENC national standards; these lessons could be easily adapted for all levels. The *Technology Strategies for Music Education* book contains 31 music production strategies listed by level and organized by the MENC National Standards as well.

Also consider David Franz's *Recording and Producing in the Home Studio: A Complete Guide* and Tom Rudolph and Vincent Leonard's *Recording in the Digital World: Complete Guide to Studio Gear and Software* (both Berklee Press). These books are packed with detailed information to help you further with making the best choices for your studio needs.

A membership in TI:ME offers you free subscriptions to four valuable magazines: *Music Education Technology, Electronic Musician, Keyboard Magazine*, and *Mix*. These publications often feature articles relating to music production and provide a wealth of information including product reviews, user tips, tutorials, and spotlights on the use technology in music programs at many levels.

Section 5: Reference Materials

Books

Anderton, Craig. *Home Recording for Musicians*. New York: Amsco Publications, 2004.

Franz, David. *Producing in the Home Studio with Pro Tools (Second Edition)*. Boston, MA: Berklee Press, 2005.

Franz, David. *Recording and Producing in the Home Studio: A Complete Guide*. Boston, MA: Berklee Press, 2005.

Garrigus, Scott. *SONAR 4 Power*. Cincinnati: Muska & Lipman, 2004.

Milstead, Ben. *Home Recording Power*. Cincinnati: Muska & Lipman, 2001.

Purse, Bill. *Home Recording Basics*. Miami: Warner Bros. Publications, 1998.

Rudolph, Tom and Leonard, Vincent. *Recording in the Digital World: Complete Guide to Studio Gear and Software*. Boston, MA: Berklee Press, 2001.

Wilkerson, Scott and Oppenheimer, Steve. *Anatomy Of A Home Studio: How Everything Really Works, From Microphones To MIDI*. Emerysville: EM Books, 1998.

PropellerHead. *Teaching Music With Reason: A Curriculum for the Classroom Teacher*. PropellerHead, 2004. (Download at www.propellerheads.se)

Shure. *Audio Systems Guide for Music Educators*. (Download at www.shure.com/booklets/default.asp)

M-Audio. *Choosing & Using Microphones*. (Download at www.MIDIman.de/files/pdf/Record_Now_Mic.pdf)

Articles

Fein, Michael. "Teaching Song Form with Audio Software." (http://metmagazine.com/mag/teaching_song_form/)

Frankel, James. "Recording the future at Dr. Phillips High." (http://metmagazine.com/mag/recording_future_dr/)

"*GarageBand* Tutorial for *Band-in-a-Box* on a Macintosh" (www.pgmusic.com/garagebandtutorial.htm)

Miller, Dennis; Smithers, Brian; and Yelton, Geary. "Sequencing on a Shoestring."*Electronic Musician*, Vol. 21, No. 9 (September), 2005.

Rudolph, Thomas E. *"Band-in-a-Box: Makes Great Computer Music 'Too Easy!'"* (www.lentine.com/articles/bandinabox.htm)

Rudolph, Tom. "Using your Mac to Convert *Band-in-a-Box* Files to Burn to a CD." (www.pgmusic.com/article_convert.htm)

Rudolph, Tom. "Your New Accompanist." (http://metmagazine.com/mag/new_accompanist)

Vail, Mark. *"Reason* in Class." (http://metmagazine.com/mag/reason_class)

Watson, Scott. "A Return to Modernism: Teaching Electronic Art Music Composition with Today's Recording Technology," *Music Education Technology*, Feb 1, 2005.

Watson, Scott. "Producing Music and Smiles at McCallum High." (http://metmagazine.com/mag/producing_music_smiles/)

Watson, Scott. "Sequence-stration." (http://metmagazine.com/mag/sequencestration)

Video

Making Music Tools. *GarageBand Video Tutorial*—Beginners. (www.musicmakingtools.com/)

Making Music Tools. *GarageBand Video Tutorial*—Pro. (www.musicmakingtools.com/)

Making Music Tools. *Songwriting for GarageBand.* (www.music-makingtools.com/)

Muro, Don. *The Art of Sequencing.* JD Wall Publishing.

Internet Resources

Berklee Music Online (www.berkleemusic.com)

Desktop Music Production for Mac. Michael Bierylo and David Mash

Desktop Music Production for PC. Michael Bierylo, Steve MacLean, and David Mash

Sound Design for the Electronic Musician. Michael Bierylo and David Mash

Sampling and Audio Production. David Doms

Pro Tools 101. Digidesign and Andy Edelstein

Producing with Pro Tools. David Franz

Mixing and Mastering with Pro Tools. Jeff Baust

Production Workshop. Mitchell Benoff

MIDI Sequencing Basics. Michael Moss

MIDI Sequencing Intermediate. Michael Moss

Making Music with GarageBand. Stefani Langol

Producing Music with Reason. Erik Hawkins

Producing Music with Digital Performer. Benjamin Newhouse

Producing Music with Ableton Live. Kai Turnbull

Recording and Producing in the Home Studio. David Franz

Helpful Web Sites

HomeRecording.com (www.homerecording.com)

Norton Music, the #1 producer of Band-in-a-Box aftermarket products (www.nortonmusic.com)

The Recording FAQ (www.phys.tue.nl/people/etimmerman/RecordingFAQ.html)

Professional Microphone Solutions (www.dpamicrophones.com/)

MiniDisc.org, the MiniDisc Community Portal (www.minidisc.org/)

SAE Reference Material Center (www.saecollege.de/reference_material/index.html)

Software/Hardware Resources

Ableton (www.ableton.com)
Adobe (www.adobe.com)
AKG (www.akg.com)
Apple (www.apple.com)

Audacity (http://audacity.sourceforge.net/)
Audio Technica (www.audio-technica.com)
Behringer (www.behringer.com)
Bias (www.bias-inc.com)
Blue Microphones (www.bluemic.com)
Boss (http://rolandus.com)
Cakewalk (www.cakewalk.com)
DigiDesign (www.digidesign.com)
Edirol (www.edirol.com)
FeltTip (www.felttip.com)
FLStudio (www.e-officedirect.com/FLStudio/English/frames.html)
Garritan (www.garritan.com)
G-Vox (www.gvox.com)
Intuem (http://intuem.com)
Korg (www.korg.com)
Marantz (www.d-mpro.com)
Mark of the Unicorn (www.motu.com)
M-Audio (http://m-audio.com)
Native Instruments (www.native-instruments.com)
Neumann (www.neumann.com)
PG Music (www.pgmusic.com)
PropellerHead (www.propellerheads.se)
Roland (http://rolandus.com)
Roxio (www.roxio.com)
Sagan Technologies (http://sagantech.biz)
Sennheiser (www.sennheiserusa.com)
Shure (www.shure.com)
Sony Media Software (www.sonyMedia Software.com)
SoundTree (www.soundtree.com)
SuperScope Technologies (www.superscopetechnologies.com)
Steinberg (www.steinberg.de)
Tascam (www.tascam.com)

Music Production*
SOFTWARE
AUDIO EDITORS

Manufacturer	Product	Web Site	Entry	Advanced	Platform	Minimum System Requirements
Adobe	Adobe Audition 1.5	www.adobe.com/products/audition/main.html		X	Windows	Windows 2000, XP, 400MHz, 64MB RAM
HairerSoft	Amadeus II	www.hairersoft.com	X		Mac	Mac OS 8.6 and later
Sourceforge	Audacity 1.2.3	http://audacity.sourceforge.net/	X		Mac/Windows/Linux	Windows 98, ME, 2000, XP, or later, 64MB RAM, 300MHz processor; Mac OS 9.0 or later, 64MB RAM, 300MHz processor
Bias-Inc	Peak	www.bias-inc.com/products/peak/		X	Mac	Mac OS X 10.2/10.3, 256MB RAM
Bias-Inc	Peak LE	www.bias-inc.com/products/peakLe/	X		Mac	Mac OS 10.3.9 minimum, G3, G4 & G5, iBook or PowerBook, 400MHz processor, 256MB RAM, 80MB QuickTime 6.0 or later
Sony	Sound Forge 8	http://mediasoftware.sonypictures.com/products/showproduct.asp?PID=961		X	Windows	Windows 98SE, ME, 2000, XP, 200MHz, 32MB RAM
Sony	Sound Forge Audio Studio 8	http://mediasoftware.sonypictures.com/products/showproduct.asp?PID=945	X		Windows	Windows 98SE, ME, 2000, XP, 200MHz, 32MB RAM
FeltTip	SoundStudio 2.1.1	www.felttip.com/products/soundstudio/	X		Mac	Mac OS X 10.2.8 (Jaguar) G20 or later, 400MHz or faster; PowerPC G3, G4, or G5 processor; QuickTime 6.0.2 or later
Steinberg	WaveLab5	www.steinberg.de/Category_sb0a02-1.html		X	Windows	Pentium/AMD III 500MHz, 256RAM, Windows XP/2000

Number of Audio Tracks	Record Resolution (word length in bits)	Sampling Rates (KHz)	Audio File Formats Supported	Plug-in Formats Supported	Special Features	List Price
128	32-bit	192+ kHz	WAV, AIFF, MP3, MP3PRO, WMA, CEL, AU, VOX, PCM	DirectX, VST	Stereo and multitrack editor, real-time effects and EQ, looping, data analysis, mastering, batch process	$299
2	16, 24-bit	192 kHz	AIFF, AIFC, FLAC, WAV, MP3, mp4, m4a, AAC, CAF, Ogg Vorbis, QuickTime, AVI, SoundDesigner II, u-law	DirectX, VST	Multiple undoing, fadings, transitions, normalization, split files, join several files together, real-time spectral analysis and oscilloscope, several sound generators	$30
Unlimited	16, 24, 32-bit	192 kHz	AIFF, WAV, MP3, MPEG-4, OG VORBIS, AU	VST	Record live audio; convert tapes and records into digital recordings or CDs; edit Ogg Vorbis, MP3, and WAV sound files; cut, copy, splice, and mix sounds together; hange the speed or pitch of a recording	Free
2	32-bit	192 kHz	AIFF, SDII, WAV, MP3, MPEG-4, SND, AU, JAM image, SONIC AIFF, PARIS (.PAF)	VST, AU	ImpulseVerb sample-based reverb, Direct Red Book CD burning; includes JAM 6 and Sound FX Machine LT	$600
2	24-bit	192 kHz	AIFF, SDII, WAV, MP3, MPEG-4, SND, AU, JAM image, SONIC AIFF, PARIS (.PAF)	VST, AU	Supports QuickTime/DV clip synchronization; play virtual instruments from virtual keyboard, Mac keyboard, or external MIDI keyboard during stereo audio playback.	$130
2	24-bit, 32-bit	192 kHz	WAV, MP3, AIFF, AVI, MOV, WMV, RM, OGG, PCA, WMA, AU/SND, DIG/SD, RAW, MPEG-1&2, VOX	DirectX		$300
2	24-bit, 32-bit	192 kHz	WAV, MP3, AIFF, AVI, MOV, WMV, RM, OGG, PCA, WMA, AU/SND, DIG/SD, RAW, MPEG-1&2, VOX	DirectX	Real-time nondestructive editing	$70
2	24-bit	192 kHz	AIFF, AIFF-C with compression including IMA 4:1, AAC, MP3 (importing only), Sound Designer II, WAV (PCM only)	VST		$50
2	32-bit	384 kHz	WAV, AIFF, AU, RAW, SDII, Paris 24-bit, uLaw, MP3, Sun/Java, more	VST, DirectX, WaveLab	DVD authoring, surround support, Audio Montage multi-track editing, video thumbnail, audio anaylsis	$699

Manufacturer	Product	Web Site	Entry	Intermediate	Advanced	MIDI	Audio	Looping	Platform	Minimum System Requirements
Media Software	Acid Music Studio 5	http://mediasoftware.sonypictures.com/Products/ShowProduct.asp?PID=926		X		X	X	X	Windows	Windows 2000, XP, 500MHz, 128MB RAM
Media Software	Acid Pro 5	http://mediasoftware.sonypictures.com/Products/ShowProduct.asp?PID=928			X	X	X	X	Windows	Windows 98SE, ME, 2000, XP, 300MHz CPU, 64MB RAM (128MB recomm.)
Media Software	Acid Xpress	http://mediasoftware.sonypictures.com/download/step2.asp?DID=551	X				X	X	Windows	Windows 98SE, ME, 2000, XP, 300MHz CPU, 64MB RAM (128MB recomm.)
PG Music	Band In A Box	www.pgmusic.com/products_bb.htm	X	X		X	X	X	Mac/Windows	Windows 2000, XP; Mac OS X 10.2
Steinberg	Cubase SE	www.steinberg.de/ProductPage_sb4b2a.html?Product_ID=2124&Langue_ID=4		X		X	X	X	Mac/Windows	Windows 2000, XP; Mac OS X 10.2
Steinberg	Cubase SX3	www.steinberg.de/ProductPage_sb51ba.html?Product_ID=2442&Langue_ID=4			X	X	X	X	Mac/Windows	Windows XP, Mac OS X
Bias-Inc	DeckLE 3.5	www.bias-inc.com/products/deckLe/	X	X			X		Mac	Mac OS 8.6 and later, PowerPC, G3, G4, or G5 desktop Apple Macintosh or PowerBook, 266MHz processor, 64MB RAM, 10MB, QuickTime 3.0 or later
Bias-Inc	Deck 3.5	www.bias-inc.com/products/deck/features.html			X		X		Mac	Mac OS 8.6 and later, PowerPC, G3, G4, or G5 desktop Apple Macintosh or PowerBook, 266MHz processor, 64MB RAM, 10MB, QuickTime 3.0 or later
MOTU	Digital Performer 4.5	www.MOTU.com/products/software/dp/				X	X	X	Mac	Mac OS X
Image Line Software	FLStudio	www.fruityloops.com/		X		X	X		Windows	Windows 9X, 2000, XP
Apple	GarageBand 2	www.apple.com/ilife/garageband/	X	X		X	X	X	Mac	Mac OS X 10.2.6 or later, 600MHz G3 CPU, 256MB RAM, QuickTime 6.4 or later, 1024 x 768 display (minimum), DVD drive
Cakewalk	Home Studio 2	www.cakewalk.com/Products/HomeStudio/default.asp	X	X		X	X	X	Windows	Windows 98/SE/ME/2000/XP
Intuem	Intuem RW	http://intuem.com/main/index.html	X	X		X	X		Mac	Mac OS X version 10.2.6 (Jaguar) and later, G3 Macintosh, 500MHz or faster, 512MB RAM
Ableton	Live 4	www.ableton.com/index.php?main=live	X	X		X	X	X	Mac/Windows	Windows 98, 2000, XP; Mac OS 9.2+ OS X 10.1.5+
Apple	Logic Express 7	www.apple.com/logicexpress/	X	X		X	X	X	Mac	Mac OS 9, OS X
Apple	Logic Pro 7	www.apple.com/logic/			X	X	X	X	Mac	Mac OS 9, OS X
Gvox	MastertracksPro 6.8.3	http://www.gvox.com/	X	X	X	X	X		Mac/Windows	Windows 98, ME, 2000, XP; Mac OS 9.x and Mac OSX 10.2 or higher
Sagan Tech	Metro 6	http://sagantech.biz/metro/metro6.htm			X	X	X		Mac	Mac OS 9.2.1, OS X, 10.2, 400Mhz processor, 64MB RAM, 10MB
Sagan Tech	Metro 6LX	http://sagantech.biz/metro/metro6lx.htm		X		X	X		Mac	Mac OS 9.2.1, OS X, 10.2, 400Mhz processor, 64MB RAM, 10MB
Sagan Tech	Metro 6SE	http://sagantech.biz/metro/metro6se.htm	X			X	X		Mac	Mac OS 9.2.1, OS X, 10.2, 400Mhz processor, 64MB RAM, 10MB
PG Music	PowerTracks Pro Audio 9	www.pgmusic.com/powertracks.htm		X		X	X		Windows	Windows 9x/NT/2000/2002/XP
DigiDesign	ProTools HD	http://www.digidesign.com/products/hd/menu.cfm#			X	X	X		Mac/Windows	Windows XP, Mac OS 10.2 and later
DigiDesign	ProTools LE	http://www.digidesign.com/products/le/		X	X	X	X		Mac/Windows	Windows XP, Mac OS 10.2 and later
DigiDesign	ProTools M-Powered	http://www.digidesign.com/products/le/		X					Mac/Windows	Windows XP, Mac OS 10.2 and later
Cakewalk	SONAR 4 Studio Edition	www.cakewalk.com/Products/SONAR/default.asp			X	X	X	X	Windows	Windows 2000/XP
Cakewalk	SONAR 4 Producer Edition	www.cakewalk.com/Products/SONAR/default.asp			X	X	X	X	Windows	Windows XP/2000
Media Software	Super Duper Music Looper	http://mediasoftware.sonypictures.com/products/showproduct.asp?pid=535	X				X	X	Windows	Windows 98SE, Me, 2000, XP Home, or XP Professional, 133MHz processor, 10MB hard-disk space, 32MB RAM, Windows-compatible sound card

Editing Views	Graphic Faders	Audio Effects	Dynamics Processing	DSP Plug-in Formats	Special Features	List Price
Piano roll, track, envelopes, and events	No	Delays, dynamics, de-esser, overdrive, lange, phase, rotary, chorus, reverb	Yes	VST, DirectX	1,000 music loops, Disc-at-once CD burning, Chopper editing tool	$70
Piano roll, track, envelopes, and events	No	Delays, dynamics, de-esser, overdrive, lange, phase, rotary, chorus, reverb	Yes	VST, DirectX	5.1 surround mixing, ASIO, MIDI piano-roll editing, alternate time signatures, Yamaha OPT support	$500
Track, envelopes, and events	No	No	No			Free
Chord, event, piano roll, notation	No	Reverbs, delays, chorus, pan	No	VST, DirectX	Soloist, melodist, CD burning, ear-training, lyrics	$88
Key, list, drum, score	Unlimited	Reverbs, delays, chorus, flange, more	Yes	VST, DirectX	Special bundle includes Virtual Guitarist SE, The Grand SE, Groove Agent SE, D'Cota SE, HALion SE	$299
Key, piano roll, list, drum, logical, sample, part, loop, score	Unlimited	Delays, dynamics, de-esser, overdrive, quadra fuzz, flange, phase, rotary, chorus, symphonic, reverb	No	VST, DirectX	Audio warp, play order track, inplace editor, MIDI device maps, external plug-ins, freeze, surround	$799
Track, wave, video, envelopes, and events	12	Gain, EQ, Delay 1 & 2, Chorus	Yes	9 built-in plus over 20 VST effects		$99
Track, wave, video, envelopes, and events	64	Gain, EQ, Delay 1 & 2, Chorus	Yes	9 built-in plus over 20 VST effects		$399
Track overview, graphic, drum editor, event list, notation	Unlimited	50+ incl. plug-ins, EQ, dynamics, filters, reverbs, etc.; MasterWorks 64-bit premium series	Yes	TDM, MAS, AU, Premiere	Supports Pro Tools HD as DAE host, supports 3rd-party AU/MAS plug-ins, virtual inst.	$795
Piano roll, track, envelopes and events	69	VST(i), DX(i), Buzz & FL	Yes	VST(i), DX(i), Buzz & FL	Speech synth, drum machine	$149
Track, notation, piano roll, tempo	Unlimited	Virtual instruments, 50+ real-time effects	Yes	VST	Share files with Logic and iTunes, import audio	$80
Piano roll, SysEx, event, notation, console, studioware, tempo, markers	Unlimited	Reverb, chorus, flange, delay, parametric EQ	Yes	DirectX, DXi 2.0	24-bit/96 kHz support, ReWire 2.0, ASIO hardware support, multiport drum grid editing	$129
Track, event, audio, notation, piano roll, tempo	Unlimited	Reverbs, delays, chorus, flange, more	Yes	VST	24-bit/96 kHz support, ReWire 2.0	$80
Arranger, session grid, piano roll, clip/waveform view	Unlimited	EQ, reverb, delay, filtering, bit reduction	Yes	VST, AU	Real-time time stretching, virtual instrument hosting, flexible routing, drag and drop sampling	$499
Event list, matrix, hyper, score	Unlimited	28 real-time effects	Yes	VST (OS 9), AU (OS X)	3-step undo/redo, track-based automation, 8 stereo busses, integrated stereo sample editor	$299
Event list, score, matrix, hyper, transform	Unlimited	Virtual instruments, 50+ real-time effects	Yes	TDM, VST (OS 9), AU (OS X)	Unlimited undo/redo, freeze tracks, advanced automation, open TL, OMF support	$999
Track, piano roll, event, notation	1		No			$100
Tracks, audio, mixer, events, bars, roll notation, SysEx editor	99	Virtual instruments, 50+ real-time effects		VST		$330
Tracks, audio, mixer, events, bars, roll notation, SysEx editor	48	Virtual instruments, 50+ real-time effects		VST		$135
Tracks, audio, mixer, events, bars, roll notation, SysEx editor	32	Virtual instruments, 50+ real-time effects		VST		$69
Tracks, audio, mixer, events, bars, roll notation, SysEx editor	Yes	Comp, gate, dist, reverb, echo, chorus, flanger, ring mod, trem, tone, EQ, exciter	Yes	Proprietary, DirectX	Detect chords from MIDI file, export to WMA and MP3, CD-RW software, guitar tuner	$49
						$1,000
					Need the M-box	$400
						$340
Track and piano roll, console view, navigator view	Unlimited	TTS-1 DXi with authentic Roland sounds	Yes	TTs-I	Universal Bus Architecture, VST support POW-r dithering	$479
Track layers and piano roll	No	31 audio effects 4 DXi soft synths, 14 MFX	Yes	DirectX VST audio, DXi and VSTi soft synths, and ReWire 1.0 & 2.0	POW-r dithering, MPEX time stretching, multiformat surround mixing	$959
			No		"Pick, paint, and play" style interface; 10 complete demo songs; unlimited tracks; 706 music loops; volume, key, and tempo controls; audio recording (microphone needed); easy song sharing via e-mail, WAV, or WMA export; online help; Quick Start manual	$20

SOUND SYNTHESIS

Manufacturer	Product	Web Site	Entry	Intermediate	Advanced	MIDI	Audio	Looping	Platform	Minimum System Requirements	Special Features	List Price
Cycling 74	Max/MSP	www.cycling74.com/products/maxmsp.html			X				Mac/Windows	Windows XP, Mac OS X	Max/MSP is a graphical programming environment, which means you create your own software using a visual toolkit of objects and connect them together with patch cords.	$495
PropellerHeads	Reason	www.propellerheads.se/			X	X	X	X	Mac/Windows	Windows XP/2000 or later, Intel Pentium III 300MHz or better, 256MB RAM, 2GB free hard disk space; Mac OS X 10.2 or later, G3, G4, or G5 processor, 256MB RAM, 2GB	Synthesizers, samplers, drum machine, REX file loop player, mastering tools, mixer, vocoder, effects, pattern sequencer	$500

MIXING/MASTERING/BURNING (CD Production)

Manufacturer	Product	Web Site	Entry	Intermediate	Advanced	Audio Input Formats	Graphic Input Formats	Video Input Formats	Audio Output Formats	Graphic Output Formats
Roxio	Easy Media Creator 7.5	www.roxio.com/en/products/emc75/index.jhtml	X	X	X	Audio CD, MP3, WAV, WMA, Dolby Digital, Ogg Vorbis, FLAC, MPEG-1/2	JPG, PNG, TIFF, BMP	AVI, DV-AVI, MPEG-1/2/4, VOB, DivX, XviD, MOV, WMV	Audio CD, MP3, WAV, WMA, Dolby Digital, Ogg Vorbis, FLAC, MPEG-1/2	JPG, PNG, TIFF, BMP
Apple	iTunes	www.apple.com/itunes/	X	X		AIFF, MP3, WAV, AAC, AU, MOV, Apple LossLess, MIDI, CDA, Audio book format.m4b	Any QuickTime image format, BMP, GIF, JPG, PICT, PDF, TIFF, PNG, or Photoshop	QuickTime-compatible videos, mov, mp4	Audio CD, MP3, WAV, WMA, MPEG4	
Roxio	Toast 6 Titanium	www.roxio.com/en/products/toast/index.jhtml	X	X	X	Any QuickTime audio format, AIFF, MP3, WAV, AAC, Dolby AC3, AU, MOV, MID	Any QuickTime image format, BMP, GIF, JPG, PICT, PDF, PSD, PNG, TIFF	Any QuickTime video format, AVI, MOV, MPEG1, MPEG2, MPEG4, DV, VOB, muxed content, iMovie project, Final Cut Pro/Express	Audio CD, MP3 Disc, DVD Music Album, Enhanced Audio CD, Mixed Mode	JPG, PNG, TIFF, BMP
Microsoft	Windows Media Player 10	www.microsoft.com/windows/windowsmedia/mp10/default.aspx	X	X		AIFF, MP3, WAV, AU, SND, CDA, WMA, M3U		MPEG, MPG, MPE, M1V, MP2, MPv2, MP2V, MPA WMV, WVX, DVR-MS	MP3, WAV, WMA, MPEG4, CDA	

HARDWARE
MIDI INTERFACES

Manufacturer	Product	Web Site	Entry	Intermediate	Advanced	MIDI I/O	Audio	Minimum System Requirements	Special Features	List Price
Creative	SoundBlaster MIDI Adapter	http://us.creative.com/products/product.asp?category=1&subcategory=16&product=251&nav=features	X	X	X	1/1	N/A	Windows	One piece cable with connection to game port on the sound card	$20
MOTU	FastLane USB	www.MOTU.com/products/midi/fastlane_usb/body.html/en	X	X	X	2/2	N/A	Mac/Windows	5 colors and charcoal Thru button passes MIDI In to Out w/ computer off	$79
M-Audio	MIDISport 1x1 USB	http://m-audio.com/products/en_us/MIDISPORT1x1-main.html	X	X	X	1/1	N/A	Mac/Windows	USB cable included, Mac/PC	$70
M-Audio	MIDISport 2x2 USB	http://m-audio.com/products/en_us/MIDISPORT2x2-main.html	X	X	X	2/2	N/A	Mac/Windows	USB cable included, Mac/PC	$90
M-Audio	Uno USB	http://m-audio.com/products/en_us/Uno-main.html	X	X	X	1/1	N/A	Mac/Windows	Compact and portable, bus-powered, with built-in cable connections	$50

Video Output Formats	Video Disc Formats	Recordable Media Formats	Platform	Minimum System Requirements	Special Features	List Price
AVI, DV-AVI, MPEG-1/2/4, VOB, DivX, XviD, MOV, WMV	DVD, Video CD (VCD), Super Video CD (SVCD), Mini DVD	CD-R/RW, DVD+R/RW, DVD-R/RW, DVD-RAM Image formats	Windows	Windows XP (service pack 1 or later) or Windows 2000 (service pack 4 or later), 500MHz Pentium III or equivalent, 128MB RAM, CD, CD-R DVD drive	Burn or copy data, audio, photo, video CDs, and DVDs; capture Internet audio; preserve music from old LPs and tapes; capture and organize pictures and video; back up files	$70
		CD-R, CD-RW	Mac/Windows	Windows XP or 2000, 500MHz Pentium processor or better, QuickTime 6.5.2, 128MB RAM (256RAM recommended); latest Windows service packs; supported CD-RW drive; Mac OS X v10.2.8 or later, QuickTime 6.5.2, 128MB RAM (256RAM recomm.); supported CD-RW	Rip, encode, and burn music files; largest legal download library; pod casting, sync to iPod; print CD inserts	Free
Video CD, Super Video CD, DVD with PCM or Dolby Digital, miniDVD	DVD, Video CD (VCD), Super Video CD (SVCD), Mini DVD	CD-R/RW, DVD+R/RW, DVD-R/RW, DVD-RAM, DLT	Mac	Mac OS X v10.2 (Jaguar) or later, Power Macintosh G3 or later, 200MB, QuickTime 6 or later, CD, CD-R, DVD drive	Burn or copy data, audio, photo, video CDs, and DVDs; capture Internet audio; preserve music from old LPs and tapes; capture and organize pictures and video; back up files	$80
AVI, MPEG-1/2/4, WMV	CD, DVD, or VCD	CD-R, CD-RW	Windows	Windows XP Home Edition, XP Professional, or XP Media Center Edition, 233 megahertz (MHz) processor, Intel Pentium II or Advanced Micro Devices (AMD) processor	Rip, encode, and burn music files; sync to MP3 players; print CD inserts	Free

AUDIO INTERFACES

Manufacturer	Product	Web Site	Entry	Intermediate	Advanced	MIDI I/O	Analog I/Os	Digital I/Os
M-Audio	M-Audio FastTrack USB	www.m-audio.com/products/en_us/FastTrackUSB-main.html	X	X	X	N/A	1 (XLR), 1 (1/4"), 1 (RCA IN), 1 (RCA OUT)	N/A
M-Audio	M-Audio MobilePre USB	www.m-audio.com/products/en_us/MobilePreUSB-main-1.html	X	X	X	N/A	2 (XLR), 2 (1/4"), 1 (1/8" Stereo IN), 2 (1/4" OUT), 1 (RCA IN), 1 (RCA OUT)	N/A
M-Audio	M-Audio FireWire Solo	www.m-audio.com/products/en_us/FireWireSolo-main.html	X	X	X	N/A	1 (XLR), 1 (1/4" Line IN), 2 (1/4" IN), 2 (1/4" OUT)	1 (S/PDIF IN), 1 S/PDIF OUT)

HYBRID AUDIO/MIDI INTERFACES

Manufacturer	Product	Web Site	Entry	Intermediate	Advanced	MIDI I/O	Analog I/Os	Digital I/Os
DigiDesign	DigiDesign Mbox	www.digidesign.com/products/mbox/main.cfm		X	X	X	2 (XLR), 1 (1/4")	1/0
Edirol	Edirol UA-20	www.edirol.com/products/info/ua20.html		X	X	1/1	2 (XLR), 2 (1/4" IN), 2 (RCA)	1/0
Edirol	Edirol UA-25	www.edirol.com/products/info/ua25.html		X	X	1/1	2 (XLR/TRS), 2 (1/4" OUT), 2 (RCA)	1/1
M-Audio	M-Audio Audiophile USB	http://m-audio.com/products/en_us/ AudiophileUSB-main.html		X	X	1/1	2 (XLR), 2 (1/4"), 2 (1/4" OUT), 2 (RCA IN), 2 (RCA OUT)	1/1
M-Audio	M-Audio FireWire 410	www.m-audio.com/products/en_us/FireWire410-main.html		X	X	1/1	2 (XLR), 8 (1/4" OUT), 2 (1/4" IN)	1 (Optical S/PDIF IN), 1 (Optical S/PDIF OUT), 1 (Coaxial S/PDIF IN), 1 (Coaxial S/PDIF OUT)
Tascam	Tascam US -122	http://tascam.com/Products/US-122.html	X	X	X	1/1	2 (XLR), 2 (1/4" IN), 2 (1/4" OUT), 2 (RCA)	N/A

Bus Type	Platform	Minimum System Requirements	Special Features	List Price
USB	Mac/Windows	Windows XP (SP1) Pentium II 350 w/64MB RAM; Mac G3 300MHz, G4 350MHz, OS X 10.2.8 or greater, 128MB RAM	Includes GT Player Express software; professional effects; guitar amp and stomp box modeling; plays standard audio files with variable speed playback; standalone operation, ReWire, or VST plug-in	$130
USB	Mac/Windows	Windows 98SE/Me/2000 (SP4)/XP (SP1), Pentium II 350 w/64MB RAM; Mac G3 300MHz, G4 350MHz OS 9.2.2, 64MB RAM; OS X 10.2.6 or greater, 128MB RAM	Includes Ableton Live Lite Phantom Power	$180
2 FireWire ports	Mac/Windows	Windows XP (SP2) with DirectX 9.0c Pentium III, 500MHz 128MB RAM, FireWire or IEEE1394 PCI card; Mac G3/G4 500MHz, OS X 10.2.8, 256MB RAM or OS X 10.3.5 or later, 512MB RAM, FireWire connection IEEE1394 PCI card	Includes Ableton Live Lite Phantom Power	$250

Bus Type	Platform	Minimum System Requirements	Special Features	List Price
USB	Mac/Windows	Windows XP Pentium IV or Athlon processor, 2.8GHz or higher; Mac OS X G5 processor 1.8GHz or higher, 512MB of RAM	Includes Pro Tools LE Phantom Power Zero Latency adjustment	$500
USB	Mac/Windows	Windows Me/98/98SE/2000/XP, Pentium Processor 200MHz or higher, 32MB RAM or more; Mac OS 8.5, 8.6, 9.x and OS X, Macintosh PowerPC G3/233MHz or higher, 64MB RAM or more, OMS 2.3.3 or later, FreeMIDI 1.35 or later	Phantom Power Zero Latency adjustment	$200
USB	Mac/Windows	Windows XP Home Edition/XP Professional/2000 Professional/Me/98 Second Edition, Pentium, Celeron, or Pentium compatible processor 600MHz or higher, 256MB or more, 200MB of free space; Mac OS 9, 10.2 or later, PowerPC G3 400MHz or higher, 256MB or more, 200MB of free space.	Phantom Power Zero Latency adjustment +4 dBu Output	$295
USB	Mac/Windows	Mac/Windows	Includes Ableton Live Lite Phantom Power	$250
2 FireWire ports	Mac/Windows	Windows 2000/XP, Mac OS 9 OS X	Includes Ableton Live Lite Phantom Power	$400
USB	Mac/Windows	Mac/Windows	Includes Cubase LE, GigaStudio 3 LE Phantom Power Zero Latency adjustment	$270

PORTABLE/DIRECT-TO-DISK RECORDERS

Manufacturer	Product	Web Site	Entry	Intermediate	Advanced	MIDI I/O	Analog I/Os	Digital I/Os
Edirol	Edirol R-1 24 bit WAV Recorder/Player	www.edirol.com/products/info/r1.html	X	X	X	N/A	1 internal microphone (stereo), 1 stereo microphone, 1 (1/8") stereo line	1 (1/8" stereo) phone jack, Headphones (1/8" stereo), 1 (S/PDIF 1/8" optical)
Korg	Korg PXR4 4-Track Digital Recorder	http://korg.com/gear/info.asp?A_PROD_NO=PXR4	X	X	X	N/A	1 (1/4") IN, 1 (1/8" OUT), 1 (1/8") stereo line	
d-mpro	Marantz CDR300	www.d-mpro.com/users/folder.asp?FolderID= 1548&CatID =18&SubCatID=170	X	X	X	N/A	2 (XLR), 1/1 (RCA)	1 (S/PDIF), 1 (S/PDIF)
Roland	Roland CD-2	http://rolandus.com/products/details.asp?CatID=12&SubCatID=52&ProdID=CD-2	X	X	X	N/A	2 (XLR)	N/A
Superscope Technologies	Superscope PSD300/300P/340	www.superscopetechnologies.com/products/psd300P/index.shtml	X	X	X	N/A	2 (XLR), 2/0 (1/4"), 2/2 (RCA), 1/1 (RCA AUX)	2 (S/PDIF), 2 (S/PDIF)
M-Audio	MicroTrack 24/96	http://www.m-audio.com/products/en_us/MicroTrack2496-main.html	X	X		N/A	1/0 (TRS), 1/1 (1/4"), 1/1 (1/8")	1 (S/PDIF)

DIGITAL AUDIO WORKSTATIONS (DAW)

Manufacturer	Product	Web Site	Entry	Intermediate	Advanced	MIDI I/O	# Tracks	Analog I/Os
Roland	BOSS BR-1600CD	http://rolandus.com/products/details.asp?catid=12&subcatid=48&prodid=BR%2D1600CD			X	1/1	16 / 256 virtual	8 (XLR), 8 (1/4")
Korg	Korg D1600 mkII	http://korg.com/gear/info.asp?A_PROD_NO=D1600MKII			X	1/1	16 / 128 virtual	3 (XLR), 5 (TRS), 6 (1/4")
Roland	Roland VS-2000CD	http://rolandus.com/products/details.asp?catid=12&subcatid=48&prodid=VS%2D2000CD			X	1/1	20 / 320 virtual	8 (XLR), 8 (TRS), 4 (TRS)
Tascam	Tascam 2488	http://tascam.com/Products/2488.html			X	1/1	24	8 (XLR), 4 (TRS), 2 (RCA)
Tascam	Tascam Portastudio DP-01FX	http://tascam.com/Products/dp01fx.html	X		X	1/1	8	2 (XLR), 2 (TRS), 2 (1/4"), 2 (RCA)
Yamaha	Yamaha AW1600	http://yamaha.com/			X	1/1	16 / 144 virtual	8 (XLR), 8 (TRS), 4 (TRS)

Bus Type	Platform	Minimum System Requirements	Special Features	List Price
USB	Mac/Windows	Windows XP/2000/Me; MacOS 9.2 or MacOS X, OS standard driver	2 Tracks (1 stereo track), recording data format WAV, MP3 built-in effects, CompactFlash card up to 2 GB capacity	$550
USB	Mac/Windows	Windows 2000/Me or later; Mac OS 9.0.4 or later	Record 4 tracks x 8 virtual, 4 tracks simultaneous playback, 2 tracks simultaneous recording; Recording format: 16-bit MPEG 1 Audio Layer 2 compressed, 32kHz; 55 different rhythm patterns PCM sounds: Rock, Funk, Big Beat, House, Reggae, Hip-Hop, R & B, Disco, Dance, Jazz, and more.	$500
N/A	Standalone	N/A	Records to CD-R/RW; Phantom Power built-in microphone, speaker; programmable mic/line EQ manual or automatic level control for recording; programmable mic/line high and band pass filtering; 3-band master EQ onboard limiter; full function IR remote included.	$900
N/A	Standalone	N/A	Records to CompactFlash and CD; onboard effects; built-in stereo mic and speakers; practice tools with tempo/key change, tuner, and metronome.	$800
N/A	Standalone	N/A	Record to CD-R/RW, change key in musical half steps, simultaneous key and tempo change, change tempo without changing key, reduce lead vocals, create A-B practice loops, plug in instruments or microphones and mix live with CD accompaniment	$850
USB	Mac/Windows	Windows 2000, XP (SP1); Mac OS X 10.3.9 or greater	Battery-operated 2-channel WAV and MP3 recording, Phantom Power storage via convenient CompactFlash or microdrives	$500

Digital I/Os	Bus Type	Platform	Minimum System Requirements	Special Features	List Price
1/1 (S/PDIF)	USB	Standalone / Mac/Windows	N/A	LCD display, PCM drums and bass w/ seq, harmony seq, pitch correction, Phantom Power, 16-track (256 V-Track), 40GB hard drive, CD-R/RW drive	$1,595
1/1 (S/PDIF)	USB	Standalone / Mac/Windows	N/A	LCD display, EQ and effects, Mix Automation, Phantom Power, editing 40GB internal hard drive, Disk-at-once CD burning	$1495
1/1 (S/PDIF)	USB	Standalone / Mac/Windows	N/A	LCD display, VGA output option, harmony sequencer, Phantom Power, PCM drums and seq, amp modeling	$2,395
1/1 (S/PDIF)	USB	Standalone / Mac/Windows	N/A	LCD display, 3-band EQ on 24 channels, Phantom Power, assignable guitar multi-effects, dedicated stereo compressor, 40GB hard drive, CD-RW drive, 64-voice General MIDI sound module	$1,499
1/1 (S/PDIF)	USB	Standalone / Mac/Windows	N/A	LCD screen, built-in effects processor with mastering reverb, one-knob-per-function design, stereo or dual mono recording capability, Phantom-powered XLR mic Ins, channel EQ, pan and digital outputs	$650
1/1 (S/PDIF)	USB	Standalone / Mac/Windows	N/A	LCD, 20GB hard disk, built-in CD-RW drive, dynamics processing and 4-band parametric EQ	$1,495

DIGITAL AUDIO WORKSTATIONS (DAW)

Manufacturer	Product	Web Site	Entry	Intermediate	Advanced	MIDI I/O	# Tracks	Analog I/Os
Roland	BOSS BR-1600CD	http://rolandus.com/products/details.asp?catid=12&subcatid=48&prodid=BR%2D1600CD			X	1/1	16 / 256 virtual	8 (XLR), 8 (1/4")
Korg	Korg D1600 mkII	http://korg.com/gear/info.asp?A_PROD_NO=D1600MKII			X	1/1	16 / 128 virtual	3 (XLR), 5 (TRS) 6 (1/4")
Roland	Roland VS-2000CD	http://rolandus.com/products/details.asp?catid=12&subcatid=48&prodid=VS%2D2000CD			X	1/1	20 / 320 virtual	8 (XLR), 8 (TRS), 4 (TRS)
Tascam	Tascam 2488	http://tascam.com/Products/2488.html			X	1/1	24	8 (XLR), 4 (TRS), 2 (RCA)
Tascam	Tascam Portastudio DP-01FX	http://tascam.com/Products/dp01fx.html	X	X	X	1/1	8	2 (XLR), 2 (TRS), 2 (1/4"), 2 (RCA)
Yamaha	Yamaha AW1600	http://yamaha.com/			X	1/1	16 / 144 virtual	8 (XLR), 8 (TRS), 4 (TRS)

MIXERS

Manufacturer	Product	Web Site	Inputs	XLR	Channels	Mono Mic/Line Channel Inputs	Stereo/Line Channel Inputs	EQ Mono/Stereo	USB	Aux Sends	Stereo Aux Returns	List Price
Behringer	UB802 Eurorack 8 Input Mixer	www.behringer.com	8	2	2 mono/ 2 stereo	2 (XLR + 1/4" TRS)	2 (1/4" TRS)	3-band/ 3-band	Yes	1 post fader	Return 1 to main mix	$65
Behringer	UB1202 Eurorack 12 Input Mixer	www.behringer.com	12	4	4 mono + 4 stereo	4 (XLR + 1/4" TRS)	4 (1/4" TRS)	3-band/ 3-band	Yes	1 post fader	Return 1 to aux send 1/main mix	$100
Behringer	PMH1000 12-Channel Powered Mixer with FX	www.behringer.com	12	6	4 mono + 4 stereo	4 (XLR + 1/4" TRS)	4 (1/4" TRS)	7-band/ 7-band	Yes	1 pre fader, 1 post fader	Return 1 to aux send 1/main mix	$360
Tascam	DM-3200	www.tascam.com	48	16	32	16 (XLR + 1/4" TRS)	4 (1/4" TRS)	128	Yes	8	8	$3,800
Mackie	1204-VLZ Pro	www.mackie.com	16	12	12	4 (XLR + 1/4" TRS)	4 (1/4" TRS)	3-band/ 3-band	Yes	2	5	$350
Yamaha	MG166FX	www.yamaha.com	16	16	16	4 (XLR + 1/4" TRS)	2 (1/4" TRS)	3-band/ 3-band	Yes	2	Return 1 to aux send 1/main mix	$420

Digital I/Os	Bus Type	Platform	Minimum System Requirements	Special Features	List Price
1/1 (S/PDIF)	USB	Standalone / Mac/Windows	N/A	LCD display, PCM drums and bass w/ seq, harmony seq, pitch correction, Phantom Power, 16-track (256 V-Track), 40GB hard drive, CD-R/RW drive	$1,595
1/1 (S/PDIF)	USB	Standalone / Mac/Windows	N/A	LCD display, EQ and effects, Mix Automation, Phantom Power, editing 40GB internal hard drive, Disk-at-once CD burning	$1495
1/1 (S/PDIF)	USB	Standalone / Mac/Windows	N/A	LCD display, VGA output option, harmony sequencer, Phantom Power, PCM drums and seq, amp modeling	$2,395
1/1 (S/PDIF)	USB	Standalone / Mac/Windows	N/A	LCD display, 3-band EQ on 24 channels, Phantom Power, assignable guitar multi-effects, dedicated stereo compressor, 40GB hard drive, CD-RW drive, 64-voice General MIDI sound module	$1,499
1/1 (S/PDIF)	USB	Standalone / Mac/Windows	N/A	LCD screen, built-in effects processor with mastering reverb, one-knob-per-function design, stereo or dual mono recording capability, Phantom-powered XLR mic Ins, channel EQ, pan and digital outputs	$650
1/1 (S/PDIF)	USB	Standalone / Mac/Windows	N/A	LCD, 20GB hard disk, built-in CD-RW drive, dynamics processing and 4-band parametric EQ	$1,495

MICROPHONES

Manufacturer	Product	Web Site	Type	Pattern	Recording Application	List Price
Audio-Technica	AT825	www.audio-technica.com	Condenser	X/Y stereo	Ensemble	$550
AKG	C 414 B-XLS	www.akg.com	Condenser	Cardioid, hypercardioid, figure eight, omni, wide cardioid	Ensemble	$1,000
AKG	D 190 E/D 190 ES	www.akg.com	Dynamic	Cardioid	Vocal	$150
AKG	D 22/XLR	www.akg.com	Dynamic	Cardioid	Instrument	$130
M-Audio	Lunar	www.m-audio.com	Condenser	Cardioid	Instrument, vocal	$250
M-Audio	Nova	www.m-audio.com	Condenser	Cardioid	Instrument, vocal	$130
M-Audio	Solaris	www.m-audio.com	Condenser	Cardioid, omni, figure-8 polar	Instrument, vocal	$350
Sennheiser USA	E835	www.sennheiserusa.com	Dynamic	Cardioid	Vocal	$260
Sennheiser USA	MD421 II	www.sennheiserusa.com	Dynamic	Cardioid	Instrument	$510
Shure	KSM32	www.shure.com	Condenser	Cardioid	Ensemble	$1,100
Shure	SM57	www.shure.com	Dynamic	Cardioid	Instrument	$145
Shure	SM58	www.shure.com	Dynamic	Cardioid	Vocal	$100
Shure	SM81	www.shure.com	Condenser	Cardioid	Instrument	$560

*Some of the data in these tables was previously published in *Electronic Musician's Computer Music Product Guide*, a product of Primedia, and is reprinted with the permission of the publisher.

CHAPTER 3

Music Notation Software

By Thomas E. Rudolph and Sandi MacLeod

Section 1: Notation Software Overview

Notation software is designed to printout out scores and parts. It can be a versatile tool for music educators. In addition, students can use notation software for composition and arranging. Notation software has a multitude of uses in the music classroom, with instrumental or vocal ensembles, and for theory/composition courses. With the familiar look of staff paper (**Fig. 1**) and common musical symbols, notation software is a program that teachers and students can learn to use with relative ease.

Names of Notation Software

Sometimes notation software is referred to in catalogs as score writing or scoring software. While the tools and menus of specific programs differ, the results are similar; music produced is in standard notation for printing, listening, and sharing. There are many types of programs that offer notation features, but are not recommended as notation software. For example, most digital audio/MIDI sequencers (discussed in Chapter 2, "Music Production") include some form of notation editing and printing. These programs are not recommended for notation printing because they lack the total feature set of notation programs mentioned in this chapter.

FIG. 1: Notation software printout

Spanish Dance No. 2

Moritz Moszkowski

Benefits to Teachers

Notation software can be used by music teachers to print out music for use in the classroom and rehearsal. Teachers can create a wide variety of materials to enhance student learning. Some of these include

▶ Composing and arranging music for ensembles.

▶ Creating warm-ups, exercises worksheets, handouts, bulletin board materials, flash cards, and tests.

▶ Creating accompaniments for classroom, choral, or instrumental practice.

▶ Creating, transposing, and arranging music to meet the varying instrumentation available or the challenges of varied ability levels in performing groups.

▶ Creating accompaniments to a melody or ensemble piece by adding drum patterns and harmony parts.

▶ Creating and saving files to import to other programs and portable keyboards.

▶ Publishing files on the Internet for home practice, assignments, and sharing of student work.

Benefits to Students

Notation software can be used by students in the classroom, the practice room, and on their computers at home. Some of the major applications include

▶ Composing and arranging music.

▶ Developing and enhancing listening skills.

▶ Using and applying musical concepts including harmony, rhythm, transposition and other skills.

▶ Practicing and preparing for performance.

See Section 4 of this chapter for a more in-depth review of student applications and notation software.

Universal Access

Notation software is also available for the sight-impaired. There are companies that offer specialized software to generate Braille music. See the list of companies in the chart below. Some programs, such as *Finale* and *Sibelius* products are available in a variety of languages including French, Spanish, and others. Since notation software offers a variety of input methods, the software can accommodate the needs of a wide variety of users.

Input Options

Notation software can be used with a stand-alone computer (Macintosh or Windows). Notes can be entered using the computer mouse and/or computer keyboard. This makes notation software an excellent program to utilize in school computer labs and with computers at home and in school. No additional hardware is needed. Sound playback is handled by the computer's built-in sound synthesis capabilities.

Notation software can also be used with MIDI piano keyboards and keyboard controllers allowing users to enter notation by playing notes on a musical keyboard. This is the fastest way to enter notation and allows for music to be played in step time and in real time with a metronome beat. For more information on MIDI and electronic instruments, see Chapter 1, "Electronic Musical Instruments." Other note input options include scanning and importing MIDI files from the Internet. These options are explained below.

MUSIC SCANNING OVERVIEW

Scanning is a viable option to input sheet music into notation software. This technology has improved significantly over the past few years and can assist educators in quickly entering notation from printed scores and parts. Currently, scanning software cannot recognize hand-written notation. Music educators who have become comfortable scanning music into their notation program will find many helpful uses for this feature. A band director may wish to create a custom part by converting an existing part for a weak or advanced student, or to bolster a weak or missing section. A choral director may wish to scan a vocal score in order to create a standard midi file of the piano part to use in rehearsals. A middle school or high school teacher may design an arranging activity in which students open a scanned hymn and orchestrate it using the software's composing/arranging features.

There are two types of scanning programs: standalone scanning software and scanning software that is integrated with some notation software. If you use *Finale* or *Sibelius*, a "lite" version of scanning software comes built in to the program. If you use other notation programs such as *Encore, Mosaic, Overture*, etc., you can purchase a standalone MIDI scanning program, such as *PhotoScore MIDI*. This program converts printed notation to Standard MIDI file format that can be opened by any notation program.

The lite versions of the scanning software that are included with both *Finale* and *Sibelius* and standalone MIDI scanning software are designed to scan only notes, clefs, and ties. There are professional scanning software versions, including *SmartScore (Finale)* and *PhotoScore Professional (Sibelius)* that will also capture slurs and text such as lyrics, expressions, and titles. *Finale* and *Sibelius* users can upgrade to the professional versions for a fee. An overview of the steps for scanning with *Finale* and *Sibelius* is listed in their respective sections below. Regardless of what scanning software option you choose, you will need to have access to a flatbed scanner (**Fig. 2**) and scanning recognition software that comes with the scanner.

FIG. 2: Canon flatbed scanner

Section 2: Selecting a Notation Program

It is important to select the best notation program for you or your students' needs. The list of the current notation programs can be found in the table at the conclusion of this chapter. This is not an exhaustive list of programs, but includes the most commonly used notation programs by students and teachers as of this writing.

Full-featured notation programs should include the following:

▶ Editing capabilities

▶ Several methods of inputting pitch and rhythm

▶ Live (real-time) recording capabilities

▶ Play back of pitches, rhythms, dynamics, articulations, repeats, and so forth

▶ Individual parts that can be easily transposed and extracted

▶ Music that can be printed in a variety of ways (scores and parts)

▶ Files saved for publication on the Internet

▶ Scanning printed (sheet) music

▶ Options for the number of staves and instrument voices

▶ Lyrics

▶ Guitar TAB

▶ Export the file in a variety of graphics formats

▶ Conversion to other file formats such as Standard MIDI File and Audio (WAV and AIFF)

MakeMusic! and Sibelius

Two companies have emerged as leaders in the notation software field: *Sibelius* and *MakeMusic!*, the publisher of the *Finale* family of products. If you are looking for notation software for the first time, we recommend selecting a package from one of these two companies as they are currently the most powerful on the market. The majority of professional development workshops utilize programs from these two companies and a wide range of support is readily available. *Finale* and *Sibelius* set the standard for notation software features that can be used by both educators and students. They are also the most used by composers and arrangers in the music field.

Because of the dominance of *Sibelius* and *Finale* related packages, we provide detailed information about the various programs from these two companies. If you're not using a *Sibelius* or *Finale* product and you are satisfied with the notation program you currently use, then stick with it. As with most software, it's best to learn a program well so you can take full advantage of the multiple features it offers. If you're not satisfied with your current notation program, then look for something that matches your needs and the new areas you'd like to explore.

NOTATION INPUT OPTIONS

Both *Finale* and *Sibelius* offer a variety of input options that include

▶ A menu or keypad to input notes one at a time (called step-time entry) by selecting the rhythm and clicking on the staff to select the pitch.

▶ Some programs come with a small piano keyboard graphic or guitar fretboard interface in the program itself for entering pitches. With others, the letter keys (QWERTY) on the computer relate to pitches; G is G on the staff, F is F, and so forth. Often computer keyboard strokes and shortcuts can be combined with the step approaches described above for faster note input.

▶ Another method of step-entry is available if a MIDI keyboard or MIDI controller device is connected to the computer. Pitches can be entered by playing the keys of the MIDI keyboard or controller.

- ▶ All programs provide the option of recording directly in real-time (along with a metronome click) with an attached MIDI keyboard, or some other MIDI instrument or controller.

- ▶ Scanned music can be imported and edited and arranged.

- ▶ MIDI files can be purchased from music vendors or downloaded from Internet Web sites.

Section 3: List and Description of Recommended Notation Programs

There are many notation programs from which to choose. Although this section will focus on *Finale* and *Sibelius* products, there are many other programs that can achieve similar results. The table that follows lists some of the popular music notation software applications that are available. This is by no means an exhaustive list; rather, it is a list of the programs we have found to be most used by teachers and students. As stated previously, the programs offered by *MakeMusic!* and *Sibelius* will be featured. For more specific information about other titles, consult the Web sites listed.

The Sibelius Family

The *Sibelius* company (www.sibelius.com) offers several notation software products. These include *Sibelius, Sibelius Student Edition, G7* and the Web posting/viewing program, *Scorch*.

SIBELIUS

Sibelius is a full-featured professional level notation program that's easy to use in the music classroom with students. Some teachers have used this program with third grade or younger students. *Sibelius* is intuitive and relates to other common software commands making it easy to learn the basics.

Unique to *Sibelius* is page layout. Instead of scrolling bars on the right hand of the screen, *Sibelius* pages move when you click and drag. The navigator window has a diminutive score, and clicking and dragging across this navigator is a fast way to get to any location in your work. *Sibelius* scores reformat quickly, usually in less than 1/10th of a second, so redrawing the screen happens instantly.

There are several features that are particularly helpful in classroom settings. *Sibelius* automatically creates and saves back-up scores. There is also a limitless multiple undo feature. Noteheads on the score turn color when notes are out of range for the selected instrument. This feature indicates both normal range and professional range and can be adjusted by the user.

Sibelius uses a feature called flexi-time for real-time recording that follows the user as they input notes from a portable keyboard or other MIDI device. This feature can be set to entry at a strict tempo or any level up to *molto rubato* as desired.

An exhaustive listing of *Sibelius* features is impossible, but other noteworthy aspects are plug-ins that include additional features such as proofreading tools for detecting parallel fifths and octaves, adding cautionary accidentals, adding simple accompaniments for piano or guitar, supplying brass or string fingerings, creating worksheets for scales and arpeggios, adding chord names, and sol-fa or solfeggio syllables. Technical support is available by phone, e-mail, or through a users chat page on the *Sibelius* Web site.

Sibelius has a Student Feature list that a teacher can set allowing certain advanced features to be turned off. Options such as changing the playback device and recording through a MIDI device can be disabled if desired. Any individual feature, such as Transpose, can be disabled if a teacher chooses.

Sibelius comes with *PhotoScore Lite* scanning software and *Kontakt Silver Player*, a software synthesizer. *Kontakt Silver* includes 20 high-quality orchestral and band sounds and can be used for saving *Sibelius* files in audio file format for burning to a CD or as an mp3 file. Professional versions of both *PhotoScore* and *Kontakt Player* may be purchased if desired for increased power for *Sibelius* users.

The Worksheet Creator feature in *Sibelius 4* includes over 1700 worksheets, exercises, projects, pieces, posters, flashcards, games, and reference information for educators. Many customizable features in the Workshop Creator are designed to save teachers valuable time and provide an extensive collection of ready-made materials. Topics include theory and musicianship; composing, arranging, and improvising; reference materials about scales, modes, instrument ranges, and chords.

Sibelius has a dedicated education Web site: www.sibeliuseducation.com is used to encourage teachers to publish worksheets for students to view, play and print. Educators can also share worksheets, resources, and other teaching materials they've created.

Dynamic Parts in *Sibelius 4* eliminates the need to extract individual instrumental parts. Parts are automatically created when the score is first set up, and editing can be done in either an individual part or the entire score with the changes appearing in both the score and the parts.

Sibelius 4 introduced a truly unique feature. It allows users to import a video and write music to the video in *Sibelius*. You can add any video file to a score. *Sibelius* displays the video in a window and plays it back in sync with the music. This is ideal for student multimedia projects and professional film scoring.

There are many satisfied *Sibelius* users who praise the product for its smart, professional looking output and initial ease of use. (see **Fig. 3** for an example of music typeset with *Sibelius*).

FIG. 3: Sibelius notation software

SIBELIUS STUDENT EDITION

Sibelius Student Edition is available at a list price of $99. This program is designed for homework and assignments such as completing worksheets or composing and arranging. Using the same easy and intuitive interface as *Sibelius*, the student edition is an ideal compliment to the full version of the program. Note input is accomplished with the mouse, with the computer keyboard, or with a MIDI device. *Sibelius Student Edition* is limited to 8 staves, does not extract parts, does not include scanning, and files cannot be saved in *Scorch* format. However, if advanced features are needed, files from the student edition can easily convert to the full version of *Sibelius*. This an excellent entry level program for elementary students through high school. View the comparison list of features at www.sibelius.com/products/sibelius_student/features.html.

G7 BY SIBELIUS

G7 Kontakt Edition is notation software designed for guitarists and songwriters. With an easy to use interface similar to *Sibelius* described above, this program provides features for guitarists such as bending, sliding and tremolo picking for a wide variety of guitars: acoustic, classical, and electric in standard guitar tunings and various number of strings. Users will appreciate the drum pattern generator and how easy it is to add lyrics. A virtual fretboard allows the user to add notes directly to the score, a useful feature for someone not familiar with standard notation.

Files can be imported from ASCII tab files, MIDI files, or scanned in using *PhotoScore Lite,* which is included with the program. Files can be saved in audio format for burning to a CD, exported to *Sibelius*, MIDI file format, a guitar tab file, or to a Web score (see *Scorch* description below). The Internet site (www.g7music.net) encourages students and teachers to publish their music. Also included in the program is a comprehensive Guitar Guide highlighting playing techniques and musical styles with illustrations and audio examples designed to help players improve their writing and playing skills.

Sibelius Web Posting Using Scorch

Sibelius Scorch is a free Web browser plug-in that lets you play, transpose, change instruments, save, and print *Sibelius* scores on the Internet. *Sibelius* is the industry leader in the Web posting of notation files. *Sibelius* users can create a *Scorch* Web score. Those wishing to access a *Sibelius Scorch* file do not need to have a copy of *Sibelius*.

They simply download the free *Scorch* plug-in for their Web browser. Scores for MENC's World's Largest Concert supplied by *Sibelius* in both piano/vocal accompaniment and instrumental arrangements are free and printable for music teachers. A variety of music publishers and dealers such as Hal Leonard, Boosey & Hawkes, and J.W. Pepper allow for listening and printing of music using *Scorch*.

Students and teachers can self-publish at www.sibeliusmusic. com by posting files created in *Sibelius* and saved in *Scorch* format. Sibeliusmusic.com currently lists more than 36,000 scores available both for sale and as free downloads.

Sibelius Scanning Overview

Sibelius ships with a free, entry-level scanning program *PhotoScore Lite* a scaled down version of Neuratron's *PhotoScore Professional 4* program. The free version will recognize notes, staves, and clefs. It will not recognize triplets, grace notes, and text including lyrics, expressions, and titles. *PhotoScore Professional* will recognize all music and text. Users who want to upgrade to *PhotoScore Professional* can do so for a fee at www.sibelius.com/products/photoscore/ professional.html.

Observing several guidelines will go a long way to insuring success when working with scans. *Sibelius* recommends scans be made at 300 dpi (or greater), with the scanner's color mode set to grayscale, and saved as a bitmap (.bmp) for Windows users or TIFFs for MacOS users.

Sibelius users launch the scanning utility by selecting Scan from the File menu. This launches the *PhotoScore Lite* application. Next, choose Open from *PhotoScore Lite's* File menu, select the image files you've scanned, and then click on the Read Pages icon on the toolbar. Editing many elements that may have been recognized incorrectly can be done using tools in *PhotoScore*. Once edited, click the *Sibelius* icon on the toolbar. The scanned music will now open in *Sibelius*. We suggest that you work with scanned pages that have an accuracy of 90 percent or better. If there are many errors that need to be corrected, it is best to enter the example by hand.

The Finale Family by MakeMusic!

The company *MakeMusic!* (www.makemusic.com) offers a complete line of notation products, starting with its free version, *NotePad*. This program can be used by teachers and students for basic applications. *NotePad Plus* includes all the features of *NotePad* plus the ability to save as, import, and export MIDI files. Next in line is *PrintMusic* for under $100. This program is well suited for student use at both the elementary and secondary levels. It includes basic scanning and MIDI input and output. *FinaleGuitar* is similar to *PrintMusic,* but it has added guitar tab features and improved scanning capability. The next version is *Allegro,* a high-end offering, and then the top of the line, *Finale.* For a complete listing of the prices and features of the various products consult the *Finale* Web site at www.makemusic.com/notation_software.asp.

The main advantage of the *MakeMusic!* line of notation products is it includes a free program and several affordable versions all the way up to their flagship program, *Finale.* Students and teachers can begin using basic notation features using the free version *NotePad.* Files can be shared between programs. The low cost of the middle line products makes them affordable for schools and computer labs.

FINALE 2006

The high end offering in the *Finale* family is one of the most popular notation programs. Over the past few years, it has been redesigned to be user friendly and intuitive. The program comes with a complete set of video tutorials for learning virtually every aspect of the program. To review a complete list, go to the www.finalemusic.com Web site.

Finale offers a wide range of note entry tools including mouse entry and typing the letter names on the computer typewriter keyboard. MIDI input is also possible using HyperScribe technology that allows the user to play to a metronome click or to control the tempo with a footpedal. *Finale* also includes MicNotator that allows singers and instrumentalists to enter notation using a microphone connected to the computer.

There are a host of arranging and composition tools available in *Finale 2006.* These include an auto-arrange option featuring *Band-in-a-Box* auto harmonizing, a rhythm section generator based on MiBac software technology, instant drum grooves, creation of a piano reduction, checking the range of instruments, adjusting the measures of extracted parts for page turns, and much more.

Finale 2006 comes with several free software synthesizers including the SmartMusic Softsynth, Integrated *Kontakt Player,*

Garritan sounds, and Row-Loff Marching Percussion Sounds. These impressive playback options allow you to save *Finale* files as MP3, WAV, or AIFF and burn an audio CD to create practice CDs for students. The combination of *Finale*'s built-in software synthesis instruments and its Human Playback feature, which realizes every marking in the score (i.e., trills, rolls, dynamic expressions, and so on), make playback of *Finale* files sonically impressive.

Finale has many features of interest to music educators. It includes a unique Exercise Wizard for creating custom exercises including scales, arpeggios, patterns, and more for any ensemble. There are also helpful templates for education including Kodaly stick notation.

FINALE PERFORMANCE ASSESSMENT

Teachers can use *Finale* to create assessment files that students open in a downloadable shareware application called *Finale Performance Assessment*, or *FPA*. Here students can practice the music, adjusting the tempo, and hear how it is supposed to be played. Then they can record the file and save it to disk for their portfolio, or e-mail it to their teacher. Their performance is assessed on-screen: notes they played correctly appear in green and incorrect notes appear in red. *FPA* is available for MIDI keyboard, woodwind, and brass players.

FINALE AND SMARTMUSIC

SmartMusic is also published by *MakeMusic!*. This program is covered in Chapter 4, "Technology-Assisted Learning." *Finale* users can create solo and accompaniment files that can be opened in *SmartMusic*. This allows teachers who use *Finale* to create an unlimited number of practice files for their students.

FINALE SCANNING OVERVIEW

Finale 2006 comes with *SmartScore Lite*, a scaled down version of Mustek's *SmartScore Pro 3* professional scanning program. The free, lite version will scan notes, rests, clefs, time signatures, and staves. It will not recognize triplets, grace notes, or text of any kind. For those who would like the professional features of *SmartScore Pro 3*, it is available as an upgrade to *Finale* users at a 30 percent discount.

To scan in a page of printed music in *Finale*, there are four steps: create a blank file with the correct staves, key, and time signature; use the scanning software that came with your scanner and scan the pages; import the scanned pages into *Finale*; then copy and paste the scanned document into the template you created. Windows users in *Finale 2006* can scan directly into *Finale* saving two of the above steps.

Finale 2006 files must be scanned in black and white or grayscale and at 300 dpi (dots per inch) saved in TIFF graphic file format. View the *Finale* QuickStart Video: Note Entry > Scanning for more information on the specific steps in the process. We suggest that you work with scanned pages that have an accuracy of 90 percent or better. If there are many errors that need to be corrected, it is best to enter the example by hand.

Finale's many satisfied users praise this program for its highly customizable output and its integration for educators with other *MakeMusic!* products such as *NotePad*, *SmartMusic*, and *Finale Performance Assessment* (see **Fig. 4** for an example of music typeset with *Finale*).

FIG. 4: Finale notation software

FINALE ALLEGRO

This version has all but a few of *Finale*'s high-end features at lower cost of $199. *Allegro* gives educators and students all the MIDI and notation tools they need to create publisher-quality scores, while leaving out the detailed engraving options found in *Allegro*'s "parent," *Finale*.

FINALE PRINTMUSIC

This is a lite version of *Finale* and includes many of the advanced features. It is priced under $100 and *MakeMusic!* offers special pricing for quantity purchases making it an excellent choice for schools and labs. Many of the basic needs of students and teachers can be met with this program. It includes built-in scanning and MIDI input and output is supported

FINALE NOTEPAD

Finale NotePad is a free program that can be downloaded from www.finalemusic.com/notepad. Since it is free, it can be put on every computer in the school. Students can also download this full functioning program for free on their home computers. Note entry is limited to point-and-click style mouse entry. Nonetheless, this is an excellent entry-level program for students at all levels.

FINALE NOTEPAD PLUS

NotePad Plus includes all the features of *NotePad* plus the ability to save as, import, and export MIDI files. For this added feature, the program costs $24.95.

Finale *NotePad* and *NotePad Plus* can be used with all of the other programs in the *Finale* family. Because *Sibelius* has the capability of loading *Finale* format files, *NotePad* files can be imported into *Sibelius*.

Finale Family or Sibelius?

Finale and *Sibelius* are competitors and both offer a range of programs. The *Finale* family has the edge in the variety of offerings including a free version. It also is the oldest and has a large installed base of users and support materials and books. *Sibelius* is a newer program and has the edge in ease of use at the entry level. It also offers several unique features including saving files to display on Web pages in *Scorch* format (see above). You can compare the programs by downloading a demonstration version from their respective Web sites. You can also read reviews that have appeared in magazines comparing the two programs. Whichever way you choose to go, you will not be disappointed with either *Sibelius* or *Finale* family products.

For a *Finale/Sibelius* review, go to Macworld, June, 2004 at www.macworld.com/2004/06/reviews/finale2004sibelius3x1/index.php.

Section 4: Using Notation Software with Students

Notation software can be an excellent tool for students to compose, arrange, and print music. There are some recommended procedures to keep in mind as well as several excellent resource materials for teachers.

Start with the Basics

The first advice is not to start with original composition. Students need to have a structure for composition and background using the software first. Some teachers assign students music theory exercises such as notating scales and intervals, copying patterns, and creating sequences to complete using notation software. Consider asking students to view and listen to short musical compositions or write out theory assignments before bridging into the composition world.

Sibelius Notes

An excellent text is published by *Sibelius* called *Sibelius Notes*. It is a complete pack of educational resources to help you teach music in the classroom with *Sibelius*. Covering all school levels (K–12, Key Stages 1–4, and beyond), *Notes* contains ready-to-use exercises and worksheets on everything from notation to composing, plus dozens of music files on CD-ROM and other useful resources. Students can use *Notes* on computer or with pen and paper. Teachers are permitted to photocopy the worksheets. Included is a Teacher's Guide with ready-to-use graded exercises and worksheets. The exercises include notation, rhythm, harmony, composition, and the basics of music.

We recommend that non-*Sibelius* users also consider purchasing *Sibelius Notes*. The files that are supplied are only compatible with *Sibelius*, however, the teacher manual contains a wealth of excellent lesson plans and ideas that could be adapted to other notation programs.

Book Resources

There are several books that contain ideas on how to incorporate music notation with students. *Strategies for Teaching Technology* (2001) edited by Sam Reese, Kim McCord, and Kim Walls and published by MENC includes many notation lesson plans. The book is organized by the MENC national standards, and there are many lessons that could be easily adapted for all levels.

The TI:ME publication, *Technology Strategies for Music Education, 2nd edition,* contains 23 notation strategies. These are listed by level and organized by the MENC National Standards.

The text *Teaching Music with Technology* by Tom Rudolph (GIA Publications), contains a chapter on notation software and also includes several teaching strategies. There are several notation lesson plans included on the companion CD-ROM that comes with the book.

Web Resources

In addition to books, the World Wide Web offers a wealth of locations that can help teachers to develop curriculum ideas for the use of notation software.

The Vermont MIDI Project Web site (www.vtmidi.org) has devoted over 10 years to developing strategies and lessons for music composition with notation software. Many of these are shared on the Web site along with examples of student work. New resources contributed by a variety of teachers for grade levels 2–12 are continuously added at www.vtmidi.org/AtoC.html. Three tried and true lessons available with examples of student work are "Melodic Construction" by Carolyn Keck for grades 3–6, "How Can I Change My Pattern? It's Perfect!" by Anne Hamilton for grades 6-8, and "Fairy Tale Assignment" by Anne Hamilton for high school.

The Technology Institute for Music Educators, (the organization that created this resource guide) also offers lesson plans on their Web site. There are sample lessons that anyone can view. Members of TI:ME have access to hundreds of lesson plans written by teachers from throughout the country. Membership is $40.00 per year, and members can access the lesson plan database at www.ti-me.org in the member's section (**Fig. 5**). Several lessons for using notation software you might start with are "Play Ball! What's the Score" for middle school instrumental and general music score reading and expressive element exploration by Ron Dumais, "Sight Singing Duets Without a Human Partner" by David Lantz for high school, and "Beats and Accents" by George Murphy for middle school music.

FIG. 5: TI:ME Members-Only Lesson Plan section

Another excellent site is www.berkleeshares.com. This site includes free lessons shared by teachers at Berklee College of Music. The lessons are free. Additionally, both *Finale* and *Sibelius* maintain Web sites where people can share compositions. These include www.finaleshowcase.com and www.sibeliusmusic.com. Teachers and students can download pieces from these sites and post their own compositions.

Teaching Techniques

The common feature of the strategies and lesson plans that are included in the above books and Web resources is they use techniques to assist students in the composition and arranging process. Some of these techniques include

▶ Editing and modifying existing pieces. Provide the student with a partially completed file and let them fill in or adjust the empty measures.

▶ Dragging or transposing given notes to new locations.

▶ Copy and paste patterns to create a melody.

▶ Adding expressive elements to compositions.

▶ Arranging excerpts enhancing the expressive effect of the music.

▶ Adding chords—tonic and dominant—to a given melody.

▶ Transposing the tonality of an existing exercise.

▶ Arranging a piano piece for two instruments.

▶ Arranging an SATB score for four instruments.

▶ Arranging a canon for four voices (for example, *Frere Jacques*).

▶ Transcribing an instrumental piece for SATB voices.

▶ Transcribing a duet or trio for three instruments.

▶ Adding melodies, chords, and accompaniments to existing songs.

▶ Creating an accompaniment—fill in the blank measures.

▶ Composing melodies to an existing chord changes.

Copyright Considerations

When using notation software, it is important to adhere to the copyright law guidelines for educators. In general, music notation software should not be used to avoid the purchase or copyrighted music or to arrange music that is under copyright. Notation software can be used to compose original compositions, to arrange music in the public domain, or to be used in an educational setting such as arranging special parts for students. For example, the MENC guidelines state, "Music teachers can edit or simplify purchased, printed copies, provided that the fundamental character of the work is not distorted or the lyrics, if any, are not altered or lyrics added if none exist." Be sure to review the Copyright Guidelines for music educators that is available from MENC on their Web site at www.menc.org/information/copyright/copyr.html.

Section 5: Reference Materials

Books

Webster, P. and D. Williams. *Experiencing Music Technology*, 3rd Edition. New York, NY: G. Schirmer, 2005.

Rudolph, T. and V. Leonard. *Finale: An Easy Guide to Music Notation*, Second Edition. Boston, MA: Berklee Press, 2005.

Purse, B. *The Finale Primer*. San Francisco, CA: Backbeat Books, 2004.

Purse, B. *The Finale NotePad Primer*. San Francisco, CA: Backbeat Books, 2003.

Purse, B. *The PrintMusic Primer*. San Francisco, CA: Backbeat Books, 2003.

Baron, J. and V. Spiegel. *Sibelius Notes*. London: Sibelius Software, 2003.

Rudolph, T. *Teaching Music with Technology,* Second Edition. Chicago, IL: GIA Publications, 2004.

Richmond, F. ed. *Technology Strategies for Music Education, Second Edition*. Wyncote, PA: TI:ME, the Technology Institute for Music Educators. Distributed by Hal Leonard, 2005.

Articles

Watson, S., "11 Innovative Uses for Notation Software": (http://metmagazine.com/ar/innovative_uses_notation/index.htm)

Richmond, F., "Instructional Activities Using Notation Software": (http://www.vfcc.edu/frichmond/notation/)

Sibelius: Hints and Tips

PDF documents created by Robin Hudson related to various topics for users of *Sibelius* such as "Creating Worksheets," "Scanning with *PhotoScore*," "Getting Started with *Sibelius*," and many more. (www.sibelius.com/helpcenter/hintsandtips/)

Sibelius/Finale review in MacWorld, June, 2004. (www.macworld.com/2004/06/reviews/finale2004sibelius3x1/index.php)

Online Courses

Writing Music with Finale by Jonathan Feist, Berklee Online Course, www.berkleemusic.com

MUSIC NOTATION SOFTWARE*

Manufacturer	Product	Web Site	Minimum System Requirements	Software Type
MakeMusic! Inc.	Finale NotePad	www.finalemusic.com/notepad/	Mac 10.2; Windows 98, 128MB RAM	Music Notation Software
MakeMusic! Inc.	NotePad Plus	www.finalemusic.com/notepad/	Mac 10.2; Windows 98, 128MB RAM	Music Notation Software
MakeMusic! Inc.	PrintMusic!	www.finalemusic.com/printmusic/	Mac 9.0.4 or 10.2; Windows 98, 128MB RAM	Music Notation Software
MakeMusic! Inc.	Finale Guitar	www.finalemusic.com/finaleguitar/	Mac 8.6; Windows 98, 64MB RAM	Music Notation Software
MakeMusic! Inc.	Finale Allegro	www.finalemusic.com/allegro/	Mac or Windows	Music Notation Software
MakeMusic! Inc.	Finale 2006	www.finalemusic.com/	Mac 10.2; Windows 98, 256MB RAM	Music Notation Software
Sibelius Software	G7	www.sibelius.com	Windows 95, 98, Me, 2000, XP, NT4; Mac G4/G3/iMac, OS 8.6	Music Notation Software
Sibelius Software	Sibelius 4	www.sibelius.com	Windows 95, 98, ME, 2000, XP, NT4; Mac G4/G3/iMac, OS 8.6	Music Notation Software
Gvox	Encore	www.gvox.com	Mac OS 9.x, OS 10.2 or higher; Windows 98 or higher, 32MB RAM	Music Notation Software
Gvox	Music Time Deluxe	www.gvox.com	Mac OS 9.x, OS 10.2 or higher; Windows 98 or higher, 32MB RAM	Music Notation Software
GenieSoft Music Software	Overture 3	www.geniesoft.com/	Windows or Mac (including OS X)	Music Notation Software
GenieSoft Music Software	Score Writer 2	www.geniesoft.com/	Windows or Mac (including OS X)	Music Notation Software
Notation Technologies	Play Music	www.notationtechnologies.com	Windows 95, 98, 2000, ME, XP, 16MB RAM	Music Notation Software
MOTU	Mosaic	www.motu.com	Mac Only	Music Notation Software
Dancing Dots	GOODFEEL (Braile Music)	www.dancingdots.com/	Windows Only	Music Notation Software
Myriad	Melody Assistant	www.myriad-online.com/en/products/melody.htm	Mac or Windows	Music Notation Software
Noteworthy Composer	Noteworthy Software	www.noteworthysoftware.com	Windows Only	Music Notation Software
Neuratron	Photoscore MIDI	www.neuratron.com/photoscore.htm	Mac or Windows	Scanning Software
Neuratron	Photoscore Professional	www.neuratron.com/photoscore.htm	Mac or Windows	Scanning Software
Musitek	SmartScore Pro 3 Edition	www.musitek.com/smartscore.html	Windows 98, NT, ME, 2000, XP; Mac: OS 9, OS 10.2+, 24MB RAM	Scanning Software
Musitek	SmartScore MIDI		Mac or Windows	Scanning Software
Visiv Co., UK	SharpEye	www.visiv.co.uk	Windows Only	Scanning Software

*Some of the data in these tables was previously published in *Electronic Musician's Computer Music Product Guide*, a product of Primedia, and is reprinted with the permission of the publisher.

Entry Level	Advanced Use	Music Input via Mouse	Input via QWERTY Keyboard	Guitar Tab	Extracts Parts	Parts Dynamically Linked to Score	Free Scanning	Softsynth Sounds Included	Special Features	List Price
Y	N	Y	N	N	Y	N	No	No	Opens any same or earlier version Finale family file; exports as SmartMusic Accompaniment	Free
Y	N	Y	N	N	Y	N	No	No	Exports as SmartMusic Accompaniment	$25
Y	N	Y	Y	N	N	N	Yes	No	Engraver slurs, MicNotator (real-time entry from acoustic inst.); exports as SmartMusic Accompaniment	$70
Y	N	Y	Y	Y		N	Yes		Exports as TIFF, MicNotator, Rhyming Dictionary, SmartMusic Accompaniment	$100
Y	Y			Y	Y	N				
Y	Y	Y	Y	Y	Y	N	Yes	Yes	Save as audio file, exercise wizard, auto-harmonize, instant orchestration, rhythm-section generator; save as SmartMusic, Finale Prerformance Assessment, Exercise Wizard	$300/$600
Y	N	Y	Y	Y		N	No		Internet publishing; sample library included.	$149
Y	Y	Y	Y	Y	Y	Y	Yes	Yes	Internet publishing, enhanced playback, OS X carbonized, auto-arrange, Flexitime note entry, score to video, worksheets, Scorch	$299/$599
Y	N	Y	Y	N	N	N	No	No	Easy to use	$400
Y	N	Y	Y	N	N	N	No	No	Easy to use	$120
Y	Y	Y	Y	N	Y	N	No		Full graphical editing of all MIDI data in Graphic window	$349
Y	N	Y	Y	N	Y	N	No		Opens Overture 3 files; scores are cross-platform compatible.	$59
Y	N	Y	Y	N		N	No	No		$50
N	Y	Y	N	N	Y	Y	No			
Y	Y	Y	N	N	N/A	N/A	N/A			
N	N	Y	N	N		N				
N	N	Y	N	N		N				
Y	N			N	N/A	N/A	N/A			
N	Y	Y	Y	Y	N/A	N/A	N/A		Reads PDF files	
N	Y	Y	Y	Y	N/A	N/A	N/A		Processes up to 32 staff lines per system; exports finished music pages into Finale and Sibelius.	$399/$299
	N	Y	N	N	N/A	N/A				
N	Y	Y	N	Y		N	N/A			

CHAPTER 4

Technology-Assisted Learning

By Floyd Richmond

Section 1: Introduction to Technology-Assisted Learning

This chapter will present a list and overview of the best and most used instructional software titles and Internet sites designed for music education. Although terms such as "Instructional Software" and "Computer-Assisted Instruction" are still in use and very relevant, the term "Technology-Assisted Instruction" is used in order to create a larger umbrella under which interactive Internet sites, as well as several unique software applications, can fall.

The chapter is divided into four sections. Following this overview, the next section is for Internet Web sites and is followed by a roundup of outstanding instructional software. In these sections, many notable Web sites and programs are featured with descriptions of their features, screen shots, and generic ideas for using them in music education. In the Internet section, sites are grouped by concept and topic, moving from simple to advanced levels. In the instructional software section, the titles are listed alphabetically. A final section provides a number of resources to find out more about this topic.

A table summarizing software and Web sites highlighted in this chapter, and many others we recommend, appears at the conclusion of the chapter for easy reference. These programs appear and disappear quickly, primarily because of the quick pace of hardware development by computer manufacturers and of software development, especially by those who write computer operating system software. Publishers of instructional software frequently choose to update software that is profitable and let other titles fall out of print. This means that a number of excellent programs are no longer available, or no longer available for current computer systems.

Section 2: Instructional Internet Sites

Web sites include text, pictures, recordings, and movies as common elements. Recently sites have expanded to include interactive lessons and activities. Because these lessons are created to run within an Internet browser, they work on all platforms (Windows and Macintosh). Because these lessons are available on the Internet, they are accessible from any Internet connection in or out of the classroom. In contrast to most instructional software, which must be purchased, these sites provide resources to augment or deliver the music curriculum at no cost.

This section identifies several interactive sites with useful lessons for music students and teachers. Because of the enormity of the World Wide Web, and because its content is constantly evolving, it would be impossible to generate a comprehensive list. Instead this section provides a sample of the types of resources that can be found on the Internet.

Recommended Representative Web Sites
Note Reading with Score
(http://courses.wcupa.edu/frichmon/usetech/musicalflashcards/aaaindex.html)
This site offers practice identifying notes in the treble, bass, alto and tenor clefs (**Fig. 1**). The computer maintains a score that the students may print and submit as proof of having completed the assignment. This site is useful for beginning musicians of all ages. Also available at this site are lessons on major and minor key signatures. This site requires JavaScript.

FIG. 1: Note reading with Score

Intervals, Chords, and Scales

(www.teoria.com/exercises/index.htm)

This site offers practice identifying and writing intervals, chords, and scales. A score is maintained in the window as the student works (**Fig. 2**). This site is ideal for students in music theory classes or for those preparing for undergraduate entrance exams in music. Java is required.

FIG. 2: Intervals, chords, and scales

ETheory

(www.emusictheory.com)

This site provides practice on note reading, piano note reading, paced note reading, C-Clef note reading, key signatures, interval drills, scale building, and chord drills (**Fig. 3**). Students in theory classes will find useful practice on fundamentals at this site.

FIG. 3: ETheory

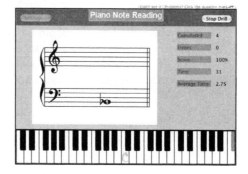

Music Theory
(www.musictheory.net)
This site is one of the most comprehensive and well-constructed presentations of music theory on the World Wide Web! The site provides explanations of and practice on simple concepts such as note identification, intervals (**Fig. 4**), scales, and chords up through advanced topics such as Neapolitan and augmented sixth chords. Gladly, there are a few unrelated activities such as drills for brass instrument fingerings.

FIG. 4: Musictheory.net

Steps and Accidentals

· A **whole step** is the same distance as two half steps.
· Key 1 to Key 3 is a whole step. (The first half step is from 1 to 2, the second from 2 to 3)

Big Ears
(www.ossmann.com/bigears/)
This site offers practice in the aural identification of intervals (**Fig. 5**). Also available is a piano keyboard that, when clicked, plays notes and announces the intervals played. Java is required.

FIG. 5: Big Ears

Earplane
(http://earplane.com/modules/earplane_main/)
This site provides ear-training practice identifying intervals, chords, rhythms, modes, and melody (**Fig. 6**). It is excellent for students taking aurals classes or theory classes in which aural skills are also taught.

FIG. 6: Earplane

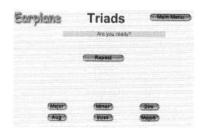

Blues Jam
(www.stevenestrella.com/IWP/bluesjam/bluesjam.html)
This site allows students to create real-time musical performances
in a blues style. The computer plays a 12 bar blues progressions
while the student selects melodic phrases ("licks") to be used
at various times in the performance (**Fig. 7**). This site requires
QuickTime. Students studying the blues will enjoy visiting this site.

FIG. 7: Blues Jam

Creating Music
(www.creatingmusic.com)
This Web site offers six activities for young children. The Musical
Sketch Pad (shown in **Fig. 8**) allows children to trace the contour
of a melody using a variety of timbres. Once written, the melody
may be played in a slow, medium or fast tempo. Also available on
this site are Music Puzzles, Playing with Music, Rhythm Band,
Cartoon Conductor, and Melodic Contours activities. The lessons
on this site are abbreviated versions of CD-ROM lessons in the
MakingMusic! series that is described in more detail in the next section. Both this site and the CD-ROM series provide opportunities
for students to compose and manipulate musical elements. This
Web site requires Java and the *Shockwave* and *QuickTime* plug-ins.

FIG. 8: Creating Music

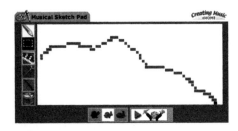

Musical Call Charts
(http://courses.wcupa.edu/frichmon/tdml99/index.html)
This site contains a number of formal call charts for familiar
pieces. Included are excerpts from the *Nutcracker* ballet (see **Fig. 9**
below), Bach's *Little Fugue in G minor*, Scott Joplin's *Entertainer*,
and more. Most of the files use MIDI for playback. For better
results, play a CD recording of the music and use the forward and
backward buttons on the movie control bar to advance in time
with the music. This site requires *QuickTime*. These lessons are
approachable by students of all ages, but especially third grade and
higher.

FIG. 9: Musical Call Charts—
"Trepak" from the Nutcracker
Ballet

Groove Builder
(www.wholenote.com)
(Click on the Groove Builder link near the top of the page, or type
the complete URL:
www.wholenote.com/default.asp?iTarget=http%3A//www.whole-
note.com/builder/builder.asp)
Groove Builder is a page within Wholenote.com, an online guitar
community. This page allows the user to enter chords that the
computer uses to generate accompaniments in various styles (**Fig.**
10). This is a nice tool for exploring chord progressions and musical style, and for practicing improvising or singing melodies over
an accompaniment. This site is similar to *Band-in-a-Box*. This site
requires JavaScript.

FIG. 10: Groove Builder

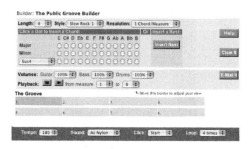

Chord Find
(www.chordfind.com)
This site, which provides guitar fingerings for chords in various positions (**Fig. 11**), is perfect for helping that "garage band" guitarist just recruited for jazz band make the transition into the more sophisticated chords and voicings required of him or her. It also contains a "chord finder" for four string instruments.

FIG. 11: Chord Find

Classical Music Archives
(www.prs.net)
It's 15 minutes before class and you need a particular piece to play for your students. Do you panic? No . . . you visit the Classical Music Archives! This site provides access to over 12,000 MIDI, mp3, and other audio files by over 500 composers (**Fig. 12**) and allows for up to five free MIDI downloads per day. Additional downloads require a subscription.

FIG. 12: Classical Music Archives

These files may be opened in notation programs for study, or played by any MIDI software or media player for listening activities. These standard MIDI files (SMFs) also serve well for activities introducing the basic features of software sequencers and notation programs by allowing students to open them and alter parameters such as tempo, timbre (instrument, program/patch), and dynamics (volume, velocity). The site also contains biographies of numerous classical composers.

File Helpers and Plug-Ins

Browser resources required to run these lessons are listed below. In most cases, these will have come pre-installed on current computers.

JAVASCRIPT

JavaScript is a programming language currently built into *Netscape* and *Internet Explorer*. Support for JavaScript exists in these browsers to some degree down to version 2 and 3 respectively. If a browser does not properly display pages that require JavaScript, check the preferences in the Edit menu to confirm that JavaScript is turned on. If the browser is older (pre-version 4), the latest version of *Netscape* may be downloaded from www.netscape.com. *Internet Explorer* is available at www.microsoft.com. *Mozilla* and *Firefox* are available from www.mozilla.com. *Safari* comes as part of Mac OSX and is available at www.apple.com.

JAVA

Java is a programming language currently built into *Netscape* and *Internet Explorer*. It is similar to JavaScript in many regards. It may be turned on or off in the browser preferences. If problems occur, check to see that it is on. Because of recent changes in Microsoft's

Internet Explorer, Java may soon require a plug-in. For the latest information see the Microsoft site (www.microsoft.com) or the Sun site (http://java.sun.com).

QUICKTIME
QuickTime is a multimedia playback system that is essential for many musical applications on the Web. Developed by Apple Computer, *QuickTime* runs in both Windows and Macintosh browsers. The latest version is available at www.apple.com/quicktime/download.

FLASH AND SHOCKWAVE
Flash and *Shockwave* are plug-ins that allow interactive programs developed with Macromedia *Director* or *Flash* to run in a browser window. Learn more about these tools in the Multimedia Authoring Tools section of Chapter 5, "Multimedia." The latest version is available from www.macromedia.com.

Section 3: Instructional Software

Examples of instructional software applications most used in music teaching are highlighted in the pages that follow. In this section, titles are listed alphabetically with a brief description of their features and uses in music education. A table of recommended software appears at the end of this chapter.

Amazing Slow Downer
Publisher: Roni Music
Platform: Macintosh, Windows
(www.ronimusic.com)

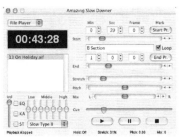

FIG. 13: Amazing Slow Downer playing back a file at almost one-third its original tempo.

Amazing Slow Downer (**Fig. 13**) allows the user to load audio from file or CD and vary the tempo without altering the pitch. Or if you want the pitch altered without varying the tempo, it does that too. This is a great little utility to have on your music room computer. When instrumental or vocal students are practicing along with performance tracks (the CD that came with your school's method book, those demo recordings that come with published music, or solos that come with recorded tracks), *Amazing Slow Downer* allows them to work at a reduced tempo. Practice loops can be set to make it easy to drill a tough passage. Simple sliders are used to make all these settings. ASD allows you to save an altered audio file with the changes you've made to it.

Auralia

Publisher: Sibelius
Platform: Macintosh, Windows
(www.sibelius.com)

FIG. 14: Auralia

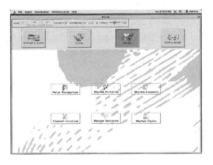

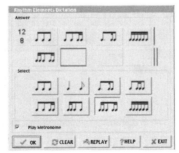

Auralia provides drill and practice on melodic, rhythmic, and harmonic dictation, and other aural skills. The program has a visually attractive user interface and its topics are well-organized (**Fig. 14**). A main menu offers choices including intervals and scales, chords, rhythms, and pitch and melody. A submenu offers up to six subtopics for practice. This program is appropriate for students studying aural theory and sight singing in high school and early college.

Some topics that can be drilled using *Auralia* include

▶ Identify and sing intervals and notes from chords

▶ Melodic and rhythmic dictation

▶ Identify cadences

▶ Recognize and correct poor tuning

▶ Sing upper or lower part of a two-part phrase

▶ Write down chord progressions

The computer calculates a score for each lesson. The teacher may set a minimum level of proficiency for each lesson that students must achieve before advancing to the next level.

Band-in-a-Box

Publisher: PG Music
Platform: Macintosh, Windows
(www.pgmusic.com)

FIG. 15: Band-in-a-Box

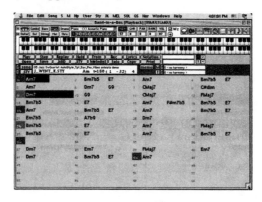

Band-in-a-Box (BIAB) is deservedly one of the best-selling music software programs and includes numerous opportunities for instructional use. Chord progressions entered by students or teachers are realized by *BIAB* using a combo instrumentation (lead, piano, bass, drum set, etc.). The software allows the user to choose from literally hundreds of jazz, rock, and popular styles. Tempo, length of song (and sections), and other parameters can be programmed as well (**Fig. 15**).

BIAB is great for simple song form composition projects with students, individually or in groups. Students can experiment with chord progressions, auditioning them as they program them, and study and apply the various musical styles at their disposal.

Teachers can use *BIAB* to generate accompaniments for classroom singing, instrumental lessons, or for jazz students to use in practicing improvisation (standards, ride choruses, tutorial loops). The software is also capable of generating solos in the style of a number of famous soloists such as Miles Davis and Charlie Parker. One feature of the solo generator permits the software to generate a "trading four" solo, in which the computer plays four measures, then the student answers with a four measure musical reply. There are opportunities for students to record their performances and burn them to CD. The software, although not structured in a tutorial or drill manner, may be used in an instructional manner. Because the software does not contain "lessons," there is no record keeping, but students may use the software to create projects demonstrating their learning. PG Music makes numerous programs supplementing *Band-in-a-Box*.

Classroom Maestro

Publisher: TimeWarp Technologies
Platform: Macintosh, Windows
(www.timewarptech.com)

FIG. 16: Classroom Maestro

This program displays a staff and keyboard and then notates and highlights the notes played on an attached MIDI keyboard. It has a mode for displaying a single note or chord or several notes or chords (**Fig. 16**). While it does not contain structured lesson or score keeping, it is useful in piano and keyboard classes as well as theory classes. The teacher may quickly show the location of notes, intervals, chords, and short melodies. Required are a MIDI interface, an electronic instrument, and a projector.

Compass and Tracker

Publisher: Sibelius
Platform: Macintosh, Windows
(www.sibelius.com)

FIG. 17: Compass (above) and its partner program, Tracker (below).

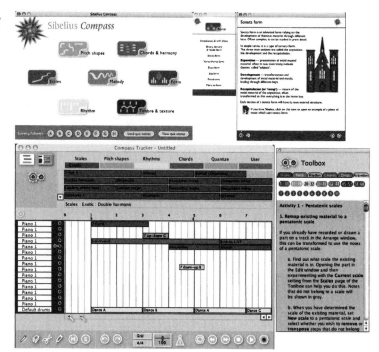

Compass, and its partner program *Tracker*, may be used to present and explore numerous compositional techniques (**Fig. 17**). It is organized according to the elements of music (melody, harmony, rhythm, etc). Each element includes sub-concepts. The melody section, for example, explains contour, variation, inversion, retrograde, and more. The unique feature of this program is that its lessons are connected to hands-on activities using the *Tracker*

program. *Tracker* is a musical sequencer with numerous building blocks. *Tracker* also permits musical elements to be manipulated in unique ways. For instance, a melody may be created or recorded, and then various scales may be applied to the melody. The melody will be rewritten using that scale. Various rhythms may also be applied, so that a plain quarter note scale can become quite syncopated. The ability to drag and drop scales and rhythms onto existing musical material provides the opportunity to create themes and variation and new compositions. The integration of these two programs is unique.

Essentials of Music Theory

Publisher: Alfred
Platform: Macintosh, Windows
(www.alfred.com)

FIG. 18: Alfred's Essentials of Music Theory

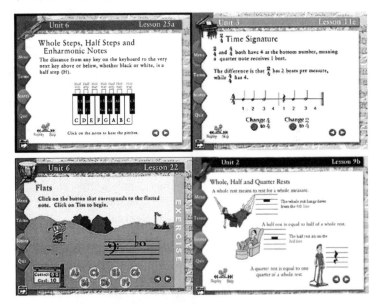

Alfred's *Essentials of Music Theory* is one of the most comprehensive and thoughtful presentations of its subject available. The curricular content is supported by a truly first-rate production (sound, images, animations, and so on) by Alfred. This software contains tutorial lessons on the fundamentals of music (**Fig. 18**). It is organized into three sequential volumes of six units each. The tutorials are interactive and include practice activities for the concepts presented (**Table 4.1**). Record keeping is included. The software would be appropriate for grades four through a college music fundamentals course. Purchase options include single-station licenses and network licenses.

Table 4.1

Volume I (Beginner): Lessons 1–25	Volume II (Intermediate): Lessons 26–50	Volume III (Late Intermediate): Lessons 51–75
Treble and Bass clefs	Major scales	1st and 2nd inversions of triads
Optional Alto and Tenor clefs	Key signatures	Figured bass
4/4, 3/4, and 2/4 time signatures	Intervals	Chord progressions
Flats, sharps, and naturals	3/8 and 6/8 time signatures	Minor scales and triads
Whole and half steps	Triads and V7 chords	Modes
Dynamic signs, tempo markings, and articulation		Harmonizing and composing melodies
Up to 8th notes and rests		12-bar blues chord progression and blues scale
		Basic forms of music

GarageBand

Publisher: Apple
Platform: Macintosh
(www.apple.com)

FIG. 19: The main GarageBand window

GarageBand is one of the newest loop-based programs and includes numerous opportunities for composition and arranging projects by students with limited music reading skills (**Fig. 19**). Students may browse musical excerpts from the bottom of the screen played by a number of instruments and in various styles. When the student selects one to be a part of their composition, they drag it into their composition window at the top of the screen. They may layer parts for a polyphonic construction, or place them one after the other in a call-and-response style. After placing the building-blocks into their composition, students may play the combination and decide whether the materials work together or not. Students make numerous musical decisions as they delete and replace parts. *GarageBand* also interfaces nicely with audio and MIDI equipment attached to the computer. The student may record their own digital audio and MIDI loops into additional tracks in the program. Some editing of MIDI tracks is possible (wrong notes and rhythms can be corrected). Digital audio tracks may have various effects (chorus, reverb, compression) applied to enhance the sound of the recording. A slider near the left middle of the screen lets the student zoom in or out so they can focus on specific parts, or the entire composition. When viewing the entire project, students can make formal decisions (whether to copy and paste the A section in again, or to end the piece). When zoomed in, students can make decisions about the timing of the entrances of the various instruments. When a project is finished, the student may use the "export to iTunes" option to burn it to CD, or integrate it into video projects using *iMovie* and *iDVD*.

One of the great strengths of *GarageBand* is its approachable interface. After just a few minutes of explanation of the program operation, students can begin composing and arranging. As with all programs which focus on creativity, no score keeping is included, but the program does generate projects that can be easily burned to CD for inclusion in electronic or traditional portfolios.

GarageBand2, released in spring 2005, includes some major improvements. Foremost among these is a traditional notation view and the ability to import standard MIDI files (SMFs) into a project. Although you still can't export *GarageBand* MIDI tracks as SMFs, these additions improve what is already an extremely useful and popular program for educators.

Guitropolis

Publisher: Alfred
Macintosh/Windows
(www.alfred.com)

FIG. 20: Guitropolis

Guitropolis is a series of lessons introducing students to the guitar. The software uses an "adventure" game format. In the game students visit a music store where they purchase a guitar and learn to tune it, a practice space where they learn songs, a recital hall in which they perform, a recording studio and a talk show. In addition to knowledge about the guitar, students learn to read notes and guitar tablature and play chords. The program is rich with multimedia (**Fig. 20**) and would be excellent for students learning individually or as part of a middle or high school course.

HomeConcert

Publisher: TimeWarp Technologies
Platform: Macintosh, Windows
(www.timewarptech.com)

FIG. 21: HomeConcert

HomeConcert provides performance practice for keyboard students (**Fig. 21**). Standard MIDI files downloaded from the Internet or created using notation or music production software may be used. The student designates tracks in the MIDI file as ones that the student should play or as accompaniment tracks. The student then practices in one of three modes: learn, perform, and jam. In learn mode, the computer plays the accompaniment and displays the notes that the student should play on a staff and on an onscreen keyboard. The computer waits for the student to play each note before continuing. In jam mode, the student must play with the computer's tempo, although the computer will follow the student's dynamics. In performance mode, the computer plays a performance level accompaniment, but following the student completely with tempo and dynamics. The computer permits the student to skip or repeat sections of the piece. *HomeConcert* is similar in many regards to *SmartMusic* (see the section "SmartMusic" later in this chapter), but for MIDI instruments only. *HomeConcert* requires a MIDI interface and keyboard.

Instruments

Publisher: Sibelius
Platform: Macintosh, Windows
(www.sibelius.com)

FIG. 22: Sibelius Instruments

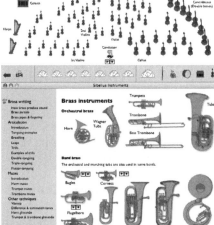

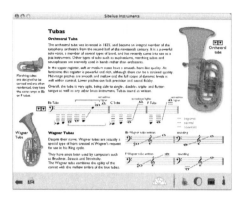

Instruments, a multimedia orchestration resource by Sibelius, contains a wealth of information about strings, woodwind, brass, percussion, and keyboard instruments, and ensembles of instruments (**Fig. 22**). It holds many uses for teachers and their students. The main menu allows students to explore the families of instruments, the history of the orchestra, and to take a quiz on the instruments. The explanation of each instrument includes pictures of the instrument, examples of how each instrument sounds, and information on related instruments (e.g., the Trumpet page includes pictures and sounds of the cornet, bugle, piccolo trumpet, and so on). Listening examples vary and include a scale over the commonly used range of the instrument, excerpts of commonly performed solos and orchestral pieces featuring those instruments. Students may explore the software in a non-sequenced, unstructured manner, following their interests, or they may complete teacher-generated worksheets as they seek specific information. Teachers may use this program to teach the sounds of the instruments to elementary students, or to recruit students for band or orchestra.

This program follows in the steps of a well-known, similarly titled, program by Microsoft called *Musical Instruments*. Unfortunately this program, with its bright graphics and excellent musical examples, is no longer produced (though copies may be found on suppliers shelves or on eBay). A notable distinction between the two programs is that Microsoft *Musical Instruments* included many non-orchestral instruments from around the world, whereas Sibelius *Instruments* does not. Sibelius *Instruments* is the most significant effort to fill the void created by the absence of Microsoft *Musical Instruments*.

Interactive Musician

Publisher: Alfred
Platform: Macintosh, Windows
(www.alfred.com)

FIG. 23: Interactive Musician

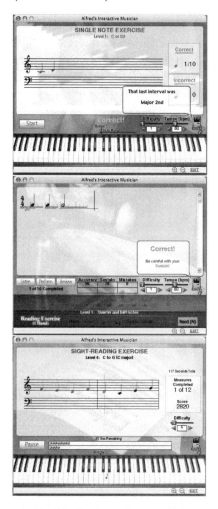

Interactive Musician is a series of instructional programs that permit the student to practice pitch, rhythm, and sight-reading performance (**Fig. 23**). As the title indicates, all activities provide students with the opportunity to interact musically with the software, usually by playing an attached electronic instrument or by tapping a rhythm on the computer keyboard. The pitch exercises include identifying intervals, and melodic dictation. The sight-reading exercises permit the student to play musical examples on an attached MIDI keyboard and to have the performance graded. Correct notes are green. Incorrect are red. The rhythm exercises require the student to tap a rhythm in time with a metronome. In all programs, there are a number of levels from beginning to advanced. In the sight-reading and rhythm exercises, the lower and middle levels are most useful. The higher levels provide great practice, but on figures that will seldom be encountered in musical performance (almost random notes in some cases). Still the program groups even the most complex rhythms properly according to the beat and contains numerous useful activities.

Jazz

Publisher: MiBac
Platform: Macintosh, Windows
(www.mibac.com)

FIG. 24: MiBac Jazz

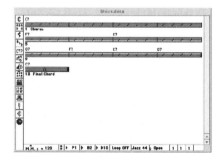

This software permits students to enter a chord progression then they hear it played on piano, bass, and drums (**Fig. 24**). This permits students to experiment with chord progressions as they compose songs. The software is able to perform the music in numerous jazz, rock, and popular styles. The student has the opportunity to study the various styles of music as well as to experiment with different styles in their own compositions. Students may also use the generated accompaniments to practice their improvisation skills. Because the software does not contain "lessons," there is no record keeping, but students may use the software to create projects demonstrating their learning.

MacGAMUT

Publisher: MacGAMUT Music Software
Platform: Macintosh, Windows
(www.macgamut.com)

FIG. 25: MacGAMUT

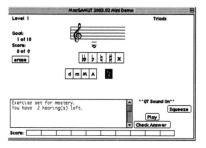

MacGAMUT (**Fig. 25**) is ear-training and music theory software appropriate for high-school and college classes. The software offers practice constructing intervals, scales, and chords on a staff and onscreen keyboard. The software also provides drill and practice in aural skills in the following areas:

▶ Intervals

▶ Scales

▶ Chords

▶ Rhythmic dictation

▶ Melodic dictation

▶ Harmonic dictation

MacGAMUT tracks student mastery of the skills above and has extensive score keeping and reporting functions. The publishers encourage adoption of this software as a text or resource for college aural theory classes. Those locations that have adopted the text frequently require the student to submit the records from their disk to demonstrate their progress through the software. The software also comes in a multiple-license version, but with more limited recordkeeping.

Making Music

Publisher: Creating Music
Platform: Macintosh, Windows
(www.creatingmusic.com)

FIG. 26: Arranging and composing views in Making Music

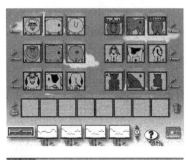

Making Music, with its non-traditional approach to creating music, enables very young students to compose and arrange. Additionally, all instructions in the program are verbal, making the program approachable to non-readers. Some of the musical concepts such as inversion and retrograde, however, could be used on a much higher level. Still the program, developed by electronic art music composer Morton Subotnik, presents them in a way that is approachable by young students.

In this program, students navigate to a main menu where they may select from a musical building-block activity (they arrange musical phrases into familiar and new melodies), a composition activity (they draw notes using various scales and instruments on an artists canvas and the computer plays the contour), a rhythm generator (they create rhythms by dragging sounds onto a timeline), and games (**Fig. 26**). Since the primary purpose of the software is composition and arranging, record keeping is not included. The software would be appropriate for grades one through six, although it would be most useful in grades three through six. *Making More Music* is similar in organization and content to *Making Music*, but with additional compositional activities and games. A third program in the series, *Hearing Music*, encourages students to experiment with sounds and encourages their ability to recognize contrast and repetition in music.

MiDisaurus

Publisher: Macmillian - McGraw Hill
Platform: Macintosh, Windows
(www.town4kids.com/us_ecom/products/midi_about.htm)

FIG. 27: MiDisaurus has great appeal for young children.

MiDisaurus is a collection of music lessons and games in 12 volumes (**Table 4.2**). The software is organized so that a tutorial movie is followed by an interactive activity. The lessons start with contrasting concepts such as loud and soft and advance through more complex content including instruments of the orchestra. The lessons would be most appropriate for grades one through six, with younger students finding them most valuable (**Fig. 27**). This software includes a printable grade report on each child.

Table 4.2

Volumes 1–4 (Selected Topics)	Volumes 5–8 (Selected Topics)	Volumes 9–12 Focus Volumes
Listening skills	Time and key signatures	Rhythm
Music composition	Musical notation of intervals; tempos; articulations: legato, staccato, and fermata	Notation
Keyboard fundamentals	Keyboard accompaniment patterns	Musical instruments
Note reading fundamentals	Scales (major, blues, pentatonic)	The great composers and their music
Intervals	Introduction to the great composers	
Accidentals	Chords (major, minor, diminished, and augmented)	
Binary and ternary forms	I-IV-V7 and i-iv-V7 chords	
I-V7 chords	Introduction to musical instruments of the world	
Introduction to orchestral instruments	Musical form (introduction, question and answer, sequence, theme and variation)	
Sing-along songs		

Music Ace I and II

Publisher: Harmonic Vision
Platform: Macintosh, Windows
(www.harmonicvision.com)

FIG. 28: Music Ace

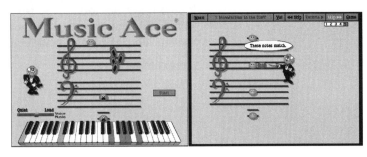

Music Ace is one of the best-loved and most used instructional titles for teaching the fundamentals of music to elementary school children. *Music Ace I* contains tutorial lessons which focus on learning the symbols of music notation and the keyboard. Each unit begins with an animation featuring engaging musical tunes, and Maestro Max, a cartoon conductor who dances and speaks with an Austrian accent (**Fig. 28**). The lessons are organized into approximately 24 units, with three to six activities and games per unit.

A Doodle Pad is available where students may listen to and manipulate existing tunes and compose and save their own. Record keeping is included in the lessons. The software would be appropriate for grades three through 12, although it would be most appealing to younger students. Purchase options include plans for a varying number of users. *Music Ace II* is similar in organization and content to *Music Ace I*, but with an increased emphasis on rhythmic skills (**Table 4.3**).

Table 4.3

Music Ace I (Selected Topics)	Music Ace II (Selected Topics)
Staff and keyboard relationship	Standard notation
Pitch identification	Music fundamentals including key signatures, intervals, major and minor scales, and harmony.
Note reading	Rhythmic concepts including tempo, note values, rests, counting, measures, time signatures, and syncopation.
Listening skills	Musical skills including echoing, comparing rhythms, rhythmic dictation, ear training, and distinguishing melodies and harmonies.
Sharps and flats	Rhythmic and melodic composition
Intro to key signature	
Keyboard basics	
Major scales	
Octaves	
Treble, bass, and grand staff	
Whole and half steps	

Music Lessons I and II

Publisher: MiBac
Platform: Macintosh, Windows
(www.mibac.com)

FIG. 29: Learning about the major scale in Music Lessons

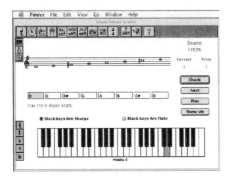

This software is appropriate for high school or university music theory classes. *Music Lessons I* features basic concepts such as note recognition, but also includes key signatures and the circle of fifths (**Fig. 29**). *Music Lessons II* includes additional work with chords. Students are graded on each lesson and must achieve mastery on each level. The program includes record keeping (**Table 4.4**).

Table 4.4	
Music Lessons I **(Selected Topics)**	**Music Lessons II** **(Selected Topics)**
Note reading	Chord elements
Circle of fifths	Triads
Key signatures	Triads ear training
Five finger positions	Seventh chords
Major and minor scales	Seventh chords ear training
Modes	Roman numeral chord identification
Jazz scales	
Scale degrees	
Intervals	
Note and rest durations	
Scales, modes, and jazz scales ear training	
Intervals ear training	

Performance Assessment by Finale

Publisher: MakeMusic!
Platform: Macintosh, Windows
(www.makemusic.com)

FIG. 30: Finale Performance Assessment reacting to a keyboard performance.

Finale Performance Assessment (FPA) is a free program from MakeMusic! It provides students with the opportunity to sing or play their instruments to exercises generated using *Finale 2005* (or later) notation software and receive immediate visual feedback on the accuracy of their performance. *FPA* employs the same user interface as *SmartMusic*, MakeMusic!'s popular intelligent accompaniment software.

Students must perform in time with the beat into a microphone, following a cursor that guides them through the music on their computer screen. Students can choose to hear a metronome and their part doubled as they play. At the end of the performance, the computer parses the performance and indicates which notes were correct and which were incorrect. Correct notes are displayed in green, incorrect in red, and missed notes in black (**Fig. 30**). The computer shows both rhythm and pitch errors. The computer also calculates a score, based on the percentage of notes performed correctly. When properly configured, the computer can e-mail the score to the instructor.

Files for use with *FPA* are created first in *Finale* notation software, saved as *FPA* files, then opened and used by students in the free *FPA* program. There are limitations on the types of musical content that can be converted from *Finale* for use with *FPA*. For instance, *FPA* doesn't support multiple staves (except MIDI keyboard), layers, polyphony (more than one simultaneous note), trills, or repeats.

149

Piano and Keyboard Method

Publisher: eMedia
Platform: Macintosh, Windows
(http://emediamusic.com)

FIG. 31: Guitar Method

The eMedia series contains computer-based lessons for beginners on various instruments including piano and keyboards, electric bass, and guitar (**Fig. 31**). Each program contains over 150 lessons on the instrument. Lessons contain sequenced pieces that progress from easy to more difficult. The software tracks the progress of students. Specific titles in the series include *Piano and Keyboard Method*, *Bass Method*, *Guitar Method* (Vol. 1), *Intermediate Guitar Method* (Vol. 2), *Rock Guitar*, *Guitar Songs*, and *Blues Guitar Legends*.

Practica Musica

Publisher: Ars Nova
Platform: Macintosh, Windows
www.ars-nova.com

FIG. 32: Practica Musica

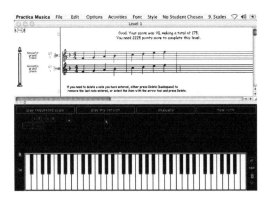

Practica Musica contains an excellent collection of music theory lessons (**Fig. 32**). The lessons are appropriate for high school or college theory, with some lessons that could be used on lower levels. The program requires that the student choose an activity from the top-right menu (note reading, intervals, chords, scales, etc.) and then a level from the submenu that appears. The student then completes a series of questions in that activity until they achieve mastery. The software is available in a number of versions including those that allow record keeping of large and small classes. The student may answer the questions using the onscreen keyboard, an attached MIDI instrument, or using a point-and-click notation entry, as the kind of question dictates.

Rock Rap 'N Roll

Publisher: Silver Burdette and Ginn
Platform: Macintosh, Windows

FIG. 33: Rock Rap 'N Roll

Rock Rap 'N Roll is a one of the earliest and most notable examples that permits loop-based composition and arranging (**Fig. 33**). In this program, students build a composition on any of 10 available styles by dragging musical building blocks into the order desired. They may then play the piece and add additional melodic elements. The styles include African, Big Band, Blues, Street Jazz, Latin, Reggae, Techno Pop, Rock, and Rap.

Buttons on the left edge of the screen represent musical building blocks. Students may click these to hear them. They can then drag these into the empty slots at the bottom of the screen in the order desired. At any time, the student may play their piece and experiment with adding melodies by clicking the buttons on the right of the screen and by typing various numbers and letters.

The musical compositions may be saved for future performance. Students may also record their own melodies or voice for inclusion in the composition.

Because the student composes with this tool, no record keeping is included. The student can, however, save projects in the *Rock Rap 'N Roll* format for including in a portfolio.

This software is increasingly hard to find, but it is still listed in the catalogs of some vendors. If this software can be found, it is worthy of serious consideration.

SmartMusic

Publisher: MakeMusic!
Platform: Macintosh, Windows
(www.makemusic.com)

FIG. 34: SmartMusic's main window

SmartMusic provides accompaniments to well-known instrumental and vocal literature, as well as the major band and string instrument method books. The performers practicing with these accompaniments may play or sing into a microphone, and when the software is properly configured, the computer-generated accompaniment will follow them. *SmartMusic* may also be used in a strict metronomic mode for students who are not ready to be expressive with tempo. The program allows the user to select to hear the melody, accompaniment, and/or a metronome for playback. A tempo slider allows for variable speeds (**Fig. 34**). *SmartMusic* may be used in evaluation mode to provide feedback to students on their performance. Practice loops can be set for drilling tough passages, and when students click on any note a pop-up fingering chart appears.

A demo of the program may be downloaded or requested free of charge from MakeMusic! The program requires a subscription and Internet connection for full use. Once the subscription is activated, the user of the program may take advantage of the accompaniments for method books, solos, many contest lists, and standard classical repertoire. Even without an active subscription, *SmartMusic's* metronome and visual tuner may be found to be very valuable in the rehearsal room.

The software includes a special microphone that provides the best results. It also offers an optional foot pedal for advancing the accompaniment should it fall behind. Given the scarcity of accompanists in many school districts, and its ability to help students evaluate and improve their performance, the software provides a useful service.

StarClass

Publisher: Sibelius
Platform: Macintosh, Windows
(www.sibelius.com/products/starclass/)

FIG. 35: Opening window of StarClass

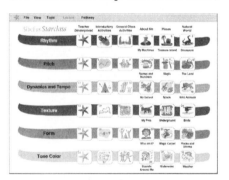

StarClass is a complete curriculum with lesson plans for elementary through middle school general music teachers (**Fig. 35**). The lessons are organized according to the elements of music: rhythm, pitch, dynamics and tempo, texture, form, and tone color. The lessons may also be searched according to the MENC National Standards for Music Education, and by their relationship to other disciplines such as Drama, Dance, Literacy, Math ("Numeracy"), Technology, and Visual Art.

Many of the lessons contain illustrations of concepts useful for presentation to students via handout, overhead, or projection. *StarClass* is a great resource to augment elementary music textbooks such as those by Silver-Burdett or Macmillan, and—since the lessons plans are already done—they are great when time is short. An audio CD containing musical examples for the various lessons is also included.

StarClass is an interactive PDF (portable document file) and requires a PDF reader, such as the free Adobe *Acrobat Reader*, to run it.

Teach Yourself to Play Guitar/Piano

Publisher: Alfred
Platform: Macintosh, Windows
(www.alfred.com)

FIG. 36: Alfred's Teach Yourself to Play Guitar (top), and Teach Yourself to Play Piano (bottom)

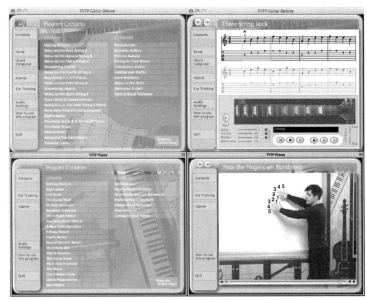

Teach Yourself to Play Piano and *Teach Yourself to Play Guitar* are CD-ROMs produced to accompany Alfred's instructional books of the same name (**Fig. 36**). They provide an introduction to reading standard music notation and a familiarity with each instrument. Songs in a variety of styles are included. Topics also include scales and play-along exercises. The student may adjust the tempo for their practice sessions and may record their performance. Numerous videos of an instructor demonstrating various techniques are included. The guitar software includes a tuner. As of this writing, there is no OSX version of *Teach Yourself to Play Piano*.

Various Lessons by ECS

Publisher: Electronic Courseware Systems
Platform: Macintosh, Windows
(www.ecsmedia.com)

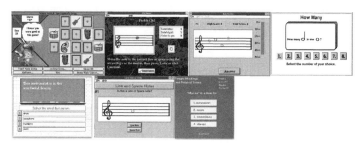

FIG. 37: Several ECS titles (clockwise, from top left)— Adventures in Musicland, Clef Notes, Note Speller, Musical Flash Cards, Spell and Define, Early Music Skills, and Music Terminology

Educational Courseware Systems (ECS) was a pioneer in the development of instructional software for music education. Although many of their titles have been around for some time, and look a little dated, their longevity is a testament to their usefulness in the classroom. All ECS games provide reinforcement of music fundamentals through a drill and practice format. Record keeping is through a hall of fame in which students compete to maintain the top scores. This software is generally appropriate for students ranging in age from grade three to twelve, with occasional exceptions for programs such as *Functional Harmony* and *Harmonic Progressions*. Because of the narrow focus of each title, these programs are easy and fun to use, and the learning is clear and direct (**Fig. 37**).

The *Adventures in Musicland* series varies somewhat from the traditional ECS format. This program provides a game format for the practice of musical memory. It includes three games. In one, the student hears a series of pitches of increasing length and must repeat them. Various modes of play permit the student to work on an easy level (visual and aural clues with only four notes) to the most difficult level (only aural cues and using all eight notes of the diatonic scale). Other games include a musical game resembling the television show, *Concentration*, and a game in which students must identify instruments and composers by viewing just a part of them. Each game has levels ranging from easy to difficult.

Various Lessons by ECS

Adventures in Musicland	Early Music Skills
Elements of Music	Music Flash Cards
KIDS (Keyboard Introductory Dev)	Musical Stairs
Smack-a-note	Rhythm Factory
Clef Notes	Echos
Note Detective	Note Speller
Musicus	Super Musicus
Aural Skills Trainer	Tap-It (I and II)
Tune-It (I and II)	Super Ear Challenger
Functional Harmony	Harmonic Progressions
Music Terminology	Musique
Keyboard Arpeggios	Keyboard Blues
Keyboard Chords	Keyboard Fingerings
Keyboard Intervals	Keyboard Jazz Harmony
Keyboard Kapers	Keyboard Notegame
Keyboard Speed Reading	Keyboard Tutor
Early Keyboard Skills	

Section 4: Resources

Books

Mash, David, C. Floyd Richmond, and Stefani Langol. *Basic Skills in Music Technology: Technology Assisted Learning Software and Multimedia* (TI:ME 2B Workbook). Wyncote, PA: TI:ME, 2005.

Reese, S., K. McCord, and K. Walls. *Strategies for Teaching: Music Technology.* Reston, VA: MENC, 2001.

Rudolph, Thomas. *General Music Curriculum.* New York: SoundTree, 1995.

Rudolph, Thomas. *Teaching Music with Technology, 2nd Edition.* Chicago: GIA Publications, 2005.

Williams, D and P. Webster. *Experiencing Music Technology, 3rd Edition*. New York: Schirmer Books, 2005.

Articles

Frankel, James. "The One-Computer Music Classroom," *Music Education Technology*. Nov 1, 2004.

Richmond, C. Floyd, "Music Technology and the National Standards, Part 2," *Music Education Technology*. Jun 01, 2004.

Rudolph, Thomas. "Music-Theory and Ear-Training Tools," *Music Education Technology*. Feb 1, 2005.

Rudolph, Thomas. "The Wonderful World of WebQuests," *Music Education Technology*. Sep 1, 2004.

Watson, Scott. "A Return to Modernism: Teaching Electronic Art Music Composition with Today's Recording Technology," *Music Education Technology*. Feb 1, 2005.

TECHNOLOGY-ASSISTED LEARNING*
INTERNET

Manufacturer	Product	Web Site	Category	Level‡
Adams, Ricci	musictheory.net	www.musictheory.net/	Aural and/or Written Theory	9-12, College
ChordFind.com	Chord Find	www.chordfind.com	Guitar Studies	6-12, College
Classical Archives LLC	Classical MIDI Archive	www.classicalarchives.com/	Resource/Reference	3-12, College, Teacher use
Estrella, Steven	Blues Jam	www.stevenestrella.com/IWP/bluesjam/bluesjam.html	Creativity (Music Production)	3-12, College
KLMusic (Norway)	Ear Plane	earplane.com/modules/earplane_main/	Aural and/or Written Theory	9-12, College
MusicTheory.com	eMusicTheory	www.emusictheory.com/	Aural and/or Written Theory	9-12, College
Ossmann, Michael	Big Ears	www.ossmann.com/bigears/	Aural and/or Written Theory	9-12, College
Richmond, Floyd	Musical Flashcards	http://courses.wcupa.edu/frichmon/usetech/musicalflashcards/aaaindex.html	Aural and/or Written Theory	3-12, College
Richmond, Floyd	Musical Call Charts	http://courses.wcupa.edu/frichmon/tdml99/index.html	Music Appreciation & History	3-12, College, Teacher use
Subotnick, Morton	Creating Music	www.creatingmusic.com/	Early Childhood	K-6
teoría	Music Theory web	www.teoria.com/	Aural and/or Written Theory	9-12, College
Wholenote.com	Groove Builder	www.wholenote.com	Creativity (Music Production)	3-12, College

Platform	Minimum System Requirements	Special Features	Notes	List Price
N/A				Free
N/A		Contains a chord finder for all 4-stringed instruments (lute, mandolin, banjo, etc.).		Free
N/A				Free for 6 MIDI files a day, $25 a year for more
N/A				Free
N/A				Free
N/A				Free
N/A		Parallel sites in Spanish, French, Italian, and Norwegian		Free
N/A				Free
N/A				Free
N/A				Free
N/A		There is a parallel Spanish language version.		Free
N/A				Free

SOFTWARE

Manufacturer	Product	Web Site	Category	Level
Alfred	Theory Games (1A, 1B, 2)	www.alfred.com	Aural and/or Written Theory	3-8
Alfred	Theory Games (3,4,5)	www.alfred.com	Aural and/or Written Theory	3-8
Alfred	Essentials of Music Theory (Vol. 1)	www.alfred.com	Aural and/or Written Theory	6-12, College
Alfred	Essentials of Music Theory (Vol. 2 & 3 - packaged together)	www.alfred.com	Aural and/or Written Theory	6-12, College
Alfred	Guitropolis	www.alfred.com	Guitar Studies	6-12, College
Alfred	Teach Yourself to Play Guitar	www.alfred.com	Guitar Studies	6-12, College
Alfred	Teach Yourself to Play Piano	www.alfred.com	Keyboard Skills & Studies	6-12, College
Alfred	Interactive Musician	www.alfred.com	Keyboard Skills & Studies, Aural and/or Written Theory	3-12, College
Apple	GarageBand	www.apple.com	Creativity (Music Production)	All levels
Ars Nova	Practica Musica	www.ars-nova.com/practica.html	Aural and/or Written Theory	6-12, College
Ars Nova	Songworks II	www.ars-nova.com/songwork.html	Performance, Keyboard Skills & Studies	3-8
Brown and Benchmark	Ear Training: A Technique For Listening	http://catalogs.mhhe.com/mhhe/search.do	Aural and/or Written Theory	9-12, College
Classical Kids	Beethoven Lives Upstairs	www.childrensgroup.com/sections/classical/bclassical_ie.html	Early Childhood, Music Appreciation & History	3-12
Clearvue/EAV	Impressionism	www.clearvue.com	Integrated and Visual Arts	6-12, College
Clearvue/EAV	The History of Jazz (CD)	www.clearvue.com	Jazz & Improvisation Studies	6-12, College
Clearvue/EAV	Instruments of the Symphony Orchestra (CD)	www.clearvue.com	Music Appreciation & History	6-12, College
Clearvue/EAV	Music & Culture (CD)	www.clearvue.com	Music Appreciation & History	6-12, College
Clearvue/EAV	The Art of Listening (CD)	www.clearvue.com	Music Appreciation & History	6-12, College
Clearvue/EAV	The History of Folk Music (CD)	www.clearvue.com	Music Appreciation & History	6-12, College
Clearvue/EAV	The History of Jazz (CD)	www.clearvue.com	Music Appreciation & History	6-12, College
Clearvue/EAV	The History of Music Part 1-2 (CD)	www.clearvue.com	Music Appreciation & History	6-12, College
Clearvue/EAV	Great Composers: Vol. 1-6 (CD)	www.clearvue.com	Music Appreciation & History	
Clearvue/EAV	Art & Music Titles Vol. 1-8 (CD)	www.clearvue.com	Music Appreciation & History, Integrated and Visual Arts	6-12, College
Creating Music	Hearing Music	www.creatingmusic.com/order.html	Early Childhood; Creativity, Composition, or Music Production	K-6
Creating Music	Making More Music	www.creatingmusic.com/order.html	Early Childhood; Creativity, Composition, or Music Production	K-6
Creating Music	Making Music	www.creatingmusic.com/order.html	Early Childhood; Creativity, Composition, or Music Production	K-6
ECS - TimeSketch Series	Bach Toccata & Fugue in Dm (CD) Sketch	www.timesketch.net/	Music Appreciation & History	6-12, College
ECS - TimeSketch Series	Beethoven Pathetique Sonata Sketch	www.timesketch.net/	Music Appreciation & History	6-12, College
ECS - TimeSketch Series	Beethoven Piano Concerto No. 3 Sketch	www.timesketch.net/	Music Appreciation & History	6-12, College
ECS - TimeSketch Series	Beethoven Symphony No. 5 Sketch	www.timesketch.net/	Music Appreciation & History	6-12, College
ECS - TimeSketch Series	Brahms Symphony No. 3 Sketch	www.timesketch.net/	Music Appreciation & History	6-12, College
ECS - TimeSketch Series	Brubeck Music Analyzed!	www.timesketch.net/	Music Appreciation & History	6-12, College
ECS - TimeSketch Series	Dvorak New World Symphony Sketch	www.timesketch.net/	Music Appreciation & History	6-12, College
ECS - TimeSketch Series	Grainger Lincolnshire Posey Sketch	www.timesketch.net/	Music Appreciation & History	6-12, College
ECS - TimeSketch Series	Miles Davis Music Analyzed!	www.timesketch.net/	Music Appreciation & History	6-12, College
ECS - TimeSketch Series	Moussorgsky Pictures at an Exhibition Sketch	www.timesketch.net/	Music Appreciation & History	6-12, College
ECS - TimeSketch Series	Mozart Symphony No. 40 Sketch	www.timesketch.net/	Music Appreciation & History	6-12, College
ECS - TimeSketch Series	Schubert Unfinished Symphony Sketch	www.timesketch.net/	Music Appreciation & History	6-12, College
ECS - TimeSketch Series	Vaughan Williams/Barber Sketches	www.timesketch.net/	Music Appreciation & History	6-12, College

Platform	Minimum System Requirements	Special Features	Notes	List Price
Mac/Windows				$19.95
Windows only				$19.95
Mac/Windows				$29.95 student, $259.95 lab pack for 10
Mac/Windows				$39.95 student, $399.95 lab pack for 10
Mac/Windows				$24.95
Mac/Windows				$19.95
Mac/Windows				$19.95
Mac/Windows				$39.95 student version $99.95 educator version, $249.95 lab pack for 5 ($30 each additional user)
Mac				$79 as part of iLife package
Mac/Windows	Mac OS X 9.1-10.4.x, PowerMac, 64MB RAM, CD Drive; Windows 95, 98, 2000, ME, XP, 133mhz CPU, 64MB RAM, CD Drive			$100 single $600 site
Mac/Windows	Mac OS X 9.1-10.4.x, PowerMac, 64MB RAM, CD Drive; Windows 95, 98, 2000, ME, XP, 133mhz CPU, 64MB RAM, CD Drive			$125 CD single / $95 download single; $900 site
Mac				
Windows only for enhanced DVD-ROM features				$24.98
Mac/Windows				$79.95 single $239.95 lab (5) $959.95 lab (30)
Mac/Windows				$60.00 single
Mac/Windows				$80 single, $240 lab (5), $960 lab (30)
Mac/Windows				$60 single, $180 lab (5), $720 lab (30)
Mac/Windows				$60 single, $180 lab (5), $720 lab (30)
Mac/Windows				$75 single, $225 lab (5), $900 lab (30)
Mac/Windows				$60 single, $180 lab (5), $720 lab (30)
Mac/Windows				Each volume: $80 single, $240 lab (5), $960 lab (30)
Mac/Windows				Each of 6 Volumes: $60 single, $180 lab (5), $720 lab (30)
Mac/Windows				$574.95 single $1724.95 lab (5) $6899.95 lab (30)
Mac/Windows	Mac OS 7 or later, carbonized for OS X; Windows 95/98/NT/XP			$30
Mac/Windows	Mac OS 7 or later, carbonized for OS X; Windows 95/98/NT/XP			$30
Mac/Windows	Mac OS 7 or later, carbonized for OS X; Windows 95/98/NT/XP			$30
	Windows 98/2000/XP; Mac OS 8, 9 and 10	See the form analysis of this work as you listen to the performance.		$40
	Windows 98/2000/XP; Mac OS 8, 9 and 10 (in classic mode).	See the form analysis of this piece as you listen to the performance.		$40
	Windows 98/2000/XP; Mac OS 8, 9 and 10	See the form analysis of this piece as you listen to the performance.		$40
	Windows 98/2000/XP; Mac OS 8, 9 and 10 (in classic mode).	See the form analysis of this work as you listen to the performance.		$40
	Windows 98/2000/XP; Mac OS 8, 9 and 10	See the form analysis of this piece as you listen to the performance.		$40
	Windows 98/2000/XP; Mac OS 8, 9 and 10 (in classic mode).	See the form analysis of each piece as you listen to the performances from the Time Out album.		$40
	Windows 98/2000/XP; Mac OS 8, 9 and 10	See the form analysis of this piece as you listen to the performance.		$40
	Windows 98/2000/XP; Mac OS 8, 9 and 10	See the form analysis of this piece as you listen to the performance.		$40
	Windows 98/2000/XP; Mac OS 8, 9 and 10	See the form analysis of each piece as you listen to the performances from the Kind of Blue album.		$40
	Windows 98/2000/XP; Mac OS 8, 9 and 10 (in classic mode).	See the form analysis of this piece as you listen to the performance.		$40
	Windows 98/2000/XP; Mac OS 8, 9 and 10	See the form analysis of this piece as you listen to the performance.		$40
	Windows 98/2000/XP; Mac OS 8, 9 and 10 (in classic mode).	See the form analysis of this piece as you listen to the performance.		$40
	Windows 98/2000/XP; Mac OS 8, 9 and 10	See the form analysis of each piece as you listen to the performances.		$40

SOFTWARE (Continued)

Manufacturer	Product	Web Site	Category	Level
Electronic Courseware Systems, Inc.	Musicus	www.ecsmedia.com	Aural and/or Written Theory	3-12
Electronic Courseware Systems, Inc.	Spell and Define	www.ecsmedia.com	Aural and/or Written Theory	3-12
Electronic Courseware Systems, Inc.	Super Ear Challenger	www.ecsmedia.com	Aural and/or Written Theory	3-12
Electronic Courseware Systems, Inc.	Tap It	www.ecsmedia.com	Aural and/or Written Theory	3-12
Electronic Courseware Systems, Inc.	Tap It II	www.ecsmedia.com	Aural and/or Written Theory	3-12
Electronic Courseware Systems, Inc.	Clef Notes	www.ecsmedia.com	Aural and/or Written Theory	3-8
Electronic Courseware Systems, Inc.	Echos	www.ecsmedia.com	Aural and/or Written Theory	3-8
Electronic Courseware Systems, Inc.	Note Detective	www.ecsmedia.com	Aural and/or Written Theory	3-8
Electronic Courseware Systems, Inc.	Note Speller	www.ecsmedia.com	Aural and/or Written Theory	3-8
Electronic Courseware Systems, Inc.	Music Terminology	www.ecsmedia.com	Aural and/or Written Theory	6-12, College
Electronic Courseware Systems, Inc.	Music Terminology for Bands, Orchestras & Choirs	www.ecsmedia.com	Aural and/or Written Theory	6-12, College
Electronic Courseware Systems, Inc.	Musique	www.ecsmedia.com	Aural and/or Written Theory	9-12
Electronic Courseware Systems, Inc.	Aural Skills Trainer	www.ecsmedia.com	Aural and/or Written Theory	9-12, College
Electronic Courseware Systems, Inc.	Functional Harmony	www.ecsmedia.com	Aural and/or Written Theory	9-12, College
Electronic Courseware Systems, Inc.	Harmonic Progressions	www.ecsmedia.com	Aural and/or Written Theory	9-12, College
Electronic Courseware Systems, Inc.	Adventures in Musicland	www.ecsmedia.com	Early Childhood, Aural and/or Written Theory	3-8
Electronic Courseware Systems, Inc.	Early Music Skills	www.ecsmedia.com	Early Childhood, Aural and/or Written Theory	3-8
Electronic Courseware Systems, Inc.	Elements of Music	www.ecsmedia.com	Early Childhood, Aural and/or Written Theory	3-8
Electronic Courseware Systems, Inc.	Music Flash Cards	www.ecsmedia.com	Early Childhood, Aural and/or Written Theory	3-8
Electronic Courseware Systems, Inc.	Musical Stairs	www.ecsmedia.com	Early Childhood, Aural and/or Written Theory	3-8
Electronic Courseware Systems, Inc.	Smack-a-Note	www.ecsmedia.com	Early Childhood, Aural and/or Written Theory	3-8
Electronic Courseware Systems, Inc.	KIDS (Keyboard Introductory Development Series)	www.ecsmedia.com	Early Childhood, Keyboard Skills & Studies	3-12, College
Electronic Courseware Systems, Inc.	MIDI Jazz Improvisation I	www.ecsmedia.com	Jazz & Improvisation Studies	6-12, College
Electronic Courseware Systems, Inc.	MIDI Jazz Improvisation II	www.ecsmedia.com	Jazz & Improvisation Studies	9-12, College
Electronic Courseware Systems, Inc.	Early Keyboard Skills	www.ecsmedia.com	Keyboard Skills & Studies	3-12, College
Electronic Courseware Systems, Inc.	Keyboard Arpeggios	www.ecsmedia.com	Keyboard Skills & Studies	3-12, College
Electronic Courseware Systems, Inc.	Keyboard Chords	www.ecsmedia.com	Keyboard Skills & Studies	3-12, College
Electronic Courseware Systems, Inc.	Keyboard Fingerings	www.ecsmedia.com	Keyboard Skills & Studies	3-12, College
Electronic Courseware Systems, Inc.	Keyboard Intervals	www.ecsmedia.com	Keyboard Skills & Studies	3-12, College
Electronic Courseware Systems, Inc.	Keyboard Note Drill	www.ecsmedia.com	Keyboard Skills & Studies	3-8
Electronic Courseware Systems, Inc.	Keyboard Speed Reading	www.ecsmedia.com	Keyboard Skills & Studies	6-12, College
Electronic Courseware Systems, Inc.	Keyboard Kapers	www.ecsmedia.com	Keyboard Skills & Studies	All levels
Electronic Courseware Systems, Inc.	Keyboard Blues	www.emediamusic.com	Keyboard Skills & Studies, Jazz & Improvisation Studies	6-12, College
Electronic Courseware Systems, Inc.	Keyboard Extended Jazz Harmonies	www.ecsmedia.com	Keyboard Skills & Studies, Jazz & Improvisation Studies	6-12, College

Platform	Minimum System Requirements	Special Features	Notes	List Price
Mac/Windows	Windows 98/2000/XP; Mac OS 8, 9 and 10.	May be used in Spanish or English. Fun and colorful games teach note values and musical meter.		$29.95 single / Lab Pack (5) $105.00 Network/Site (24) $240.00
Mac/Windows	Windows 98/2000/XP; Mac OS 8, 9 and 10 (in classic mode).	Teachers can create and customize vocabularies for student studies.		$39.95 single / Lab Pack (5) $140.00 Network/Site (24) $320.00
Mac	Mac OS 8, 9 and 10 (in classic mode)	Designed to develop ear training skills through memory and color.		$39.95 single / Lab Pack (5) $140.00 Network/Site (24) $320.00
Mac/Windows	Windows 98/2000/XP; Mac OS 7, 8, 9 and 10. MIDI optional.	Learn to keep a steady beat by listening or reading random rhythms; full record keeping.		$39.95 single / Lab Pack (5) $140.00 Network/Site (24) $320.00
Mac/Windows	Windows 98/2000/XP, Mac OS 7, 8, 9 and 10. MIDI optional.	Tapping drills include syncopation, eighth and sixteenth note values. Varying tempos available.		$39.95 single / Lab Pack (5) $140.00 Network/Site (24) $320.00
Mac/Windows	Windows 98/2000/XP; Mac OS 8, 9 and 10	Includes note reading on treble, bass, alto, or tenor clef.		$39.95 single / Lab Pack (5) $140.00 Network/Site (24) $320.00
Windows only	Windows 98/2000/XP	Implements concepts of sight-reading using MIDI keyboard.		$59.95 single / Lab Pack (5) $160.00 Network/Site (24) $480.00
Mac/Windows	Windows 98/2000/XP; Mac OS 8, 9 and 10 (in classic mode). MIDI optional.	Discover basic piano skills with the help of Sherlock.		$59.95 single / Lab Pack (5) $160.00 Network/Site (24) $480.00
Mac/Windows	Windows 98/2000/XP; Mac OS 8, 9 and 10. MIDI optional.	Timed games that develop note reading skills. Treble, bass, or alto clef.		$39.95 single / Lab Pack (5) $140.00 Network/Site (24) $320.00
Mac/Windows	Windows 98/2000/XP; Mac OS 8, 9 and 10 (in classic mode).	Glossary of terms included along with five different types of testing.		$39.95 single / Lab Pack (5) $140.00 Network/Site (24) $320.00
Mac/Windows	Windows 98/2000/XP; Mac OS 8, 9 and 10 (in classic mode).	Quizzes on terms specific to each ensemble, general musical terms with definitions		$39.95 single / Lab Pack (5) $140.00 Network/Site (24) $320.00
Mac/Windows	Windows 98/2000/XP; Mac OS 8, 9 and 10 (in classic mode). MIDI optional.	Collection of software with self-paced exercises for theory instruction		$595 single / Lab Pack (5) unknown Network/Site (24) $4760
Mac/Windows	Windows 98/2000/XP; Mac OS 8, 9 and 10 (in classic mode). MIDI required.	Choose intervals, basic chords or seventh chords for studies and quizzing; keeps records.		$99.95 single / Lab Pack (5) $365.00 Network/Site (24) $800.00
Mac/Windows	Windows 98/2000/XP; Mac OS 8, 9 and 10 (in classic mode). MIDI required.	Choose studies: basic chords, diatonic 7ths, secondary dominants, or borrowed/altered chords.		$149.95 single / Lab Pack (5) $560.00 Network/Site (24) $1200.00
Mac/Windows	Windows 98/2000/XP; Mac OS 8, 9 and 10 (in classic mode). MIDI required.	Analyze chords, harmonic dictation, and aural identification; keeps records.		$200 single / Lab Pack (5) $700.00 Network/Site (24) $1600.00
Mac/Windows	Windows 98/2000/XP; Mac OS 8, 9 and 10 (in classic mode).	Features characters from *Alice in Wonderland* by Lewis Carroll. For ages 4 through 12.		$49.95 single / Lab Pack (5) $150.00 Network/Site (24) $400.00
Mac/Windows	Windows 98/2000/XP; Mac OS 8, 9 and 10	Introduces pre-note reading concepts to young children		$39.95 single / Lab Pack (5) $140.00 Network/Site (24) $320.00
Mac/Windows	Windows 98/2000/XP; Mac OS 8, 9 and 10 (in classic mode).	May be used by children or adults for entry-level studies in music		$79.95 single / Lab Pack (5) $200.00 Network/Site (24) $640.00
Mac/Windows	Windows 98/2000/XP; Mac OS 8, 9 and 10 (in classic mode).	Includes drills on note naming, scales, key signatures, intervals and basic chords		$99.95 single / Lab Pack (5) $365.00 Network/Site (24) $800.00
Mac/Windows	Windows 95/98/2000/XP; Mac OS 7, 8, 9 and 10 (in classic mode). MIDI optional.	Aural-visual game introduces intervallic relationships to young students.		$49.95 single / Lab Pack (5) $150.00 Network/Site (24) $400.00
Mac/Windows	Windows 98/2000/XP; Mac OS 8, 9 and 10	Click on the "critters" that match the note names presented. Variety of skills included.		$19.95 single / Lab Pack (5) $50.00 Network/Site (24) $160.00
Mac/Windows	Windows 98/2000/XP; Mac OS 8, 9. MIDI optional.	Includes studies in solfege, note reading, and finger numbers for piano playing; many activities.		$49.95 single / Lab Pack (5) $150.00 Network/Site (24) $400.00
Mac/Windows	Windows 98/2000/XP; Mac OS 7, 8, 9 and 10. MIDI required.	Develop improvisational skills. Requires software sequencer that can read standard MIDI files.		$59.95 single / Lab Pack (5) $160.00 Network/Site (24) $480.00
Mac/Windows	Windows 98/2000/XP; Mac OS 8, 9 and 10. MIDI required.	Develop improvisational skills. Requires software sequencer that can read standard MIDI files.		$59.95 single / Lab Pack (5) $160.00 Network/Site (24) $480.00
Mac/Windows	Windows 98/2000/XP; Mac OS 8, 9 and 10	Introduction to basic piano skills such as note reading and piano key names		$39.95 single / Lab Pack (5) $140.00 Network/Site (24) $320.00
Mac/Windows	Windows 98/2000/XP; Mac OS 8, 9. Requires MIDI	Review piano arpeggio performance and fingerings to increase performance skills.		$39.95 single / Lab Pack (5) $140.00 Network/Site (24) $320.00
Mac/Windows	Windows 98/2000/XP; Mac OS 8, 9 and 10 (in classic mode). MIDI optional	Drill and practice program that teaches major, minor, diminished, and augmented chords; keeps records.		$79.95 single / Lab Pack (5) $200.00 Network/Site (24) $640.00
Windows	Windows 98/2000/XP. Requires MIDI.	Review standard and special fingerings for major, natural minor, and harmonic minor scales.		$39.95 single / Lab Pack (5) $140.00 Network/Site (24) $320.00
Mac/Windows	Windows 98/2000/XP; Mac OS 8, 9 and 10 (in classic mode). MIDI optional.	Learn major, minor, diminished, and augmented intervals; keeps student records.		$39.95 single / Lab Pack (5) $140.00 Network/Site (24) $320.00
Mac/Windows	Windows 98/2000/XP; Mac OS 8, 9 and 10 (in classic mode). MIDI optional.	Varying levels of difficulty, helps develop note reading skills. May be used with or without MIDI.		$39.95 single / Lab Pack (5) $140.00 Network/Site (24) $320.00
Mac/Windows	Windows 95/98/2000/XP; Mac OS 7, 8, 9. MIDI optional.	Timed drills help develop quicker note reading skills; keeps student records.		$39.95 single / Lab Pack (5) $140.00 Network/Site (24) $320.00
Mac/Windows	Windows 98/2000/XP; Mac OS 8, 9 and 10. MIDI optional.	Note reading, ear training, piano skill development games. Hall of Fame displays high scores.		$39.95 single / Lab Pack (5) $140.00 Network/Site (24) $320.00
Mac/Windows	Windows 98/2000/XP; Mac OS 8, 9. MIDI required.	Introduces simple blues chords; user can practice improvising with background chords.		$49.95 single / Lab Pack (5) $150.00 Network/Site (24) $400.00
Mac/Windows	Windows 98/2000/XP; Mac OS 8, 9 and 10 (in classic mode). MIDI optional.	Learn 9th, 11th, and 13th chords both aurally and visually; keeps records.		$79.95 single / Lab Pack (5) $200.00 Network/Site (24) $640.00

Manufacturer	Product	Web Site	Category	Level
Electronic Courseware Systems, Inc.	Keyboard Jazz Harmonies	www.ecsmedia.com	Keyboard Skills & Studies, Jazz & Improvisation Studies	9-12, College
eMedia Music Corporation	eMedia Rock Guitar Method	www.emediamusic.com	Guitar Studies	3-12, College
eMedia Music Corporation	eMedia Bass Method	www.emediamusic.com	Guitar Studies	6-12, College
eMedia Music Corporation	eMedia Blues Guitar Legends	www.emediamusic.com	Guitar Studies	6-12, College
eMedia Music Corporation	eMedia Guitar Method	www.emediamusic.com	Guitar Studies	6-12, College
eMedia Music Corporation	eMedia Guitar Songs	www.emediamusic.com	Guitar Studies	6-12, College
eMedia Music Corporation	eMedia Intermediate Guitar Method	www.emediamusic.com	Guitar Studies	6-12, College
eMedia Music Corporation	eMedia Piano & Keyboard Method	www.emediamusic.com	Keyboard Skills & Studies	3-8, College
ERTechnologies	Musica Analytica	www.ertechsoft.com	Aural and/or Written Theory	9-12, College
Harmonic Vision	Music Ace & Music Ace 2	www.harmonicvision.com	Early Childhood, Aural and/or Written Theory	3-12, College
Harmonic Vision	Doodle Pad (from Music Ace)	www.harmonicvision.com	Early Childhood; Creativity, Composition, or Music Production	3-12
Interactive Publishing Co. / Future Vision	Tchaikovsky's 1812 Overture		Music Appreciation & History	6-12, College
iSong / Hal Leonard	EASY Classical Piano Vol 1 Hyb	www.halleonard.com/	Keyboard Skills & Studies	3-8, College
iSong / Hal Leonard	EASY Classical Piano Vol 2 Hyb	www.halleonard.com/	Keyboard Skills & Studies	3-8, College
iSong / Hal Leonard	Popular Classical Piano	www.halleonard.com/	Keyboard Skills & Studies	6-12, College
iSong / Hal Leonard	Glen Gould Plays Bach Hyb	www.halleonard.com/	Keyboard Skills & Studies	9-12, College
Lars Peters	EarTraining	www.lpeters.de/	Aural and/or Written Theory	9-12, College
MacGAMUT Music Software	MacGAMUT	www.macgamut.com	Aural and/or Written Theory	6-12, College
Macmillan/McGraw Hill	MiDisaurus	www.town4kids.com/us_ecom/products/midi_about.htm	Early Childhood, Aural and/or Written Theory	3-12, College
MakeMusic!	SmartMusic	www.smartmusic.com/	Performance	3-12
MakeMusic!	Finale Performance Assessment	www.finalemusic.com/finale/features/educatortools/fpa.aspx	Performance	3-8
MiBAC Music Software, Inc.	Music Lessons I Fundamentals (Mac)	www.mibac.com	Aural and/or Written Theory	9-12, College
MiBAC Music Software, Inc.	Music Lessons I Fundamentals (Windows)	www.mibac.com	Aural and/or Written Theory	9-12, College
MiBAC Music Software, Inc.	Music Lessons II Chords and Harmony	www.mibac.com	Aural and/or Written Theory	9-12, College
MiBAC Music Software, Inc.	Jazz	www.mibac.com	Jazz & Improvisation Studies	6-12, College

Platform	Minimum System Requirements	Special Features	Notes	List Price
Mac/Windows	Windows 98/2000/XP; Mac OS 8, 9 and 10 (in classic mode). MIDI optional.	Study chord symbols and 7th chords; keeps records.		$79.95 single / Lab Pack (5) $200.00 Network/Site (24) $640.00
Mac/Windows	Windows 95 and higher; Mac OS 7.5 and higher	Over 100 audio and video enhanced lessons. Includes a built in tuner, metronome, and recorder.		$40
Mac/Windows	Windows 95 and higher; Mac OS 7.5 and higher	114 lessons; includes animated fretboard, video instruction, audio with tracking, and digital metronome.		$60
Mac/Windows	Windows 95 and higher; Mac OS 7.5 and higher	10 original artist recordings including The Allman Bros., Robert Cray, Stevie Ray Vaughan, and B.B. King		$30
Mac/Windows	Windows 95 and higher; Mac OS 7.5 and higher	Animated fretboard, digital metronome, chord dictionary, automatic tuner, video instruction, looping.		$60
Mac/Windows	Windows 95 and higher; Mac OS 7.5 and higher	Over 20 hit songs by The Who, Peter Frampton, Heart, Stevie Ray Vaughn, Eric Clapton, and Grateful Dead		$30
Mac/Windows	Windows 95 and higher; Mac OS 7.5 and higher	155 lessons; includes animated fretboard, automatic tuner, digital metronome, and scale dictionary.		$60
Mac/Windows	Windows 95 and higher; Mac OS 7.5 and higher	Animated keyboard displays correct fingering as music plays; features 70 full motion videos.		$60
Mac/Windows				$200 for 20, other pricing available depending on lab size.
Mac/Windows				$49.95 each
Mac/Windows				Packaged with MusicAce
Mac/Windows		Specific detailed information on each section and individual instruments with appropriate commentary.	Not readily available; can be found in some online stores.	Prices vary
Mac/Windows	Mac: PowerMac, 4MB application RAM, 1MB Video RAM, 6x CD-ROM, QuickTime 2.5 or greater; Windows: Pentium Processor, 4MB application RAM, 1MB Video RAM, 8x CD-ROM, Sound Blaster compatible, QuickTime 3.0 or greater. At the date of publication, iSong is not compatible with Mac OS 9 and higher.	Each iSong pack includes arrangements ranging from very simple to note-accurate transcriptions, a performance video, and a virtual fretboard or keyboard. iSong syncs to the original recordings of legendary musicians.		$24.95
Mac/Windows	Mac: PowerMac, 4MB application RAM, 1MB Video RAM, 6x CD-ROM, QuickTime 2.5 or greater; Windows: Pentium Processor, 4MB application RAM, 1MB Video RAM, 8x CD-ROM, Sound Blaster compatible, QuickTime 3.0 or greater. At the date of publication, iSong is not compatible with Mac OS 9 and higher.	Each iSong pack includes arrangements ranging from very simple to note-accurate transcriptions, a performance video, and a virtual fretboard or keyboard. iSong syncs to the original recordings of legendary musicians.		$24.95
Mac/Windows	Mac: PowerMac, 4MB application RAM, 1MB Video RAM, 6x CD-ROM, QuickTime 2.5 or greater; Windows: Pentium Processor, 4MB application RAM, 1MB Video RAM, 8x CD-ROM, Sound Blaster compatible, QuickTime 3.0 or greater. At the date of publication, iSong is not compatible with Mac OS 9 and higher.	Each iSong pack includes arrangements ranging from very simple to note-accurate transcriptions, a performance video, and a virtual fretboard or keyboard. iSong syncs to the original recordings of legendary musicians.		$24.95
Mac/Windows	Mac: PowerMac, 4MB application RAM, 1MB Video RAM, 6x CD-ROM, QuickTime 2.5 or greater; Windows: Pentium Processor, 4MB application RAM, 1MB Video RAM, 8x CD-ROM, Sound Blaster compatible, QuickTime 3.0 or greater. At the date of publication, iSong is not compatible with Mac OS 9 and higher.	Each iSong pack includes arrangements ranging from very simple to note-accurate transcriptions, a performance video, and a virtual fretboard or keyboard. iSong syncs to the original recordings of legendary musicians.		$24.95
Mac	Mac OS X only			Free download
Mac/Windows	Mac is OS9 only			$35
Mac/Windows				Vol. 1 only $44.95; Vols. 1-4 $149.95; Vols 5-8 $149.95
Mac/Windows	Mac: G3 or higher; 128MB RAM minimum, 256 recommended; OS X 2.8 or higher, CD-ROM drive, 400MB free disk space, microphone port or adapter. Windows: 98SE/ME/2000/XP, Pentium-class 300MHz processor, 128MB RAM, CD-ROM drive, 400MB free disk space, DirectX 9 compatible soundcard with full duplex support.	A complete music practice system with over 30,000 titles and 50,000 exercises.		School Subscriptions: $90 first computer, $60 second computer, $30 third computer, $20 each computer after three; school subscribers can offer SmartMusic to their students at home for only $20 per year (10 student minimum).
Mac/Windows				Free download; comes with Finale as well.
Mac	Mac OS X (10.2 or later); Mac OS 9, Mac OS 8. MIDI optional.	Flexible skill levels, onscreen help, built-in music theory reference, scorekeeping		$149
Windows	Windows 98, ME, NT4, 2000, XP; Sound Blaster and MIDI compatible.	Flexible skill levels, onscreen help, scorekeeping, built-in theory reference		$119
Mac/Windows	Windows/Mac Hybrid: Windows XP, 2000, ME, 98, 95. Mac OS X, OS 9, OS 8. MIDI optional.	Every drill, including ear training, can be done in naming, writing, and playing study activities.		$149
Mac/Windows		Realistic-sounding jazz accompaniments, 12 styles, flexible song forms and playback, large chord vocab.		$125

SOFTWARE (Continued)

Manufacturer	Product	Web Site	Category	Level
Norton	CD-ROM Masterworks	www.wwnorton.com/mw1.htm	Music Appreciation & History	6-12, College
PG Music, Inc.	Jazz Guitar MasterClass Vols. 1 & 2	www.pgmusic.com	Guitar Studies	6-12, College
PG Music, Inc.	Band-in-a-Box	www.pgmusic.com	Jazz & Improvisation Studies, Performance	3-12, College
Pyware	Amadeus al fine, Amadeus Tutor	www.pyware.com/Frames/amadeus.html	Performance	3-12
Queue, Inc.	Children's Treasury of Stories, Nursery Rhymes, and Songs	www.qworkbooks.com/Queueinc/lit.html	Early Childhood, Music Appreciation & History	3-8
Queue, Inc.	Apple Pie Music	www.qworkbooks.com/Queueinc/mus.html	Music Appreciation & History	6-12, College
Queue, Inc.	History of Country Music	www.qworkbooks.com/Queueinc/mus.html	Music Appreciation & History	6-12, College
Queue, Inc.	History of the Blues	www.qworkbooks.com/Queueinc/mus.html	Music Appreciation & History, Jazz & Improvisation Studies	6-12, College
Sibelius Software	Auralia	www.sibelius.com	Aural and/or Written Theory	9-12, College
Sibelius Software	Compass and Tracker	www.sibelius.com	Creativity, Composition, or Music Production	6-12, College
Sibelius Software	Instruments	http://www.sibelius.com/	Music Appreciation & History (Orchestration)	6-12, College
Sibelius Software	StarClass	www.sibelius.com	Music Curriculum	3-12
Silver Burdett	Rock Rap and Roll		Early Childhood; Creativity, Composition, or Music Production	3-12, College
TimeWarp Technologies	Home Concert Xtreme / Home Concert 2000	www.timewarptech.com	Performance	3-12, College
Voyetra	Multimedia History of Music including Great Composers	www.voyetra.com	Music Appreciation & History	6-12, College

*Some of the data in these tables was previously published in *Electronic Musician's Computer Music Product Guide*, a product of Primedia, and is reprinted with the permission of the publisher.

* Many entries in this table were adapted from the TI:ME 1B Course Workbook (*Basic Skills in Technology: Technology-Assisted Learning and Digital Media*) and are used with permission.

‡ "Level" indicates most appropriate general use grades. Note that many of these titles have value for instruction with students at other levels.

Platform	Minimum System Requirements	Special Features	Notes	List Price
Mac		Scores, historical notes, online help and glossary, and quizzes on 12 pieces from the Norton Scores and The Enjoyment of Music	Not readily available.	Prices vary
Windows only	Windows 9x/ME/NT/2000/XP, minimum 16MB RAM, PC 16 bit soundcard, CD-ROM drive	60 complete lessons, 10 songs, 5 hours of recorded audio comments, and notation; chord displays and onscreen guitar displays.		$29 each volume, $49 for both
Mac/Windows	Mac 10.2; Mac OS8 or 9 requires 16MB of available memory. (Note: OSX is a different program than earlier versions—be sure to order the correct item); Windows 9x/ME/NT/2000/XP, minimum 16MB RAM, 32MB recommended, 35-135MB hard drive space, PC Sound Card or MIDI module.	Automatic accompaniment; MegaPAK includes 49 additional style sets, 13 additional soloist sets, 5 additional melodist sets, and video tutorial.		$88 standard version or $249 MegaPAK
Mac/Windows	Mac OS 7 or 8, 8MB RAM; 166mhz or faster; Serial Port (not a USB port, for Macs with only USB: Serial Port interface cards cost around $50), MIDI box and MIDI cables. Microphone (inexpensive dynamic omni directional); Sound device such as a synthesizer or tone generator. / Windows 95 or 98; 16MB RAM; MIDI port and MIDI cables; MIDI capable sound card; Microphone (inexpensive dynamic omni directional)	Amadeus al fine is a hardware box that converts "microphone input" of any wind instrument into standard MIDI data. Amadeus Tutor is assessment and evaluation software that works with Amadeus al fine and allows you to develop a curriculum for your students.		Amadeus Harware $499 Amadeus Tutor $295
Mac/Windows		Includes a publishing program that enables children to write, illustrate, and print their own stories based on the characters in the stories.		$49.95 single / Lab Pack (5) $149.85
Mac/Windows		Over 400 complete compositions are featured, representing almost 350 years of America's history through its music. Almost half of the music comes from archival of Native Americans, coal miners, prisoners, and cowboys.	Not readily available.	Prices vary
Mac/Windows		Photographs and recordings are woven into a narration that emphasizes the genre's continuing evolution and vitality.	Not readily available.	Prices vary
Mac/Windows		The development of the blues from the music of field hollers and the chants of American slaves to the "big city" blues of the 1920s and the birth of "rhythm and blues" and "rock and roll."		$59.95 single / Lab Pack (5) $179.95 Network $599.50
Mac/Windows	Windows 95, 98, ME, NT, 2000, XP; Mac OS X	26 topics, student tracking, customizable content		$149
Mac/Windows	Windows 95/98/Me/2000/XP/NT4 or later, Pentium II or faster, 64MB RAM (128MB for Windows 2000/XP), 300MB free hard disk space; Mac OS 8.6 or later (including OS X), iMac/G3/G4/G5, 64MB RAM (128MB for OS X), 300MB free hard disk space	Includes lessons, worksheets, and self-tests covering a wide range of topics, leading to complete composition projects.		$159
Mac/Windows	Windows 95/98/Me/2000/XP/NT4 or later, Pentium II or faster, 32MB+ RAM, 170MB free hard disk space, CD-ROM drive; Mac OS 8.6 or later (including OS X), 32MB+ free RAM (128MB total RAM for OS X), 170MB free hard disk space, CD-ROM drive	Interactive encyclopedia of instruments, bands, orchestras and ensembles; includes complete information on every orchestral and band instrument with full details of their characteristics, how to write for them, and hundreds of high-quality recordings.		$119
Mac/Windows	Windows 95/98/Me/2000/XP/NT4 or later, Pentium or faster, 32MB+ RAM, 300MB free hard disk space, CD-ROM drive; Mac OS 8.6 or later (including OS X), 32MB+ free RAM, 300MB free hard disk space, CD-ROM drive	Sibelius Starclass guides you through 180 exciting, ready-to-use lesson plans that support MENC and QCA standards. Starclass includes full explanations of musical concepts for non-specialist teachers, hundreds of music clips and printable pictures, and an audio CD to play in class.		$159
Mac/Windows			Not readily available; listed here because it is a great program, and you may find used copies online.	Prices vary
Mac/Windows	Home Concert Xtreme: Mac OSX 10.3 or later; Windows XP / Home Concert 2000: Windows 98SE, ME, 2000, and XP; Mac OS 7.1-9.x			$99.00 / demo version (free download) available
Windows	Windows 95, 98, Me, 486DX2/66 or faster, 8MB of RAM, 1MB of hard disk, VGA card and monitor with 256 colors, 2X CD-ROM drive, Windows-compatible sound card	Journey through the Renaissance, Baroque, Classical, and Romantic periods of music history and examine the lives and works of 14 renowned composers.	Discontinued; may still find at online and retail outlets.	Prices vary

CHAPTER 5

Multimedia

By Scott D. Lipscomb and Kimberly C. Walls

Tell me and I'll forget;
show me and I may remember;
involve me and I'll understand.
—Variously attributed

Section 1: Overview of Multimedia

In recent years, "multimedia" has become one of the most oft-used buzzwords in education, sometimes touted as a potential solution to many education-related challenges. With the arrival of a multiplicity of tools that facilitate the creation of multimedia materials, creating these engaging instructional materials is well within the reach of any teacher willing to invest the time necessary to learn how to use this software . . . and these programs continue to get easier and easier to use with each new version. There are a wide range of tools available, varying significantly in their levels of complexity and, correspondingly, the associated learning curve. Some tools, like the presentation software discussed early in this chapter, are largely intuitive in their basic functionality and require very little time to learn the essentials. Others, like the full-fledged multimedia authoring programs discussed later, do require a greater investment of time, but the potential payoff can be great. Even these more complex programs, however, require significantly less time to learn than a formal programming language (like C++ or

Java), and it is worth emphasizing that the user need not learn how to utilize *every* capability the program has to offer. In fact, by learning just a handful of the most useful capabilities, instructors can create engaging interactive materials that have great potential for enhancing the learning experience.

Given all of the responsibilities associated with a teaching position, it is certainly reasonable to ask the obvious question: "Why would anyone want to invest the time necessary to learn how to create multimedia instructional materials?" An initial response to this query is that interactive multimedia can make the learning process more fun and engaging for the students. In a more general sense, there is evidence that such engagement results in deeper learning (Barnett, 2003). At a more anecdotal level, this sentiment is expressed beautifully in the oft-quoted statement provided at the beginning of this chapter, variously attributed to Aristotle, to Confucius, as a Chinese proverb, or as a Native American proverb. This same basic tenet has been a driving force in recent years as more educational programs are devoted to student-centered learning, group learning activities, and problem-based learning contexts. Interactive multimedia provide computer-based technologies that can provide students with many of these same active, engaging learning experiences as these "in person" pedagogical approaches.

Section 2: Categories of Multimedia Software, Representative Examples, and Teaching Applications

Creating Presentations

Presentation programs such as *PowerPoint* (Mac/Windows) and *Keynote* (Mac) are used to coordinate the display of text, images, and media on the computer in an interactive manner. A presentation consists of a series of "slides," the term used to describe each screen of content. Many different types of media—including files imported directly from a video camera or captured using image manipulation software (such as Adobe *Photoshop* or Macromedia *Fireworks*)—can be incorporated into a presentation. The amount of interactivity incorporated into a presentation can vary widely, as represented here:

▶ A non-interactive presentation that utilizes the timing capabilities of the software to create a presentation that runs automatically (like informational museum kiosks).

▶ A situation that simply requires a mouse click or key press to initiate the display of each element contained on every slide.

▶ A non-linear presentation in which the actions of the user determine the order in which information is presented.

▶ Any combination of the types listed above.

Presentations can also be converted to a series of digital images or saved to a Web-ready format, allowing online access.

Often, presentations created using this software are projected onto a screen to accompany a teacher's lectures. However, there are many other uses for presentations in the music classroom: teacher-centered activities, group processes, lessons for individualized learning, and performances. Specific examples for each of these types of educational activities are as follows:

TEACHER CENTERED

▶ Display text, play recordings, and show graphics to accompany a lecture, such as introducing a new composition to an ensemble or a new unit theme to a class.

Playing a musical example, using either a digital audio file or audio CD, from within a presentation is easily accomplished: **Insert→Movies and Sounds→[select sound source].**

▶ Display classroom rules or the daily agenda.

▶ Display and play a teacher-created listening guide.

Graphics or text can be synchronized to a recording, using the timing features of the presentation software: **Slide Show→ Custom Animation[select object on slide, then set timing].**

▶ Display questions for a timed test incorporating text, graphics, and/or musical examples.

▶ Playback and/or display sight singing or rhythmic dictation exercises.

▶ Convey program or course overview for parent night, open house, etc.

Can be set to run automatically and/or loop continually.

▶ Use in class in lieu of a chalk or whiteboard to interactively take notes on discussion content.

These notes can then be posted to the Web, along with the agenda for the day's class, homework assignments, and so on.

GROUP

▶ Small groups research a topic, organize their content into a series of slides, then present their report to the class.

▶ Groups record collaborative musical compositions into *PowerPoint*, allowing you to provide your evaluation of their work.

▶ Groups work together to create an interactive listening guide themselves.

INDIVIDUALIZED LEARNING

▶ Students review materials from missed classes.

▶ Students practice a displayed exercise, recording their practice sessions.

▶ Students create a presentation analyzing a composition they listened to or composed.

PERFORMANCES

▶ Display student artwork during performance.

▶ Provide information about music being performed, including information about the composer, contemporaneous events, and so on.

▶ Display photos of students participating in activities as an end-of-the-year presentation or yearbook.

▶ Display pre-concert announcements regarding upcoming music department activities such as concerts, trips, summer programs, and so on.

MICROSOFT POWERPOINT (MAC/WINDOWS)

By far the most popular presentation software in this category is Microsoft's *PowerPoint* ($99.95 upgrade), currently in the 2004 version for Macintosh computers and 2003 version for Windows. The versions leapfrog, such that one platform is always a version ahead of (or behind) the other. *PowerPoint* can be purchased as a standalone product or as part of the Microsoft Office Suite of applications, including *Word* (word processor), *Excel* (spreadsheet), *PowerPoint* (presentation), and *Access*, a powerful relational database program available only on the Windows platform.

PowerPoint facilitates the creation of slides containing instructional content with the Slide Layout panel (**Fig. 1**). To add a slide to your presentation, simply click on the New Slide icon in the toolbar (or use the program menus to choose **Insert→New Slide**), then select the appropriate type of slide from the Slide Layout panel (**Format→Slide Layout**). This collection of layouts includes various combinations of titles, bullet points, graphics, charts, and many other media types. You can easily create your own slide layout or add to a slide's default content by selecting items from the Insert menu. Every object on the slide can be assigned an animated entrance and/or exit from the main content area, using the Custom Animation panel (**Slide Show→Custom Animation**). In addition, *PowerPoint* comes with a large selection of predefined templates—found in the Slide Design panel (**Format→Slide Design**)—that include color schemes, font selection, and slide formatting to ensure that the slides within your presentation maintain a consistent look and feel. As you become more comfortable with the program, you can create your own templates by editing the Slide Master (**View→Master→Slide Master**). There is even an AutoContent wizard (**File→New**, then click on From AutoContent wizard in the New Presentation panel) that will provide a basic skeleton of a presentation for you based on the type of presentation you select, though be aware of the fact that you trade a significant amount of control over the design and organizational structure of your presentation for this convenience. We recommend avoiding this latter "convenience" and utilizing the Templates and Slide

Layout panel to create your presentations, with the following caveat.

FIG. 1: Adding a new slide and selecting a slide layout in Microsoft PowerPoint.

Though the templates do facilitate the speed of development and consistency of look and feel, some serve as (unintentional) examples of poor design in their lack of color contrast, formal makeup, and other design-oriented attributes. The best advice, from Dave Williams, co-author of *Experiencing Music Technology* (2006), is to "keep it simple," using basic backgrounds and fonts.

APPLE KEYNOTE 2 (MAC)

Keynote 2 is a Macintosh-only presentation software package. It is very similar in function to *PowerPoint*, but comes as part of the $79 iWork suite, including *Pages* (word processor) and *Keynote 2* (presentation). Like *PowerPoint*, this program comes with numerous predefined templates and an impressive set of slide transitions and animations (**Fig. 2**), making the creation of an interactive presentation highly intuitive. As shown in **Fig. 3**, when you create a presentation, the Inspector window (**View→Show Inspector**) allows direct access to many of the most commonly used functions, including settings related to the presentation document, the current slide (transitions and layout), animations for building items of a list, text formatting and lists (both bulleted and numbered), adding or editing graphic symbols, charts, or tables, and many other useful components. It is quite easy to move information between *PowerPoint* and *Keynote*. The latter program will import and export files in *PowerPoint* format, and both *Keynote* and *PowerPoint* export to *QuickTime* format.

FIG. 2: Selecting a Transition effect in Apple's Keynote

FIG. 3: Selecting a Build effect using the Inspector in Apple's Keynote

FINAL COMMENTS REGARDING THE USE OF PRESENTATION SOFTWARE

Before concluding this section about presentation software, we should mention the fact that, while many believe these packages provide a very powerful tool to assist the teacher/presenter engaged in the process of organizing material for instructional purposes, there are others who feel that the resulting style of information transfer is diluted. Edward R. Tufte (2003), for example, lambastes the bullet-point approach to presenting complex information. In support of his position, he points to an "intentional and ferocious parody" (p. 14), in which Peter Norvig (2005) provides for us an example of what Lincoln's famous *Gettysburg Address* would have been like were it presented using *PowerPoint*, including the ubiquitous banter often heard at the beginning of a presentation as the technology is being tested.

Both Tufte and Norvig provide valuable information as we consider the most effective ways to use presentation software in educational contexts. Despite some admitted weaknesses, the present authors continue to believe that the benefits provided by such technologies far outweigh any potential negative effects, many of which can be minimized, if not eliminated, simply by being aware of the pitfalls. As a result, we recommend being aware of the concerns expressed by Tufte and Norvig, so that you can make more informed decisions in the creation of your own pedagogical materials, resulting in a higher quality of instructional multimedia to enhance learning in your music classroom.

Finally, one must consider the advantages and disadvantages of various hardware setups used to display presentations (or any multimedia products). Both visual and aural aspects of the presentation must be considered. If one student or a small group of students will be viewing a multimedia product, then the computer screen may suffice. One student may listen through a pair of headphones inserted into the headphone jack. An amplified headphone splitter such as the *Boosteroo* portable audio amplifier and splitter ($29.95) allows up to three students to hear the presentation through headphones. For more than three students, amplified speakers (preferably with a sub-woofer) or a stereo system may be plugged into the computer's headphone jack. A scan converter attached to the video output of the computer can be plugged into a large television to display images for larger groups. Using a television for a presentation can work well for small classes when small visual details are not essential. A data projector can display a larger, more detailed image that is sufficient for detailed viewing by large classes or audiences. Purchasing scan converter equipment is less expensive than purchasing a high-quality computer projector, but consider the overall costs, effectiveness, uses of the equipment, and classroom management issues before deciding which option will fulfill your needs and meet your requirements most effectively.

Making Movies and Creating DVDs

Movie software is great for documenting and evaluating performances, especially those involving coordinated movement as in marching band or show choir. It is also a valuable self-assessment tool, when used to evaluate one's own teaching. Used in a well-designed lesson plan, movie software allows students to understand the role of music in motion picture experience and actually become "movie music composers" themselves. Using sequencing software or digital audio files (discussed in Chapter 2, "Music Production"), students can compose a musical soundtrack for any video sequence. Many of the current sequencing software packages integrate both audio and video capabilities and allow the integration of MIDI and various types of digital audio, greatly facilitating this creative process.

Movie-making software is a specific type of multimedia software for which great strides have been made in recent years. The exponential increase in hard drive storage space available on a typical personal computer (PC)—now measured in *giga*bytes, rather than *mega*bytes—and similar increase in processor speed—now measured in *giga*hertz, rather than *mega*hertz—have made basic video capture and amateur movie-making a possibility on most PCs.

Ideas for implementation in the music classroom include the following:

▶ Record both the audio and video of a performance or rehearsal, then playback for students' self-assessment.

▶ Students try using different soundtracks with a film clip or different film clips with a given soundtrack to see the effects on the mood and interpretation of the visual images.

▶ Students compose their own soundtrack to accompany an existing film or their own original video footage.

▶ Students record individual performance exams, over which the teacher records ("dubs") a verbal critique.

▶ Provide short video clips demonstrating instrumental/vocal techniques or dance routines.

▶ Any of the ideas from presentation software may be used, integrated into a video context.

With today's technology, putting together a video tutorial or demonstration is easier than ever, but it still takes time. To determine whether such an effort would be beneficial to you, ask yourself how many times you deliver the same message to your students throughout the year. If you find that you repeat the same information many times, year after year, it may be profitable to document your instruction in a video clip. A brief video clip that explains the basics of instrument maintenance or how to interpret time signatures are good examples.

The discussion of specific software in the following section will be divided into two subsections, based on the complexity and capabilities of the programs. We will begin by introducing three entry-level programs (*iMovie, iDVD,* and *MovieMaker 2*), and then we will proceed to a discussion of software with more advanced editing capabilities.

ENTRY-LEVEL SOFTWARE

This most basic level of movie-making software typically incorporates simple drag-and-drop techniques to easily organize a series of various media types (video, sound, still images, and so on) into an impressive, quite professional-looking movie that can be saved as a file on your computer or, optionally, burned to a recordable CD or DVD. In addition to the programs discussed below, Apple's *QuickTime* can be used as an inexpensive option for basic video editing. This unique, inexpensive program will be discussed later in the chapter as one of the multimedia authoring software packages.

Apple iMovie and iDVD (Mac)

These two programs come as part of Apple's amazingly affordable *iLife '05* suite of multimedia software ($49), including *iPhoto* (graphic image editing), *iMovie* (movie-making), *iDVD* (DVD creation), *GarageBand* (loop-based digital audio and MIDI sequencer), and *iTunes* (media player). Movie clips, photos, sound files, and other media can be imported into the program, then assembled and rearranged using a "timeline" at the bottom of the program window. With *iMovie* (**Fig. 4**), the user can easily create titles for the movie and include numerous built-in transitions and effects to provide an added sense of professionalism to the final product.

FIG. 4: The interface for Apple's iMovie software

iMovie makes it especially easy to incorporate content from applications in the *iLife* suite. For instance, a section of an *iMovie* may feature still images imported from *iPhoto* with a soundtrack from your *iTunes* library but originally created with *GarageBand*. There is one *iMovie* audio glitch you may encounter that is worth mentioning. The audio soundtrack of longer movies can gradually become out of sync with the video. This happens when the audio bit resolution of the camera that captured the movie is at a different setting than the 16-bit playback used by *iMovie*. If your camera allows for multiple settings, just choose 16-bit. If not, a workaround is to extract the audio from the video (**Advanced→Extract Audio**) and lock it in place (**Advanced→Lock Audio Clip at Playhead**).

Once the movie is created, *iDVD* can be used to write the complete movie (or a collection of movies) to a recordable DVD. *iDVD* also makes creation of a DVD menu a snap.

For those who wish to produce even more professional-looking DVD media, there are many products available for this purpose, varying in their level of sophistication, complexity, and price. Some of the many products available are Roxio's *Toast 6 Titanium* (Mac; $99.95), Roxio's *Easy Media Creator 7.5* (Windows; $99.95), Apple's *DVD Studio Pro* shown in **Fig. 5** (Mac; $499), and Sony's *DVD Architect 3* (Windows; $299.95 packaged with Sony's *Vegas 6*, professional-grade movie creation software, discussed below).

FIG. 5: Creating an interactive menu in Apple's DVD Studio Pro

Windows MovieMaker 2

For the Windows platform, Microsoft has provided a very easy-to-use entry level piece of movie creation software. *MovieMaker 2* (**Fig. 6**) is included as part of the Windows XP operating system with free upgrades available from Microsoft's Web site. This software has the same basic capabilities as *iMovie* for the Mac platform, including a timeline-based assembly method for combining various movies, graphic images, sound files, and other media into a self-contained movie. Once finished, your movie can be saved to your computer's hard drive, a recordable data CD or DVD, emailed as an attachment, sent to a server via the Internet, or recorded to a tape on a digital video (DV) camera.

FIG. 6: Adding media to the timeline in Windows Movie Maker

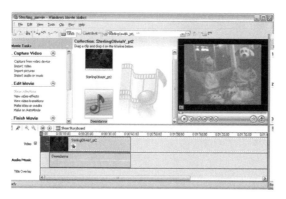

MORE ADVANCED EDITING

When a more advanced video editing system is required, there are many options available. Though significantly more expensive than the entry level software discussed above, two of the more affordable advanced video editing options include Apple's *Final Cut Express* (Mac; $299) and Sony's *Vegas Pro 6* (Windows $199.95 or $299.95 packaged with Sony's *DVD Architect 3*, a professional-grade program for DVD authoring). Typically, these programs offer the user a significantly enhanced level of creative freedom in the movie-making process and include higher precision editing tools, more complex transitions, more advanced effects, improved sound handling capabilities (e.g., multi-channel audio, 5.1 surround sound mixdown, and so on), improved rendering, increased compatibility with more media types, to name just a few of the many enhancements.

Final Cut Express (Mac)

Final Cut Express is a limited version of Apple's professional-level program, *Final Cut Pro 5* (Mac; $999), but it is a full-featured video editing package that should provide educators with all the power they need. In addition to the enhanced capabilities available in these higher-level software packages, the user also has a great deal of flexibility to alter the interface by showing or hiding various windows or panels, depending upon what task needs to be completed at any given time. For example, in **Fig. 7** you will notice the

179

timeline at the bottom of the *Final Cut Express* window. In addition, I have chosen to reveal a list of effects, such as (from left to right) the Cross Zoom panel (for adjusting the effect parameters) and a preview panel that displays the resulting video at the current point of the playback head (represented by the vertical line that scrolls horizontally across the timeline as the movie plays back).

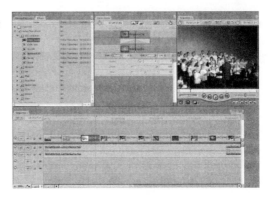

FIG. 7: Editing video in Apple's Final Cut Pro

Final Cut Express and other advanced video editing programs provide the user greater flexibility, a more customizable interface, and more choices of transitions and effects. One of the primary reasons for stepping up to this next level of software is the capability to handle a greater number of tracks (both audio and video). While some of the entry level software is quite limited in their ability to handle anything beyond basic two channel audio and a limited number of video tracks, with *Final Cut Express* and similar software, the designer can utilize multiple audio and video tracks, creating a complex multimedia experience. Advanced video editing software also typically affords compatibility with a greater number of file types for both importing into a project and exporting the finished project, using any one of a growing number of compression schemes to reduce the file size without sacrificing an unacceptable amount of the image or sound quality. Apple's *Soundtrack Pro* ($99) is an impressive audio editor that shares a highly integrated relationship with *Final Cut Express*, allowing the user to move back and forth between the two applications for quick and easy audio editing or for recording new audio material for a given visual sequence.

Vegas Pro 6

Originally created by Sonic Foundry, *Vegas Pro* (**Fig. 8**) was recently purchased by Sony Corporation, along with its sister programs *Sound Forge* (digital audio editing) and *ACID* (a loop-based music creation package). Similar to *Final Cut Pro* in its level of sophistication and ease of use, this Windows-based, movie-making package provides the user with the capability to create very professional-looking movies, incorporating multiple media sources, impressive transitions, video effects, titles, and musical soundtracks. Like the programs discussed above, various media are imported into the program and then assembly and (re)arrangement of these components of the movie are accomplished using a simple drag-and-drop technique. In *Vegas Pro*, whenever two audio or video sources overlap on the same track, a crossfade is automatically inserted so that the first sound fades out as the second fades in. It is extremely easy to edit these default behaviors so that the resulting movie looks exactly the way the user intends.

FIG. 8: Video editing using Sony's Vegas Pro

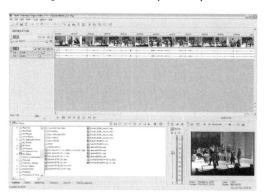

Another advanced video editing option—formerly a cross-platform solution, but now available only on the Windows platform—is Adobe's *Premiere Pro 1.5* ($219.95; *Premiere Elements*, a reduced package, is available for only $69.95), offering many of the same functions as *Vegas Pro*, but including tight integration with other Adobe software such as *Photoshop* (graphic image editor), *Audition* (digital audio editor), *After Effects* (motion graphics and visual effects), and *Encore* (DVD authoring).

Capturing Digital Images

Digital image capturing software provides a method for the creation of image files that can be integrated easily into a presentation, a movie, or in printed materials (e.g., flyer or newsletter). Many photo editing and graphics programs include a "slide show mode," allowing the user to display a sequence of images, often even providing an easy method for adding a musical soundtrack to the slideshow. Some of these programs also provide a way to export a sequence of images as a movie for playback using one of the popular media players (e.g., QuickTime, Windows MediaPlayer, RealPlayer). Though there are many ways to capture images, two of the most commonly used methods will be discussed below: scanning images and importing images from a digital camera or digital video camera.

SCANNING

When you purchase a flatbed scanner, you should receive a CD-ROM containing software compatible with the operating system of your computer. In order to get full functionality from your scanner, you will need to install this software. Typically, two sets of functionality will be included with this installation. There will likely be a stand-alone program that allows you to scan text documents, graphic images, or a combination of the two into an appropriate format. Some of the more advanced software even includes optical character recognition (OCR) capability so that the document text is converted from a graphic image into text format, reducing the file size dramatically and allowing the text to be edited in a word processing application such as *Word* or *AppleWorks*. In addition to providing the standalone software, most scanners will also include drivers (utility programs that remain largely invisible to the user) that allow your scanner to be accessed by programs that have the capability to integrate scanned images into their functionality. Two of the most prominent types of programs that benefit from such connectivity include graphic editing software (e.g., Adobe *Photoshop*, Macromedia *Fireworks*) and music notation software (*MakeMusic! Finale, Sibelius*). Both of these types of programs can import images either for the purpose of editing the image content or for converting the graphic symbols into music notation, a very powerful capability indeed for the music teacher. Another prominent program that may include access to scanning drivers is Adobe *Acrobat*, which allows documents to be saved as PDF files (portable document format) for Internet delivery.

Software Packaged with Scanners

The software that comes with a Hewlett-Packard Scanjet 3970, a moderately priced, consumer-level scanner owned by one of the present authors, allows the user to select one of the following options: scan picture, scan document (can include text *and* images), or make photocopies of the scanned document (**Fig. 9**). Once the appropriate document type has been selected, it is possible to set a number of properties that will determine the quality of the scanned file and how large the resulting image will be. The two most important settings are the *resolution* and *number of colors*.

The *resolution* setting determines how many dots per inch (dpi) will be captured. The higher the resolution, the clearer and more accurate the captured image will appear. Higher resolutions also result in significantly larger file sizes. If you plan to use your images for a high-quality print, you will probably want to set the resolution to 600 dpi (or higher). If, however, you intend to use the image only on the World Wide Web (WWW) where it will be viewed on a computer screen, there is no reason to set the resolution any higher than 72 dpi. This will keep your file sizes much smaller, resulting in significantly less "waiting time" for visitors to your Web site. Similarly, the *number of colors* can be set to monochrome (black and white only), grayscale, or any of a number of predefined color settings, including 256 colors (8-bit), 65 thousand colors (16-bit), and millions of colors (24-bit). Once again, the purpose for which you are scanning should determine your needs. If you want a high quality color print, you may want to go with the highest 24-bit (millions of colors) setting. If the print copy will be black and white, you can reduce the file size significantly by using a grayscale setting instead. Likewise, if your image will be viewed solely via the WWW, you will ensure consistency between viewers using different browsers on varying operating systems by selecting the 8-bit (256 color), Web palette setting.

FIG. 9: The interface for scanning software provided with the HP Scanjet 3970 printer.

Typically, the scanning software requires only a very few highly intuitive steps:

1. Start the program.

2. Insert the document or picture face down on the glass of the scanner.

3. Choose the appropriate settings as described above.

4. Initiate the scanning process.

5. Provide a file name for the scanned document or image file.

Most scanning applications allow you to scan multiple pages before saving them to a file on your hard drive. In addition, it is often possible to save files in any number of formats, including as a graphic image (TIFF, JPG, GIF), text only, and rich text format (RTF), the latter of which can be opened and edited directly in a word processor. PNG graphic images are more commonly being incorporated into Web pages, though the level of cross-platform and cross-browser compatibility inherent in JPG and GIF images for online use remains unrivaled at present. Another highly compatible means of transferring graphic images between applications is the Adobe *Acrobat* (PDF) format.

Using Scanned Images in Other Software Applications

To scan an image into *Photoshop*, after successfully installing the driver from your scanner's CD-ROM, one need only select the appropriate device from the Import submenu (**File→Import→ [select device]**; see **Fig. 10**). If you do not see your scanner listed here, you will need to reinstall the driver or call technical support for assistance. Once you have selected your scanner, a window will open that looks almost identical to the standalone version of your scanner software, allowing you to perform the exact same steps enumerated above to capture the image. Once the scanning is complete, however, the scanned image will appear as a new document in *Photoshop*, where you can save it as a *Photoshop* document (PSD), export in a Web-ready format (**File→Save for Web**), or edit the image.

FIG. 10: Importing a scanned image directly into Photoshop

The procedure for scanning musical notation into computer music notation programs such as *Finale* or *Sibelius* (**Fig. 11**) is relatively easy and is described in detail in Chapter 3 "Music Notation Software" in the present volume. Though a powerful capability, it is apparent that there is still room for improvement in OMR technology—Optical Music Recognition—and a certain amount of editing is required to convert a scanned image accurately to music notation. The level of accuracy will undoubtedly continue to improve, but we still appear to be years away from a 100 percent input-output accuracy for scanning music notation. Nonetheless, Chapter 3 offers several ideas for classroom implementation of scanning with music notation software that music educators have found successful in the process of enhancing the music learning experience.

FIG. 11: Scanning music notation into Sibelius using PhotoScore

CAMERAS

Another method for getting images from a remote source to your computer is to use a digital camera or video camera to capture the images, then transfer them to the computer hard drive. The most common means of transferring files is via a USB 2.0 or FireWire port, since the file size can be quite large and these transfer protocols are fast enough to suffice, where a parallel or USB 1.0 port would take significantly longer. Even faster data transfer rates can be achieved for transferring images from a digital camera by purchasing an adapter that allows you to remove the flash memory card from the camera and insert it directly into the computer.

The most important specification to identify when purchasing a camera is the number of pixels used when storing each image, typically reported in terms of megapixels (one megapixel equals approximately one million pixels). At the time of publication, 5.1 megapixel cameras were the standard, while 8 megapixel cameras were considered state-of-the-art. In many contexts, depending on the intended use for your pictures—especially if they will be viewed only via the Intenet—a lower resolution (3.2 or even 2.0 megapixels) might suffice. Also, you will want to be aware of the format in which your images will be saved, since most cameras compress the images immediately upon capture, sacrificing some of the image quality in order to economically utilize the finite space available on the memory stick or flash drive.

Digital cameras and video cameras that are able to transfer data to a computer typically come with the software required to complete this task. Because each camera manufacturer provides software that varies significantly, we will focus on the basic steps required to capture the images and then to transfer them to your computer. You should, of course, carefully read the documentation that comes with your own camera and/or software to ensure that you are doing it correctly for your specific equipment setup.

The basic steps involved are as follows:

▶ Capture your still images (digital camera) or motion pictures (video camera).

▶ With your computer turned on, connect your camera to the USB or FireWire port on your computer, then turn the camera on.

▶ In many instances this will automatically initiate the data transfer; if not, you will need to refer to your owner's manual to determine the appropriate steps to be taken.

▶ Make sure that you know where the pictures will be saved on your computer, a property that is typically set in the configuration settings of the software that came with the camera.

▶ Optionally, you can edit any of the images using a graphic image editor like *Photoshop*, *Fireworks*, or *Paint Shop Pro*.

▶ Transfer images to PhotoCD, incorporate them into a Web site, an audio-visual presentation (*PowerPoint* or *Keynote*), or a multimedia movie (*iMovie* or *MovieMaker*), or store them on your computer hard drive for use at a later time.

Like the incorporation of scanned images, digital cameras and video cameras are becoming ever more user-friendly and their products easier to integrate into multimedia contexts. This is one area in which you should simply take the first step by diving in head first, since there is little chance of negative impact. After all, students love to see pictures of themselves, and you can take one step toward getting them more involved in the learning experience by recording their efforts for posterity, gaining appropriate permissions for using such images, of course.

Some uses for digital images include the following:

▶ Scanning a notation excerpt to be used in an educational handout

▶ Scanning a notation excerpt to be used in a presentation

▶ Collecting digital photos to document an activity or process

▶ Adding photos to a school music department Web site

▶ Photographs of unusual instruments (can be supplemented with digital audio files of performances on the instrument)

▶ Photos for animated listening guides (presentation or movie)

▶ Photos to generate ideas for compositional activities (presentation or movie)

▶ Prepare a brief movie clip to incorporate in a presentation or Web page

The World Wide Web

It is possible to place almost any of the media you create using multimedia software on the Internet for access via the World Wide Web. When doing so, however, it is very important that you keep in mind issues related to U.S. copyright law and that you always remain vigilant to potential violations regarding the privacy of your students and their work.

Most word processing software allows the user to easily save files in a Web-ready format. In Microsoft *Word*, for example, you can open any document. Select **File→Save as Web Page**, save the file with an ".htm" or ".html" extension, and upload the converted document to your server for immediate online access by your students, parents, and/or other teachers. While this may be the easiest and most expedient way for a novice to create a Web page, it affords the least amount of control over how the document will appear and function online. In order to gain such control, one must use one of the many Web authoring software packages that are now available. A couple of the most popular are discussed below.

WEAVING WEB PAGES

Web page authoring tools allow teachers and students to create Web pages that make multimedia projects accessible to anyone around the globe with an Internet connection. Web page software works best for creating pages that display static information such as text and still graphics. Audio and synchronized media such as movies or presentations are typically incorporated into Web pages as links to Web-compatible multimedia files. Users may need to download plug-in software to access audio, movies, or presentations, depending on the formats of the media. Web pages do not provide the designer with the same high degree of control over appearance and timing of media as presentation, movie, or word processing software, but they do have the benefit of distributing that information to anybody in the world who has an Internet connection in a format that is, in most cases, cross-platform and cross-browser compatible. Be aware that you may have students who do not have access to the Web from home, so be careful about requiring home assignments utilizing the Web.

Web pages are often used as primary communication between the music program and the program's constituents outside of class meeting time. For example, calendars and informational announcements for parents and home practice materials for students can be disseminated via the Internet. Web pages may also be used to organize research and reference material so that students can learn more about topics introduced in music class. Teachers may create course Web pages that include a syllabus, assignments (including downloadable worksheets, audio examples, and so on), and hyperlinks to valuable information resources. Student compositions and performances may also be archived to the Web, but make certain you have the students' and publishing companies' permissions to do so.

Mozilla Composer (Mac/Windows/Linux)

As a free component of the Mozilla browser, *Composer* provides a great way to start creating your own Web pages. Simply download the Mozilla Suite (free). In addition to *Composer* (the HTML editor for creating Web pages), this suite of programs includes the Mozilla *Navigator* (an Internet browser), an e-mail and newsgroup program, and chat capability. Once installed, you simply select the desired program from the Window menu. For our present purposes, we will select *Composer*, an amazingly capable HTML editor, given the fact that it is provided to you at no charge. HTML is an acronym for hypertext markup language, the code system used by Internet browsers to format the content of Web documents.

Like most HTML editors, *Composer* provides a WYSIWYG (pronounced: "wizzywig") interface, which stands for "what you see is what you get." Like *Word*, *Word Perfect*, and other present-day word processing software, you see exactly what your final document will look like as you type (**Fig. 12**), rather than entering HTML tags like **This text is bold!!** to make the text surrounded by the opening (****) and closing (****) tags appear in boldface type. Instead, like in a word processor, you simply type your text, select the text to which you wish to apply formatting, then click on the appropriate formatting button on the toolbar (the "B," in this case) to create boldface type. Think of *Composer* as a simple word processor for creating Web pages. You can also apply paragraph formatting (headings, body text, etc.) by selecting the desired format from the drop-down box on the left side of the Format toolbar. You can show and hide the various toolbars by selecting **View→ Show/Hide→[select or deselect toolbar]**. In addition to paragraph formatting, the Format toolbar gives you one-click access to the text color, font size, bold, italic, underline, paragraph indent, paragraph alignment (left, center, right, or justified), and some more advanced capabilities. The Composition toolbar provides direct access to opening, saving, and creating new HTML files. It also provides buttons for adding hyperlinks, images, and tables to your page and a spell checker to minimize the chance that typographical errors will be contained on your Web pages.

FIG. 12: Creating Web pages using Mozilla's Composer

Though the WYSIWYG interface is intended to "protect" the Web designer from having to work directly with the underlying HTML code, it is possible to view that code using the Edit Mode toolbar. Perusing the content of the Code window after using the WYSIWYG editor to create a Web page is a marvelous way to learn how to work with HTML "as you go," rather than having to learn all—or even a significant amount—of the codes before you begin the process of creating Web pages.

Macromedia Dreamweaver MX 2004 (Mac/Windows)

Dreamweaver MX 2004 ($95) is a full-featured HTML editor that has capabilities well beyond those provided by basic programs like *Composer*. All of the capabilities described above are possible in *Dreamweaver*, though the toolbar system for this program provides dozens of extra features that are accessible to the designer by default and can be readily personalized to suit the individual's preferences and needs. *Dreamweaver* allows you to work in Design mode (WYSIWYG), Code mode (HTML code), or Split mode, allowing the designer to see both views simultaneously. In addition, the Properties window allows direct access to design formatting relevant to any selected object in the document (**Fig. 13**).

FIG. 13: Using Macromedia's Dreamweaver to create a Web page.

Perhaps the most powerful aspect of *Dreamweaver* is its site management capability. Beyond its ability to provide a WYSIWYG interface for the creation of simple to extremely complex Web pages, *Dreamweaver* is an invaluable tool for the maintenance and management of a Web site. Though utilizing this capability does require an additional step—defining a "Site" for each of your Web sites—once this process is completed, the program will assist mightily with the tasks required when maintaining a Web site. For example, the Synchronize command (select **Site→Synchronize** from the File window's context menu) allows a method for updating all files that have changed since the last time files were uploaded to the server. Once the user has connected to the Internet and initiated the Synchronize process, *Dreamweaver* compares all files within the site folder on your local computer to all files on the server and provides a list of files that need to be uploaded (or downloaded) to ensure that all files on the Internet server are the newest version. With a single click, *Dreamweaver* will update all files. In addition, the Check Links Sitewide command (**Site→ Check Links Sitewide**) will search every file in your Web site and report to you the number of broken links (links to files that do not exist), external links (links to pages outside of your Web site), and orphaned files (files to which no files within the site are linked).

Any of the teaching/learning ideas from presentations can be used with Web page authoring tools, just keep in mind that audio/visual synchronization is not feasible with basic HTML Web page creation. In order to accomplish such high-level integration of multiple media types for presentation online, multimedia authoring software provides a solution and will be discussed in the coming pages.

COURSE MANAGEMENT SOFTWARE

Course management software offers many of the same possibilities as Web page authoring software regarding distributing media, presentations, movies, and Web pages. One primary distinction, a definite advantage when copyrighted materials serve an important educational purpose, is that the course management Web site is typically password-protected. This means that only students enrolled in your course(s) have access to the site. As a result, you may be able to share recordings, scores, and other published material that the school has purchased for this purpose. Though each teacher should confirm the local school and district policies regarding such matters, placing materials on a password-protected server significantly strengthens the "fair use" argument for sharing copyrighted materials with students for educational purposes.

Course management software adds features to Web sites that can enhance the learning experience. Those features include internal email, discussion forums (sometimes called bulletin boards), chat, audio conferencing, calendars, contact information, assignment uploading, an online gradebook for posting student grades, and quizzes that can be graded and entered into the online gradebook automatically. Because such programs are intended to allow access to course materials online, course management software is typically cross-platform and cross-browser compatible. Two of the most commonly used course management systems are *Blackboard* and *WebCT*. Because the present authors are most familiar with the former, we will provide details about this software package. However, most of these same capabilities are available in *WebCT* and other similar course management systems. One particularly easy-to-use course management solution, free to all educators and available online, is *TeacherWeb*. It is also worthy of note that many of the major education publishers are providing pre-packaged course content that instructors can download and customize for use in their own classes from within one of the commercial course management software systems.

Some of the ways music teachers have utilized course management software include the following:

▶ Posting recordings for students to listen to at home

▶ Encouraging further dialogue about music-related topics through bulletin board postings

▶ Having students turn in assignments consisting of typed responses or audio recordings of their performance

▶ Collecting student input via anonymous surveys

▶ Administering quizzes (graded or ungraded) to review material covered in class or online

Blackboard

Within the context of a chapter such as the present one, it would be impossible to cover all of the many capabilities of a program like *Blackboard*. As a result, we shall focus on those aspects of the program that have proven most useful in our own classes. The general purpose of "course management" is to provide easy access to a variety of course-related materials and create course areas online where students can interact with one another about the topic of study outside of the classroom in a variety of ways.

Blackboard allows the instructor an easy way to create Web-ready content, using the Visual Text Box Editor, a simple WYSIWYG interface. Using QuickEdit, the instructor can quickly switch between the instructor view and student view of the course content. The program also comes with a Syllabus Builder that facilitates the process of creating an online syllabus, either by uploading an existing syllabus or producing a brand new syllabus using the built-in syllabus creation functionality. Instructors can create sequenced lessons using *Blackboard's* Learning Units and can determine whether students can navigate through the material at will or if they must proceed through the lessons in a predetermined sequential order.

FIG. 14: Using the Discussion Board component of Blackboard

Discussion boards, an important component of most course management systems, provide a marvelous method for taking topical discussions outside of the classroom. The instructor can create multiple forums, typically organized around a specific topic, in the Discussion Board area for the purpose of allowing (or requiring) students to contribute to an ongoing discussion on any or all of the delineated topics (**Fig. 14**). Unlike chat rooms, discussion boards are an asynchronous, nested form of communication. The term "asynchronous" refers to the fact that participants need not be logged on to the system at the same time to carry on a dialogue. Rather, one person can submit a contribution (called a "post") to the discussion board, and it will be seen by other members of the class the next time they log on to *Blackboard* and access the Discussion Board area. The term "nested" refers to the manner in which a series of posts are organized visually on the computer screen. When one participant contributes a new post (called a "thread") to the discussion, other participants have the choice of either replying to that post or creating an original thread of discussion on their own. Posts that are replies to other student contributions are nested (that is, indented) underneath the original post to which the message was intended as a response. This provides a very clear visual representation of the virtual conversation in which the students are participating and greatly facilitates the ability to follow a common thread of dialogue from its initial post through all topic-related replies.

Blackboard also facilitates group activities with the Groups tool, allowing the instructor to create multiple subgroups of students. Each group can be assigned to its own file exchange area (for collaboration on group projects), discussion board, virtual classroom (chat), and group e-mail. Instructors can create Assignment items within *Blackboard* that allow students to submit their assignment electronically. When using this method, the assignments for an entire class can be downloaded simultaneously by the instructor. An online Gradebook, with calculation functionality built-in, allows the instructor to maintain student grades in a safe location, where each student has direct access to their own grades—but no one else's—for all graded assignments and quizzes. The Gradebook supports grading scales, grade weighting, and item analysis.

As these courseware management systems continue to mature, more and more third-party tools are being created to assist teachers in the process of creating educational online materials. Many of these products can be found by perusing the *Blackboard* and *WebCT* sites. Two particularly useful additions are Respondus (for the creation and management of exams) and StudyMate (for the creation of interactive activities and games).

FTP CLIENTS

Once you have created your multimedia materials, you can begin integrating them into your music classroom and instruction. In addition to making these interactive learning materials available on computers located in the school, many of the programs mentioned in this chapter allow you to create Web-ready versions of the software that can be accessed via the Internet. However, in order to allow students access to these materials online, you must upload the Web-compatible files to a server. If you do not own *Dreamweaver* or simply have not yet learned how to use its site management capabilities, you will need to use a utility program to upload the files to the Internet, using *file transfer protocol* (FTP). The programs mentioned in this section (and many others) provide the capability of transferring files from your local computer (the computer you used to create the materials) to a remote server (a computer typically located at a different location) that is connected to the World Wide Web.

Because the primary function of these programs is simply to transfer files from one computer to another for the purpose of making them available via the World Wide Web, we will make no specific suggestions for integration of this software into the classroom. Instead, these programs should be considered absolutely essential tools, required to place your files on the Internet. The most common FTP clients are platform-specific, so we will provide a brief introduction to one of the most used programs for each of the two major platforms, Macintosh and Windows.

Fetch 5 (Mac)

Fetch 5 (free for educators) is a Macintosh-based program for transferring files using FTP. The interface for this program is extremely simple, providing only the most essential options (**Fig. 15**). When the program starts, the user connects to the desired server by either entering the appropriate URL, username, and password or using a previously saved "shortcut." The program allows users to transfer files from a remote server to their local computer (download) by clicking on the Get button on the toolbar and selecting the file(s) to transfer. Similarly, in order to upload files (i.e., transfer files from the local computer to a remote server), the user simply clicks on the Put button on the toolbar and selects the files to be transferred. Alternatively, users can simply drag and drop files from their hard drive onto icons representing folders on the server.

FIG. 15: The basic interface for Fetch, an FTP utility for the Macintosh computer.

AbsoluteFTP (Windows)

VanDyke Software's *AbsoluteFTP* ($29.95) is a Windows-based program that facilitates the process of transferring files in much the same way that *Fetch* accomplishes the task on the Mac platform. This software incorporates a very familiar design, allowing the user to copy files to or from the server by dragging and dropping them from one window to another ... exactly the same method one uses to copy files between folders on the local hard drive using Windows *Explorer* (**Fig. 16**). The only difference is that the user must log on to the server with a username and password before files can be copied or moved. Like *Fetch*,

AbsoluteFTP allows the user to save logon information (including passwords) for multiple sites and/or servers. Using this capability, the process of logging on can be accomplished with a single mouse click. There are many similar programs that can be used to accomplish the task of transferring files on both the Windows and Macintosh platforms.

FIG. 16: Van Dyke's AbsoluteFTP, an FTP program for Windows-based computers.

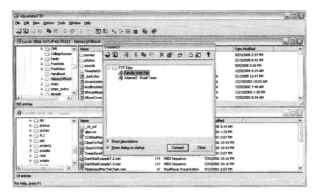

MULTIMEDIA AUTHORING TOOLS

Multimedia authoring tools constitute one of the most advanced types of software discussed in this chapter, allowing the creation of truly interactive and engaging instructional materials. Many interactive programs—commercial, shareware, and freeware—have been created to fulfill a variety of specific needs for music teachers. For example, the creation of interactive listening guides has been greatly facilitated by programs like ECS Media's *Timesketch Editor* ($99.95) and Scott Lipscomb and Marc Jacoby's *BubbleMachine* (free download; **Fig. 17**). The authoring tools described in the following paragraphs, however, provide the flexibility necessary to create interactive multimedia educational materials individually suited to a specific teacher's needs. Like all programs, of course, one does not have to know and understand *all* of the capabilities available before making effective use of a subset of these functions. In fact, both of the cross-platform programs discussed below offer the user a streamlined method for the creation of interactive multimedia. It is possible to learn the basics that will allow you to get up and running in a matter of hours. For those willing to take the time to learn how to utilize some of the more complex capabilities, however, these programs offer an infinite set of possibilities.

FIG. 17: An interactive listening guide created with BubbleMachine.

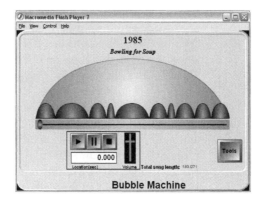

Potential instructional applications of multimedia instructional materials created with these authoring tools include

▶ Incorporating sound, images, and animation into an engaging presentation of topical information.

▶ Creating animations and demos to illustrate complex concepts.

▶ Creating interactive instructional units that require active student engagement in making selections, dragging objects with the mouse, etc.

▶ Providing online quizzes that provide the instructor with formative assessment of student learning well in advance of a concluding summative evaluation (e.g., final exam) so necessary pedagogical adjustments can be made.

▶ Creating interactive listening guides for musical compositions, allowing students to navigate from section to section as they wish, providing a true "exploratory environment" for musical learning.

▶ Offering advanced students an opportunity to use the authoring tools to create their own interactive materials to present to the class or submit as assignments.

Apple QuickTime Pro 7 (Mac/Windows)

QuickTime is a familiar program to most Internet users who have come into contact with multimedia on the Internet. As one of the earliest multimedia options, it has truly retained an important place in the online community. The *QuickTime Player* is available for free download from the Apple Web site. In order to create and/or edit your own multimedia, however, you must purchase the "Pro" version of the software. It is certainly an economical option since, at $29.99, this program offers some impressive capabilities. *QuickTime* can be used as a basic file conversion utility to convert one type of audio, video, or audio-video file to another type. The list of compatible file formats is simply too extensive to include in this chapter, but it includes all of the most frequently used types, and more. One of the most useful conversion possibilities available is the conversion from MIDI files to digital audio (WAV, AIFF, or MP3). Though the size of the resulting file will be much larger than the original MIDI file, the digital audio file can be easily burned to an audio CD. *QuickTime* movies can include sound (MIDI or digital audio), images, video, animation, text, or any combination of compatible media types (**Fig. 18**). The program also includes remarkable compression technology, allowing the user to determine the appropriate compromise between sound and image quality and file size.

FIG. 18: An interactive listening guide created in Apple's QuickTime Pro.

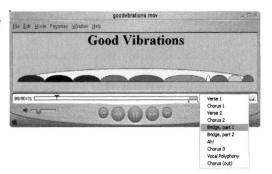

Beyond basic file conversion, *QuickTime* affords the intermediate-to-advanced user some powerful editing capabilities that, with some effort, can result in impressively interactive instructional media. This program provides an economical alternative to the more expensive options discussed below and the video editing software discussed in a preceding section, though its simplistic interface makes creating more complex multimedia a bit difficult. Many programs, such as Macromedia *Flash* and Adobe *GoLive* or *LiveMotion*, provide an option to save files in *QuickTime* format. Though this requires purchase of one of these more expensive programs, the creation of complex multimedia is made substantially easier and the process is significantly streamlined. Even *PowerPoint* and *Keynote* allow you to export the slides in a presentation as a series of images that can then be imported into *QuickTime* where an audio soundtrack can be added. *QuickTime* can also import any set of digital photos, such as a folder of family or classroom photos, or a photo album from *iPhoto*. That said, investing a bit of effort toward learning how to use the *QuickTime* interface will result in substantial payoff without significantly taxing your technology budget.

Macromedia Flash (Mac/Windows)

Macromedia *Flash MX 2004* provides an authoring environment for the creation of truly interactive multimedia materials. The free browser plug-in and player available from the company's Web site have established a near-ubiquitous presence on the Internet—over 95 percent of the computers used to surf the Internet have the plug-in installed, making this program one of the most reliable ways to ensure that your users will be able to utilize your interactive instructional materials to their fullest extent. *Flash* provides a marvelous balance between user-friendliness and complexity (**Fig. 19**). It is possible to learn the program's most basic capabilities and put these to work almost immediately in the creation of interactive instructional materials. The inclusion of "Behaviors" in the most recent versions of the program greatly facilitate the integration of interactivity and the ease with which more complex movies can be created. For those willing to spend the extra time to learn ActionScript, the scripting language that is part of *Flash*, the program's potential is almost limitless. Though there are still some multimedia tasks that Macromedia *Director* accomplishes better—with its Lingo scripting language and *Shockwave* movie creation for online access—in recent years, *Flash* has become the program of choice for many Web developers. One obvious reason is the cost: academic pricing for *Flash* is less than $100, while *Director* still costs about $500. One area in which *Director* retains a distinct advantage over *Flash* is in the handling of MIDI—*Flash* does not include MIDI capability, while *Director* can be used to create some very impressive MIDI-based materials that even incorporate music notation. In order to do so, however, a third-party package (such as Sibelius' *SequenceXtra* [$249]) is required.

Though it does not allow the direct import of MIDI files, *Flash* offers many other attractive and useful capabilities. Its tight integration with other Macromedia products in the *Studio MX 2004* suite ($195; including *Flash*, *Dreamweaver*, *Fireworks*, and *Freehand*) is certainly an advantage. *Flash* allows users to import graphic images, video, sound files, and many other types of media created in other programs or downloaded from the Internet. Many types of objects (e.g., text, ovals, rectangles, lines, customized gradients, etc.) can be created directly in *Flash*, using the Tool palette. These basic shapes and objects can be combined to create professional looking graphics, buttons, or other objects for use in your own animations. In addition, *Flash* comes with several common libraries to provide many ready-to-use objects. The Buttons library contains an impressive array of buttons, sliders, knobs, faders, and other useful objects that can be readily included in your movies. The Learning Interactions library contains templates—including complex interactive capabilities—for creating various types of quiz forms: true-false, multiple choice, fill in the blank, drag-and-drop, and others. In addition, the program comes with a remarkable set of components with built-in functionality. Some of the most commonly-used components—Macromedia's built-in, interactive objects—include the checkbox, radio button, progress bar, list box, combo box, text input, and many others. The professional version of *Flash* (costs $50 more than the standard version) also provides advanced features for creating forms, database connectivity, high-quality video, advanced components (media playback, data grid, calendar, menu, and more), and many other impressive capabilities.

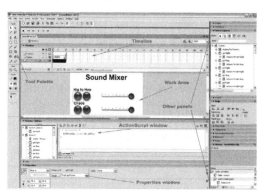

FIG. 19: Creating an interactive music mixer in Macromedia's Flash MX 2004.

Like many Macromedia programs, *Flash* uses a timeline metaphor to facilitate the creation of animations. This allows complex animations to be created without necessitating the frame-by-frame creation of each individual image. Instead, the user marks important locations (called "keyframes") along the Timeline and sets the desired location of each object in the movie at this point in time. *Flash* then automatically calculates the appropriate location for each object in every intervening frame, a process known as "tweening." Because *Flash* utilizes vector graphics instead of bitmaps (or raster graphics), the resulting files are much smaller and take less time for online visitors to download. The context-sensitive Properties window allows users direct access to the most common attributes of any object selected in the work area (or Stage). Other panels (accessible from the Windows menu) allow the user to set the alignment of objects on the Stage, transform and skew objects, mix colors, use pre-made components, view all objects in the present movie, along with many other possibilities.

For those who wish to move to more advanced levels of interactivity, *Flash* provides a powerful programming language called ActionScript, providing many of the same capabilities that were previously only the purview of much more complex and difficult to learn programs like Java and C++. With the arrival of ActionScript 2.0 (included with *Flash MX 2004*), object-oriented programming is possible within *Flash*, providing a much higher level of control and enhanced potential for users willing to invest the time to learn these more advanced techniques. There are many helpful resources—some of which are listed in the "Resources" section at the end of this chapter—that will assist you in learning how to use this program to meet your instructional objectives and enhance the learning experience for your students.

ELECTRONIC PORTFOLIOS

In recent years, "electronic portfolio" (or "digital portfolio") has become another significant buzzword in the educational community. Using some or all of the technologies discussed in this chapter and elsewhere in the present text, students and teachers can document their academic accomplishments and development processes for dissemination to prospective employers, educators, colleagues, or other individuals with a level of ease and compatibility never before possible. Portfolios provide an opportunity to document intellectual growth, scholarly maturation, and—specific to our current objective—acquisition of technology-related skills. In addition, a portfolio typically includes foundational content, including a personal statement, teaching philosophy, specific skill sets, and evidence of scholarly work, lesson plans, and teaching ability. Bauer and Doty (2002) distinguish two different types of portfolios: the *developmental portfolio* and the *showcase portfolio*.

> The [purpose of the] developmental portfolio is to document growth across time and thus contains a multitude of materials showing various stages of progress in a person's development. A showcase portfolio is amassed for the purpose of showing the highest level of attainment as well as the professional competence of a person. (p. 3)

Typically, the highly organized structure of a portfolio document is based upon a set of goals or standards related to specific proficiencies considered desirable within the profession or field of study. The National Standards for Music Education can be used to provide a common framework for the organization of music-related portfolio materials.

The electronic portfolio retains several significant advantages over its predecessor, the hardcopy portfolio. The electronic version can be updated continuously, so that an individual's most recent accomplishments are always included. Every type of multimedia discussed in this chapter (video, animation, interactive instructional materials, etc.) can be readily incorporated into an electronic portfolio and provides the viewer with an opportunity to see these elements exactly in the manner they were intended to be used, rather than looking at still images captured for the purpose of inclusion in a hardcopy document. One of the most useful approaches is to create a Web-ready electronic portfolio that can be made available for viewing via the Internet. This allows the student or teacher to disseminate the URL (Web address) to interested individuals, so that every time the information is accessed, the most up-to-date version of the portfolio is available. Alternatively, the current set of data files (HTML, media, and other documents) can be burned onto a recordable CD or DVD and sent for review. Experience has shown that, when the latter method is chosen, it is always wise to include a hyperlink to the URL where the most current version of the portfolio can be found. One of the greatest advantages of the portfolio approach to assessment is that the student or teacher plays an active role in this process, constantly witnessing their own growth and acquisition of new skills.

FILE TYPE CONVERSION

Throughout this chapter we have referred to many multimedia file types and alluded to the desirability of saving or converting certain content to one file type or another depending on its intended use. For instance, a graphic image originally saved as a high-resolution TIFF may be converted to a compressed (smaller) JPEG file format before incorporating it into a Web page or *PowerPoint* presentation. Similarly, a teacher may want to convert a recording of a student performance saved as CD-quality audio (16-bit, stereo, 44.1kHz sample rate, and saved in either AIFF or WAV format) to a smaller, compressed format such as MP3 for storage in a digital portfolio or to e-mail to a parent.

There are many useful programs to help you convert digital audio, image, and video files from one file format to another. The free program, *iTunes,* can import most sound formats, as well as standard MIDI files and can convert to AIFF, MP3, and WAV formats. *Preview* (part of Mac OSX) and *Windows Picture and FAX Viewer* (part of Windows XP) can both be used to view many image file types and to convert from one format to another. As mentioned previously, *QuickTime Pro* can be used to convert between numerous image and audio file types and the program also allows for the creation of movies that incorporate multiple media types. These movies can then be exported in a variety of useful multimedia formats, containing both sound and image (AVI, MPEG-4, *QuickTime* movie, and so on).

Conclusion

The various technologies presented in this chapter provide an almost infinite amount of potential to the teacher willing to invest even a small amount of energy into learning at least the basic capabilities of one or more of these programs. In addition, throughout the chapter, we have attempted to suggest effective ways in which these engaging—often interactive—materials can be integrated into the music classroom. These suggestions, of course, merely scratch the surface of the potential inherent in these technologies and their practical application. We encourage you to use your own creativity to determine novel and innovative ways of integration that best suit your own teaching style. Once you have had the opportunity to discover successful methods that enhance the educational experience in your classroom, please take time to share these experiences with other teachers so that they too can benefit from your efforts. Professional conferences, both local and national, provide opportunities for disseminating this information in a manner that both earns you well-deserved recognition for your effort and benefits other colleagues who share your interest in music technology. The annual conferences of the Technology Institute for Music Educators (TI:ME; K–12), the Association for Technology in Music Instruction (ATMI; higher education), and the National Symposium for Music Instruction Technology (NSMIT; K–12) provide excellent opportunities to communicate your own experiences, learn from the experiences of others, and network with other music educators who are interested in pedagogically meaningful technology integration.

Section 3: Resources

Books

Apple Corporation. *QuickTime for the Web for Windows and Macintosh, 2nd ed.* San Diego, CA: Academic Press, 2002.

Ferguson, D. J. *Essentials for Design: Flash MX 2004* (level one). Upper Saddle River, NJ: Prentice-Hall, 2004.

Ferguson, D. J. *Essentials for Design: Flash MX 2004* (level two). Upper Saddle River, NJ: Prentice-Hall, 2004.

Kay, M. R. *The Web Wizard's Guide to Flash.* Boston, MA: Addison-Wesley, 2003.

Rickards, J. *Essentials for Design: Macromedia MX 2004* (level one). Upper Saddle River, NJ: Prentice-Hall, 2004.

Rickards, J. *Essentials for Design: Macromedia MX 2004* (level two). Upper Saddle River, NJ: Prentice-Hall, 2004.

Rosenzweig, G. *Macromedia Flash MX: ActionScript for Fun and Games.* Indianapolis, IN: Que Publishing, 2003.

Towers, J. T. *Macromedia Dreamweaver MX 2004 for Windows and Macintosh: Visual Quickstart Guide.* Berkeley, CA: Peachpit Press, 2005.

Ulrich, K. *Macromedia Flash MX 2004 for Windows and Macintosh: Visual Quickstart Guide.* Berkeley, CA: Peachpit Press, 2003.

Williams, R. *The Non-Designer's Design Book: Design and Typographic Principles for the Visual Novice, 2nd ed.* Berkeley, CA: Peachpit Press, 2004.

Williams, R. and J. Tollett. *The Non-Designer's Web Book: An Easy Guide to Creating, Designing, and Posting Your Own Web Site, 2nd ed.* Berkeley, CA: Peachpit Press, 2000.

Internet Resources

MUSIC TECHNOLOGY ORGANIZATIONS

Association for Technology in Music Instruction (http://atmionline. org—includes instructions for subscribing to the ATMI listserv)

National Symposium for Music Instruction Technology (http://nsmit.org/)

Technology Institute for Music Educators (www.ti-me.org)

SOFTWARE RESOURCES
AbsoluteFTP (www.vandyke.com/products/absoluteftp/)
Blackboard (www.blackboard.com/)
Boosteroo (www.boostaroo.com/)
BubbleMachine (www.faculty-web.at.northwestern.edu/music/lips-comb/bubblemachine/)
Dreamweaver (www.macromedia.com/software/dreamweaver/)
Fetch (www.fetchsoftworks.com/)
Final Cut Pro (www.apple.com/finalcutstudio/finalcutpro/)
Finale (www.finalemusic.com/finale/)
Fireworks (www.macromedia.com/software/fireworks/)
Flash (www.macromedia.com/software/flash/)
iDVD (www.apple.com/ilife/idvd/)
iMovie (www.apple.com/ilife/imovie/)
Keynote Home Page (www.apple.com/iwork/keynote/)
Movie Maker 2 Home Page (www.microsoft.com/moviemaker/)
Mozilla Suite (www.mozilla.org/products/mozilla1.x/)
Paint Shop Pro (www.corel.com/paintshop/)
Photoshop (www.adobe.com/products/photoshop/)
PowerPoint 2003 Home Page (www.microsoft.com/powerpoint/)
Premiere Pro (www.adobe.com/products/premiere/)
QuickTime (www.apple.com/quicktime/)
QuickTime Tutorials (www.apple.com/quicktime/authoring/tutorials.html)
Respondus (www.respondus.com/)
Silbelius' SequenceXtra (www.sibelius.com/products/sequencex-tra/)
Sibelius (www.sibelius.com/)
TeacherWeb (teacherweb.com/)
Timesketch Editor (www.ecsmedia.com/indivprods/tseditor.shtml)
Vegas Pro (www.sonymediasoftware.com/)
WebCT (www.webct.com/)

ELECTRONIC PORTFOLIO RESOURCES
Case Western Reserve University (http://music.case.edu/mused/portfolios.html)

University of Virginia's Center for Technology and Teacher Education (http://curry.edschool.virginia.edu/class/edlf/589-07/sample.html)

Helen Barrett's portfolio examples (University of Alaska) (http://helenbarrett.com/ALI/samples.html)

RESOURCES FOR INFORMATION ABOUT U.S. COPYRIGHT LAW
www.copyright.gov/
www.whatiscopyright.org/
www.utsystem.edu/OGC/IntellectualProperty/copypol2.htm
www.umuc.edu/library/copy.html
www.dese.state.mo.us/divimprove/curriculum/copyright/

ACADEMIC PRICING FOR SOFTWARE
Academic Superstore (www.academicsuperstore.com/)
Creation Engine (www.creationengine.com/)
Software Express (www.swexpress.com/)

References

Barnett, H. *Investing in Technology: The Payoff in Student Learning.* Syracuse, NY: ERIC Clearinghouse on Information and Technology, 2003.

Bauer, W. I. and A. D. Doty. "Web-Based Electronic Portfolios in Music Education." Paper presented at the Ninth International Conference on Technological Directions in Music Learning (San Antonio, TX). < http://music.utsa.edu/tdml/conf-IX/IX-Bauer&Doty.html>

Brown, M. D. "Electronic Portfolios in the K-12 Classroom." <http://www.educationworld.com/a_tech/tech/tech111.shtml>

Norvig, P. "The Gettysburg PowerPoint Presentation." <http://norvig.com/Gettysburg/>

Tufte, E. R. *The Cognitive Style of PowerPoint.* Cheshire, CT: Graphics Press LLC, 2003.

Williams, D. B. and P. R. Webster. *Experiencing Music Technology, 3rd ed.* Belmont, CA: Thomson Higher Education, 2006.

MULTIMEDIA*

Manufacturer	Product	Web Site	Type	Minimum System Requirements	Special Features	List Price
Microsoft	PowerPoint 2003/2004	www.microsoft.com/office/editions/	Presentation	Mac/Windows	Part of Microsoft Office Suite	$149 (as part of Office Student and Teacher Edition)
Apple	Keynote 2	www.apple.com/iwork/keynote/	Presentation	Mac	Part of iWork Suite	$49 (iWork Suite, Academic)
Apple	iMovie	www.apple.com/ilife/imovie/	Movie/DVD	Mac	Part of iLife Suite	$59 (iLife Suite)
Apple	iDVD	www.apple.com/ilife/idvd/	Movie/DVD	Mac	Part of iLife Suite	$59 (iLife Suite)
Roxio	Toast 6 Titanium	www.roxio.com	Movie/DVD	Mac		$99.95
Roxio	Easy Media Creator 7.5	www.roxio.com	Movie/DVD	Windows		$99.95
Apple	DVD Studio Pro	www.apple.com/finalcutstudio/ dvdstudiopro/	Movie/DVD	Mac		$499
Sony	DVD Architect 3	www.sonymediasoftware.com/	Movie/DVD	Windows		$100
Microsoft	Windows MovieMaker 2	www.microsoft.com/moviemaker/	Movie/DVD	Windows	Part of Windows XP	$199 ($99, upgrade)
Apple	Final Cut Express	www.apple.com/finalcutexpress/	Movie/DVD	Mac	Lite version of Final Cut Pro	$299
Apple	Final Cut Pro	www.apple.com/finalcutstudio/ finalcutpro/	Movie/DVD	Mac		$999
Sony	Vegas Pro	www.sonymediasoftware.com/	Movie/DVD	Windows		$199.95 ($299.95 with DVD Architect 3)
Adobe	Premiere Pro	www.adobe.com/products/premiere/	Movie/DVD	Windows		$699
Adobe	Premiere Elements	www.adobe.com/products/premiere/	Movie/DVD	Windows	Lite version of Premiere Pro	$99.99
Mozilla	Mozilla Composer	www.mozilla.org/products/ mozilla1.x/	Web Weaving	Mac/Windows/Linux		Free
Macromedia	Dreamweaver	www.macromedia.com/software/ dreamweaver/	Web Weaving	Mac/Windows	Can be purchased as part of Studio 8 Suite for $299.	$199 (Education)
Blackboard, Inc.	Blackboard	www.blackboard.com	Course Management	Mac/Windows	Purchased and implemented by your school.	N/A
WebCT, Inc.	WebCT	http://webct.com/	Course Management	Mac/Windows	Purchased and implemented by your school.	N/A
Fetch Softworks	Fetch 5	http://fetchsoftworks.com	FTP Client	Mac		$25
VanDyke Software	AbsoluteFTP	www.vandyke.com/products/ absoluteftp/	FTP Client	Windows		$29.95
ECS Media	Timesketch Editor	http://ecsmedia.com/indivprods/ tseditor.shtml	Multimedia Authoring Tool	Mac/Windows		$99.95
ECS Media	Timesketch Editor Pro	http://ecsmedia.com/indivprods/ tseditorPRO.shtml	Multimedia Authoring Tool	Mac/Windows		$499.95
Lipscomb & Jacoby	BubbleMachine	http://faculty-web.at.northwestern. edu/music/lipscomb/ bubblemachine/	Multimedia Authoring Tool	Mac/Windows		Free
Apple	QuickTime Pro 7	www.apple.com/quicktime/	Multimedia Authoring Tool	Mac/Windows		$29.99
Macromedia	Flash	www.macromedia.com/software/flash/	Multimedia Authoring Tool	Mac/Windows	Can be purchased as part of Studio 8 Suite for $299.	$149 (Education)

* As the chapter suggests, by seeking "academic pricing" and discount vendors, you can acquire many of these programs below list price.

CHAPTER 6

Productivity Tools, Classroom and Lab Management

By Lee Whitmore and Dennis Mauricio

Section 1: Overview of Productivity, Management Tools, and Resources

The applications and tools, both hardware and software, discussed in this book are sometimes instructional in nature. These tools are applied in the classroom as teacher-centered and student-centered vehicles for creation and production. As examples, a teacher may use notation software to create a worksheet, or students may use music production software to compose a piece of music.

In addition to the many music-centric hardware and software tools educators and their students use regularly, there are a host of other tools—sometimes musical, sometimes not—that make life in a classroom or lab much more productive and effective. This chapter deals with three primary types of tools and resources that can greatly enhance the quality of classroom instruction.

The first category is *data management* and deals with the record keeping and other administrative/organizational chores. This area includes tools that are used by all educators such as

▶ Grading programs

▶ Librarian and inventory databases

The second category is *computer peripherals* and deals with the hardware devices necessary to support technology-based instruction. This area includes, among other things

▶ Printers

▶ Storage devices

▶ Projectors

The third category is *lab management* and includes music-specific devices and curricula for networking many instruments together for group instruction as well as computer-networking tools that can enhance lab management.

Section 2: Data Mangement

Grading Programs

Ever considered switching from a paper grade-book to a computer-grading program? Now is a good time. Grade-book applications eliminate the necessity to do math to determine students' grades, and instantly generate class statistics and reports. In other words, a grading program will saves a lot of time. Grading programs are generally created to look, feel, and work like a traditional, paper grade-book.

Since grade-book programs are useful to all teachers in a school or district, check to see if a specific grading program has been adopted. If so use that grading program rather than selecting another program for music department use only, saving budget resources for other musical tools.

The programs described in this section can all be purchased as individual licenses, and some can be purchases by schools or districts in multi-seat licenses of dozens or hundreds of copies.

ORBIS SOFTWARE EASY GRADE PRO (MAC/WINDOWS)
Easy Grade Pro allows the user to create an electronic grade-book that can store student information for all classes and subjects in a

single file. It provides an abundance of tools to save time, provides a wealth of information, and allows educators to generate professional Internet and paper reports to communicate student data with parents, students, and administrators. *Easy Grade Pro* features a unique multi-class grade-book structure that can adapt to any teacher's schedule. It has tabs for viewing addition information such as scores, attendance, seating, student profiles, and assignments with a single mouse click. *Easy Grade Pro* allows the user to quickly and easily select different classes, subjects, or charts.

With *Easy Grade Pro* the user can score assignments with numbers, letter grades like B or C+, and other marks such as a checkmark to verify that an assignment was completed. In addition, the software features Search All Current-Term Classes and Continuous Search Mode options that let you grade without a lot of prior paper shuffling. *Easy Grade Pro* also goes beyond basic graphical seating charts with the ability to create detailed maps of your classroom—a real plus for ensemble seating and setup charts.

Easy Grade Pro's HTML features all for the creation of HTML student reports with password security for posting to a school's or teacher's Web site. Users can utilize one-click uploading of encrypted reports to *Edline*, a full-featured, Web service. With its cross-platform capabilities you can use the same grade-book on both Windows and Macintosh platforms including OSX.

JACKSON SOFTWARE GRADEQUICK 9 (MAC/WINDOWS)

GradeQuick is designed for flexibility of use to accommodate teachers with almost any grading system at any grade level. It's easy enough to use that it requires little or no training time. *GradeQuick* offers seamless integration with third-party student information systems, customized reports and report cards, attendance management at the classroom level, a seating chart with student photos, and other flexible grading options.

An intuitive layout allows users to track state standards, skills, assessments, and lesson plans within the same window. Directly enter standards and skills or import them with its StandardsBuilder feature. Simply click on the Student Assessments tab and immediately enter assessments. Clicking on the Lesson Plans tab allows the user to view all lesson plans associated within the particular skill being assessed.

One of *GradeQuick's* unique features allows customization of the main screen to display everything a user needs, so it's all in one place. The main screen can show more than just test scores and averages; with a mouse click it can display statistics and personal student data fields, full length test names instead of abbreviations, student nicknames, birthdays, and addresses.

GradeQuick provides a wide selection of ready to print reports including basic gradebook spreadsheets, report cards, missing work lists, and blank worksheets. In addition, it offers the ability to print reports that can automatically combine scores from different subject files, or from different teachers' files into one report for each student.

CHARIOT SOFTWARE GROUP MICROGRADE 6.02 (MAC/WINDOWS)

MicroGrade (**Fig. 1**) features a Quick Start wizard that simplifies the process of starting a new class file. Other features include password protected class files, attendance tracking and reporting, built-in seating chart, student notes and comments, and the ability to create grade scales using numbers or letters. *MicroGrade* does make users type in an equal sign (=) before you enter a letter grade, which is slightly awkward. Mark assignments as excused or incomplete and changed scores are flagged for easy identification. *MicroGrade* can calculate grades by total points, weighted percent, and/or relative weights automatically.

FIG. 1: Chariot Software's MicroGrade

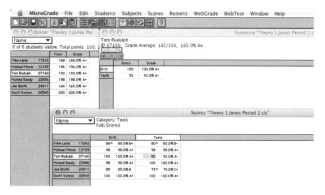

MicroGrade includes a grading period option that can combine multiple grading terms for final grade calculation. It also lets users transfer student information between class files, but unfortunately doesn't provide access to multiple classes in one file; it supports only one class per file.

MicroGrade excels in the area of Web export and e-mail features. It allows users to import student data and export final grades for use with your school wide computer system or administrative software packages such as SASI, OSIRIS, and Skyward. Keep students and parents informed of progress via *MicroGrade's* e-mail function and upload grades to their online WebGrade service. In addition, *MicroGrade* provides fourteen different configurable reports that can be printed or e-mailed to students and parents.

DANIEL ETHIER GRADEKEEPER 5.8 (MAC/WINDOWS)

Gradekeeper's grade-book is a straightforward interface that shows students, assignments, scores, and current grades for the current term. It provides two basic views of information. Choose whether to list student by name, ID number, or both. Grade averages for a class and a breakdown by letter grade are also provided, but *Gradekeeper* doesn't offer the option to curve grades. *Gradekeeper* can display a variety of reports exactly as they will be printed and can create reports from multiple classes.

The attendance grid shows students, dates, and attendance information. It also lets users choose which days of the week are displayed. *Gradekeeper* updates the number of absences and tardies automatically as entered. The student attendance report is a complete summary of a student's attendance listing every absence and tardy and the dates they occurred. The seating chart shows students assigned seats in basic user definable rows and columns. You can also take attendance using the seating chart.

Users keep students and parents informed using *Gradekeeper's* Clear Paper and online reports. *Gradekeeper* can create a Web page listing current grades and attendance totals, or a complete Web site with a Web page for each student and an authorization Web page to limit access to those with a valid student name and ID code. This allows users to provide current information to students and parents over the Internet. *Gradekeeper* is distributed as shareware. Download *Gradekeeper* and try it; but if you decide to continue using it, you must pay for it.

MAXIUM DEVELOPMENTS MASTER GRADE 1.5 (MAC/WINDOWS)

Master Grade integrates classes, students, assignments, and comments into one, easy to manage file—instantly access all classes in one file. It features a graphical toolbar that allows for quick navigation between windows. Create and modify assignment information, and enter student progress all from the same window. However,

Master Grade does require more mouse clicking and dragging to create assignment categories than the other grading programs, and then it makes you apply those categories to the specific classes.

Master Grade provides support for custom weighting of terms, final exams, assignment categories, assignment scaling, special scores, and letter grade scales. However, *Master Grade* doesn't provide the capability to drop the lowest score in an assignment category. In addition, *Master Grade* is the only one of the grading programs in this review that doesn't include a seating chart or attendance tracking features (those features should be available in the next version of the software). On the plus side *Master Grade* does have an integrated comment editor with spell checker that allows the creation and editing of freeform comments of unlimited length including intelligent word substitution. It also has the ability to generate a variety of progress reports for classes and individual students.

Master Grade is equipped with a customizable, plug-in architecture that allows for the importing and exporting of data from office administration systems. It even allows users to import or export from multiple classes in a single operation. Export grades to HTML so you can post them to a music department or school's Web site, or e-mail reports to parents and students.

In addition to the pre-packaged grade-book programs mentioned, there are simple alternatives that may not require the purchase of new or additional software. The major productivity suites, Microsoft *Office* and Apple's *AppleWorks*, both contain spreadsheet functionality that may serve your electronic grade-books needs. Users have two options, either create grade-books from scratch or use pre-packaged templates. Both Microsoft (*Excel*) and Apple's programs come with grade-book templates for educators. A simple search on the Internet will also identify a number of freeware and shareware grade-files for *Office* and *AppleWorks* that have been created by educators for educators. Frequently educators take grade-book templates from others and customize the files to meet their own classroom needs.

Databases for Music Educators

While there are a number of commercially available databases for education, including those that catalogue equipment, texts and other assets, few are specifically designed for music educators. RCI

Software publishes a "librarian" for Windows and Mac, *RCI Music Library* (**Fig. 2**), that

▶ Organizes and tracks performances.

▶ Creates program notes.

▶ Catalogues school music libraries.

▶ Inventories equipment and loans.

FIG. 2: RCI Software's Choral Music Library

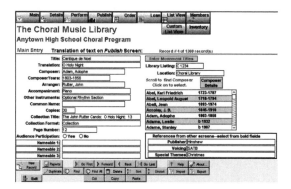

The program is made available in nine different libraries, including band, orchestra, choir, vocalist, worship/church, and more.

Just as the spreadsheets programs mentioned earlier offer alternatives to commercial grade-books, Microsoft *Access* (also part of the *Office* suite) and *AppleWorks* can also be used to create custom databases to inventory music, performances, recordings, and more. Templates that come with each program are easily customized for use in music education.

Section 3: Computer Peripherals

There are innumerable, hardware-based computer peripherals that are useful in music education—more than space or time permits in this book. With that said, given the kinds of work done in music education, from scoring music for the printed page to recording, mixing, and mastering music for high-quality playback, some computer peripherals deserve special consideration by music educators:

▶ Printers for high-quality output of music notation in scores or other instructional materials.

▶ Storage devices, from "flash drives" to external hard-disks.

▶ LCD projectors for presentation to classes.

Printers

Printers come in a wide range of shapes and sizes from portable travel companions to workgroup workhorses. There are several different types of printing technology to choose from, each suited for different needs and budgets.

SPECIFICATIONS

When investigating and evaluating different printers, the first thing you're likely to see is a list of specifications full of confusing acronyms such as "ppm" and "dpi." The main specifications for printers are resolution, print speed, connectivity, processor and memory, and paper handling.

The resolution refers to the maximum number of dots per inch (dpi) that can be printed. A printer's dpi spec is measured both horizontally and vertically. For example, a 600 x 1200 laser printer makes a one-inch square composed of 600 dots across by 1200 dots down. In theory, a printer with a higher resolution is capable of producing more-detailed images and text than a lower resolution printer. However, some manufacturers have inflated the specifications for marketing purposes so the numbers frequently no longer directly correlate with a higher image quality. In addition, the number of colors, the types of toner or ink used, how they are transferred to the paper, and the paper that's used all have an impact on the final image quality.

The print speed measures how many pages per minute (ppm) a printer can print. Although the spec appears to be pretty straightforward and can be for comparison purposes, some manufacturers test using basic text documents at the lowest quality print settings to come up with the fastest possible speeds. You can often expect to see about half the speed promised by the manufacturer in the real world of printing handouts with graphics and music scores. Laser printers print at the same ppm for all possible documents.

Connectivity refers to how a printer connects to your computer. Nearly all printers have either a USB 1.1 (Universal Serial Bus) or the newer, faster USB 2.0 connection. It's not a problem if your system doesn't have USB 2.0—it's still compatible with USB 1.1 systems, and USB 1.1 is plenty fast for printing. Workgroup printers also support printing over a network using a standard Ethernet cable. Some even support printing wirelessly, using Bluetooth, infrared, and Wi-Fi access points with built-in print servers.

Some manufacturers include information on a printer's processor and memory. These specifications are relatively unimportant for personal use, but if you intend to network the printer for multiple users or frequently print high-resolution photos or other large files, you'll want a printer with a faster processor and additional onboard memory.

The paper handling specifications on a printer typically include everything from paper size and thickness to the standard and optional paper tray input and output capacity. Nearly all personal laser writers and inkjets can print on standard paper sizes (letter and legal), accept envelopes, and have input trays that hold at least 100 sheets. Higher-end models may also provide advanced features such as printing on both sides (duplexing), tabloid-size printing, and auto document feeders for copying and faxing.

PRINTER TYPES
There are several general types of printers to choose from including inkjet, personal laser, workgroup laser, and multifunction (all-in-one).

Inkjet Printers
Inkjets can produce both crisp text and rich photo prints. They print an image by applying a precisely controlled stream of minuscule ink droplets from one or more ink cartridges to the paper. The size of the droplets and the way they are applied to the paper determine the image quality. Each manufacturer uses slightly different techniques.

Most manufacturers offer both general purpose and photo inkjet printers. Unfortunately, the inkjet printing process is relatively slow compared to that of laser printing. Inkjet printers range in price from under $100 to as much as $800, depending on image quality, features, and paper-handling capabilities. In addition, the ink cartridges and special papers for photo printing can be costly.

The print resolution for inkjets varies widely by manufacturer and model. Print speed also varies greatly—rated speeds are from 5 to 20 pages per minute. Memory is typically measured in KB rather than MB. The most common connection type is USB, but FireWire, parallel, and a few "networkable" models are available. Paper capacity is generally 100 sheets or more with a standard input tray.

Personal Laser Printers

Personal laser printers (**Fig. 3**) have been around for around 20 years and are still going strong because they combine sharp output, fast print speeds, and a low print-cost per page. Like photocopiers, laser printers use a photographic drum to attract electrically charged toner and transfer it to paper, where a heated roller fuses the image to the paper. Most laser printers are monochrome (black and white), and are best suited for printing text and basic graphics. Personal laser printers start around $200 and go up from there, typically with increased features and print speed. Until fairly recently color laser printers were too expensive for individuals and those on a limited budget, but there are now several models for less than $1,000. These color laser printers could soon become viable alternatives to color inkjets.

FIG. 3: HP laser printer

The resolution for personal laser printers is typically 600 x 600 dpi and rated print speeds range from 10 to 20 pages per minute. Personal laser printers normally connect to your computer via a USB or parallel connection. Most have 16MB of memory and provide a paper capacity of 150 to 250 sheets with a standard input tray.

Workgroup Laser Printers

As the name implies, workgroup printers are designed for use in small offices or small teams within larger organizations. Although they are based on the same laser printing technology, these printers provide additional functions and features designed specifically to meet the needs of multiple users. They have faster processors and additional memory so that they can print faster and handle multiple jobs. Workgroup printers also provide the connections to print over a network either standard or as an optional add-on. They generally more sophisticated paper-handling capabilities, including larger input and output trays. Workgroup laser printers start around $400 and go up from there.

Like personal laser printers, the vast majority of workgroup lasers are monochrome. Print resolution is normally either 600 x 600 or 1200 x 1200 dpi and rated print speeds for workgroup lasers can exceed 20 pages per minute. Memory is typically 16MB or more, and paper capacity is usually 250 sheets or more with a standard input tray. Connectivity is generally via an Ethernet network connection, but USB and parallel connections are also often provided.

Multifunction Printers

Multifunction or "all-in-one printers" are the Swiss Army knives of printers. They combine printer, copier, scanner, and, in many models, fax capabilities in one unit, making them an attractive choice. Multifunction printers are available with either inkjet or laser printing to suit different needs and budgets. The top-end models include flatbed scanners and auto-document feeders for walk-up scanning, faxing, and copying of multi-page documents. Multifunction printers start at around $100.

Multifunction printers normally provide a USB connection. The print resolution and print speed varies depending on the type of printer technology. Memory is typically 16MB, and the paper capacity is 100 sheets or more with a standard input tray.

CHOOSING A PRINTER

The best choice for a printer depends on you specific needs and budget. For printing music and class handouts, a personal laser printer provides you with fast, quality printing at an affordable price. If you need to occasionally print in color, a general-purpose color inkjet is a good choice for a second printer. A multifunction printer is a good option if you have moderate printing requirements and need the copying and faxing functions. If you plan to share a printer with other teachers in your department or do large volumes of printing, then consider investing in a workgroup laser printer that can handle network printing, has high-capacity toner cartridges, larger paper input and output trays, and other work-group features.

Storage Devices

Storage of data, from scores to recordings to grade-books and tests, is essential. Don't simply rely on the hard drive that is in your laptop or desktop computer at school or at home. Backing up your work to more than one storage medium is crucial so that precious time isn't lost. It is always better to take time to make multiple backups, or duplicates, of your files, than to have to recreate them.

Storage devices come in a variety of forms and formats—some more portable than others, but all are generally universal, meaning they can be used on both Windows and Macintosh computers.

USB FLASH DRIVES

USB flash drives are the ultimate in terms of portability and convenience for backing up files such as student grades, music scores, MIDI sequences, audio files, and just about anything else. They're fast, reliable and easily transport back and forth between school and home. If you only work with a limited number of small size files such as text files, MIDI sequences, and student grades, then a 128MB or 256MB drive should suffice. However, if you regularly need to back up and transport audio files, digital photos, and other large media files, then a 512MB or even a 1GB USB flash drive is highly recommended.

USB flash drives are very compact and easy-to-use storage devices that are similar in use to the hard drive in your computer. Also referred to as a keychain drive, thumb drive, jump drive, or pen drive, you can carry a USB flash drive attached to a keychain, around your neck, or simply in your pocket for ultimate portable storage of your important files.

USB flash drives come in several memory sizes; currently the most common are 128MB, 256MB, 512MB, and 1GB, but 2GB and greater are likely in the future. They are quite affordable, but prices can vary quite a bit depending on the manufacturer and retailer, so take time to shop around before purchasing one. As with many technology storage devices, prices decrease while the amount of memory storage increases on a regular basis.

A USB flash drive is very simple and easy to use—just plug it into the USB port of a computer and a new drive appears on your desktop within a few seconds. Besides being very portable, they're generally quite durable, have good data transfer speeds, no moving parts, and no need for batteries. With all these benefits, a USB flash drive could easily replace the need for a floppy, Zip disk, or CD-RW disc.

Earlier model USB flash drives were designed using the original and slower USB 1.1 format. Virtually all flash drives currently manufactured are USB 2.0, which provides a potentially much faster data transfer rate. However, to take full advantage of the faster speed the flash drive needs to be labeled specifically as being a USB 2.0 Hi-Speed format. In addition, if your computer is the older USB 1.1 format, it won't be able to take advantage of higher speed. Fortunately, all USB 2.0 flash drives are backwards compatible with USB 1.1 computers; you just won't be able to take advantage of the faster data transfer rate until you get a computer that is equipped with USB 2.0.

EXTERNAL HARD DRIVES

External hard drives are a great tool for backing up the important data on your computer's internal hard drive. While Zip disks, CD-R/RW discs, and USB flash drives are fine for backing up or transferring files of 1GB (gigabyte) or less, external hard drives are the best choice for large data amounts of several GB or more. Some external hard drives include backup software so you can automatically schedule one-time, daily, weekly, and monthly backups, and can even remind you if you haven't backed up recently.

The two most important hard drive specifications are storage capacity and connectivity. If you plan on using the hard drive for multi-track digital audio recording applications or digital video, you should also look at other specifications that affect its performance including the rotational speed and seek time.

The storage capacity refers to how much data the hard drive can store. The capacity is measured in GB (gigabytes) and generally speaking, bigger is better. External hard drives typically range from 80GB to 300GB or more. If you only work with text, MIDI, notation, and other files that take up relatively small amounts of space, then an 80–100GB will easily suffice. On the other hand, if you regularly work with digital audio recording files, digital videos, and digital photos, then you should purchase a larger capacity drive.

The two most common means of connecting an external hard drive to your computer are FireWire and USB 2.0. If you choose a USB drive, make sure both the hard drive and your computer are USB 2.0 compatible. The older USB 1.1 standard is too slow for digital audio and backing up large amounts of data.

The rotational speed indicates how fast the disk—a hard metal platter, hence the name hard disk—spins. The most common speeds for external drives are 5,400 RPM (revolutions per minute) and 7,200 RPM. The seek time refers to the length of time required to move a disk drive's to a particular location on the disk. A major part of a hard disk's access time is actually seek time. Seek time is measured in milliseconds (ms) and commonly ranges from 8ms to 12ms. The lower the seek time, the better.

No matter how reliable a computer is there's always the possibility that the hard drive inside the computer could "crash," meaning that is stops working. Although there are software utility programs that can fix many disk related problems, if the failure is due to a physical breakdown you could permanently lose all your data on the disk. This makes the case for backing up your files on another storage device an essential issue.

Note that recording consumes around 5MB per track minute. When using a computer for digital audio recording, it makes good sense to use an external hard drive for your audio files as they could fill up your computer's internal hard drive fairly rapidly. External hard drives are also great for storing large libraries of MP3 and digital photo files.

Projectors

Teaching with a computer, desktop, or laptop, presents a challenge—how do the students or audience you're speaking and presenting to see what is displayed on a computer screen? This question should never be answered be crowding a group of students around a small, personal computer monitor or laptop screen.

In some classrooms using a reasonably sized TV monitor that supports RGB or S-Video input from a computer may be acceptable. The best solution for classroom, lab, or auditorium-based teaching and presenting is an LCD (Liquid Crystal Display) projector (**Fig. 4**). These devices are somewhat affordable, starting at about $799 and up.

FIG. 4: InFocus LCD Projector

LCD projectors may or may not be portable. Decide on which type based on whether you need to take your teaching materials from one place to another, in school or from building to building. If the projector is to be used in a single lab or classroom have it professionally mounted in from the ceiling.

Deciding on a projector isn't easy as there are many brands and models. Some of the most popular brands include inFocus, Hitachi, Casio, NEC, HP, Epson, and many more. Select a projector based on the following:

▶ Size of the lab or classroom

▶ Distance to project, from projector to optimal wall/screen

▶ Type of device(s) to connect and project, including computer, TV, DVD player, and others

▶ Need for integrated sound and mixing capabilities

There are some key specifications to consider based on current projector technology:

▶ Native screen resolution(s) supported (for example, 800 x 600 or 1024 x 768, SVGA or XGA)

▶ Luminosity (the more lumens the better, based on budget)

▶ Availability of a zoom lens

▶ Video compatibility (including NTSC, PAL, HDTV)

Section 4: Classroom and Lab Management Tools

There are two primary classifications of music lab management tools. One is music lab controller systems, sometimes including pre-packaged curricula in print and/or software. These systems have been in existence for decades, starting with pioneering keyboard lab systems such as those made by Wurlitzer and Musictronics.

The other essential lab management tool is used in and out of group music instruction—computer network management software that allows a teacher or lab/network manager to monitor and control all computers on a network, from student instructional use to deploying, updating, and maintaining software on up to hundreds of computers.

Lab Controller Systems

Lab controller systems allow the keyboards in a lab to be connected together via a central lab controller unit that the teacher controls. Lab controllers typically allow the teacher to communicate with individual students, small groups, or the entire class. Most lab controllers also allow you to connect other external devices such as a CD player to the controller. With a group controller system in your keyboard lab, the teacher can monitor and listen to individual students practice on their instrument. The teacher can also use a lab controller to group students together so they can practice and perform in duets and quartets.

KORG GROUP EDUCATION CONTROLLER (GEC3)

The Korg *GEC3* (**Fig. 5**) is a digital, microprocessor-based teacher controlled device that interconnects 16 student workstations allowing two-way communication between students and teacher with noise-free digital audio. An expansion unit (GECEXP) may be added on to the system to provide support for up to thirty-two student interface connections. The *GEC3* comes in an easy-to-use package that integrates seamlessly into a group education environment. It's designed to provide the highest level of control for teachers and maximum flexibility for students.

The *GEC3* system consists of two major components, the *GEC3* (Teacher Controller Unit) and the Student Interface Units (SI Units). The SI Units are each connected to audio sources such as MIDI keyboards, guitars, sound modules, or computer sound cards. The SI Units also have jacks for two student headsets—stereo headphones with microphones. All of these audio sources are combined in the SI Unit, digitized, and then sent to the *GEC3* Teacher Unit. These connections allow the students to musically interact with one another and the teacher in nearly any manner imaginable.

There are three main modes of *GEC* operation:

▶ *Lecture Mode* is used when the teacher wants to present material in a lecture format. All students hear your microphone and instrument as well as their own instruments.

▶ *Practice Mode* allows students to work independently. Each student hears only his or her own instrument. You have the option of listening to the student and you can initiate two-way communication with the student.

▶ *Group Mode* allows students to work together in groups—two or more student workstations in any conceivable order. The students in a group can hear their own instruments as well as the instruments of the other members of their group.

FIG 5: Korg GEC3 Group Education Controller

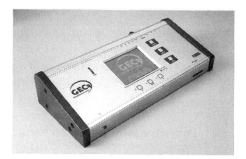

The *GEC3*'s MIDI OUT function allows the teacher to control the sound selection on all student keyboards, and a flexible grouping function enables teachers to match up students for peer learning within groups of any size. Teachers can also store custom groups by class for easy reference, and select students by name. For added flexibility, teachers can create customized teacher, class, and student lists using the QWERTY keypad on the *GEC3*'s touch screen panel, or the USB remote control from a personal computer with keyboard and mouse.

ROLAND RCS-848: MUSIC CONFERENCING SYSTEM

The Roland *RCS-848 Music Conferencing System* is an all-in-one communication solution for group piano teaching, music ensemble instruction, and even sophisticated language lab teaching. The *RCS-848 Conference Controller* is designed as a standard 19-inch rack-mountable unit rather than the common tabletop design, and it doesn't rely on external computer hardware or software. As a completely self-contained device, it's both intuitive and easy to use.

In Standard Mode, the *RCS-848* allows a teacher to monitor and communicate with up to eight students in stereo via nine supplied RCS-1 interface boxes and RCS-HS headsets. You can expand the system to accommodate up to 48 students in stereo with optional RCS-8EXP expansion kits. In addition, you can assign any student to one of four practice groups (i.e., Group [A], [B], [C], or [D]) for ensemble practice, performance, and communication. You can drill students privately, in pairs, or in groups. The result is a flexible music conferencing system that's fully expandable.

The *RCS-848* can also operate in Split Mode, allowing you to communicate with up to 16 students in mono via nine supplied RCS-1 interface boxes and RCS-HS headsets. In addition, you can communicate with up to 48 students in mono by adding optional RCS-8EXP expansion kits and optional RCS-HS headsets as needed. However, practice groups aren't available in Split Mode. The *RCS-848* also includes auxiliary and CD input, along with record and monitor output jacks for connecting other devices.

The *RCS-848* system comes packaged with the *Roland Home Concert Software Bundle*, including Time Warp Technologies *Home Concert Xtreme, Home Concert 2000,* and *Classroom Maestro*. Moreover, with the purchase of eight keyboards for the lab system, eight copies of the *Music Mentor Curriculum (Teaching Music with Technology)* are included.

SUZUKI SPL-10 PERSONAL TEACHING SYSTEM

Suzuki's *Piano Lab Teaching System* provides you with easy monitoring and communication with each student in your keyboard class. Its verbal switching network allows two-way communication and lets you monitor the progress of up to 10 students at a time. You can combine up to three systems for classes of up to 30 students. In addition, you can monitor performance on an individual basis or classes can be split into two groups based on lessons learned.

YAMAHA LC2 MUSIC LAB

Yamaha's most recent entry into the music lab arena is the *LC2 Music Lab*. This modular system can be instructed in groups of eight student instruments. Everything required to connect and teach with eight students instruments is included, from headset/ mics to student interfaces. The system includes a teacher control surface that can be used with optional *Music Lan Management (MLM)* software. The teacher control surface connects to a "hub" into which all student instrument connections are made.

YAMAHA MLC100 MUSIC LAB TEACHING CONSOLE

The *Yamaha Music Laboratory* is an integrated system that consists of the *MLC100* console, teacher's keyboard, up to 16 student keyboards, headsets with microphone, and student call boxes. *The MLC100* is a very flexible controller that lets you easily solo or combine students into groups. In addition, it provides two-way communication between you and a student with a single button-push. You can communicate with an individual student and pairs or groups of students from your own keyboard station, without disturbing other students or interrupting the entire class.

From the teacher station you can control of all activities using the *MLC100*. You can instantly change the classroom configuration by pressing a single digital control including ensemble playing, duets, one-on-one instruction, students helping students, or a student teacher assisting you with one, two, three or four groups. Although the *MLC100* will function with virtually any manufacturer's electronic keyboard, the Yamaha *Clavinova* digital piano is recommended.

YAMAHA MUSIC IN EDUCATION (MIE) CURRICULUM

Yamaha's *Music In Education* (*MIE*) is a sequential and comprehensive music curriculum that offers an innovative and contemporary focus to music teaching and learning in the general music classroom. Not just a keyboard program, the design of the *MIE* curriculum emphasizes the study of music, and provides continual opportunities for student experience and achievement as individuals and as a group so they express their own creativity. The curriculum materials, teaching strategies, listening, and review and quiz, provide a structured and comprehensive musical experience for students.

The design of *Music In Education* curriculum components and instructional activities is intended to stimulate the development of personal musical skills through four distinct areas of experience: listening, discussing and describing, making, and creating. The curriculum is organized into 80 modules, and the material found in each module reinforces these four experiential areas. Each series of learning strategies in a module focuses on the development and understanding of specific concepts, and the acquisition of musical skills, through the interaction of these four areas.

Each module is designed to allow comprehensive student understanding of specific musical concepts. Students sing, play, discuss, and listen using the new concept, then use that concept in individual and group creative activities. Because the introduction of concepts is integrative and sequential, songs, activities, and skills in succeeding modules reinforce and reapply the concepts introduced in previous modules. *Music In Education* songs and listening selections have been chosen to provide both traditional and contemporary musical examples for students. Multi-part song arrangements accommodate learners of all levels, regardless of their previous musical experience. The *Music In Education* curriculum is intended to be interactive with other methods or materials.

Network-Based Computer Management and Monitoring Tools

There are a number of software-based tools for managing and monitoring multiple computers in a lab or school building. Most of these software packages can deal with dozens or hundred of computers at a time.

All the prevailing Windows and Macintosh management and monitoring tools allow a teacher or lab manager to remotely support and update computer software and fix problems. Some of the management features of these programs include

▶ Deployment of new software and software updates to many computers.

▶ Drag-and-drop deployment of files, from text documents to notation to audio to all student desktops.

▶ Remote start up and shut down of computers.

More interesting as a teaching tool, some of these programs are designed with educators in mind. They allow a teacher to

▶ Monitor a student's work at a computer with or without their knowledge.

▶ Easily take control of student machines.

▶ Message to all student machines.

▶ Share the teacher's, or any student's screen, on all lab computers, simultaneously.

Note that with each of the software tools, listed below, a teacher/manager application is typically installed on a single computer (although sometimes it makes sense to have the teacher software on more than one computer), and "client" software is installed on each of the student computers.

The most commonly used management and monitoring software packages in the education arena are

▶ Apple Remote Desktop (Mac) (**Fig. 6**)

▶ MasterSolution MasterEye 5 (Windows)

▶ Netopia Timbuktu Pro Remote Control Software (Mac/ Windows)

FIG 6: Apple's Remote Desktop lab management software

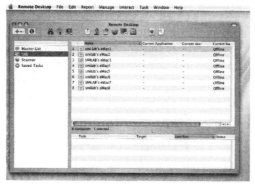

Section 5: Reference Materials

Books

Langer, Maria. *QuickBooks Pro 6 for Macintosh: Visual QuickStart Guide*. Berkeley, CA: PeachPit Press, 2004.

Miller, Michael. *Absolute Beginner's Guide to Computer Basics*. Indianapolis, IN: Que, 2002.

Articles

Maiden, Jeffrey and Nicholas J. Migliorino. "Educator Attitudes Toward Electronic Grading Software." *Journal of Research on Technology*, 2004.

Woodward, Matt. "USB 2.0 Hi-speed Flash Drive Roundup." (http://arstechnica.com/reviews/hardware/flash.ars/1)

Internet Resources

Apple (www.apple.com)
Chariot Software Group (www.chariot.com)
Daniel Ethier (www.gradekeeper.com)
InFocus (www.infocus.com)
Jackson Software (www.jacksoncorp.com)
Korg (www.korg.com)
MasterSolution (www.codework.com/classroom)
Maxium Developments Inc. (www.maxium.com)
Netopia (www.netopia.com)
Orbis Software (www.orbissoft.com)
RCI Software (www.riden.com)
Roland (www.rolandus.com)
Suzuki (www.suzukimusic.com)
USB Flash Drive Alliance (www.usbflashdrive.org)
Yamaha (www.yamaha.com)

PRODUCTIVITY TOOLS, CLASSROOM AND LAB MANAGEMENT
DATA MANAGEMENT

Manufacturer	Product	Web Site	Type	Version	Platform	Special Features	List Price
Orbis Software	Easy Grade Pro	www.orbis soft.com/	Grading Program	3.6	Mac/Windows		$49
Jackson Software	GradeQuick	www.jacksoncorp.com/gradequick.html	Grading Program	10	Mac/Windows		$69.95
Chariot Software Group	MicroGrade	www.chariot.com	Grading Program	6.02	Mac/Windows		$95
Daniel Ethier	Gradekeeper	www.gradekeeper.com	Grading Program	5.8	Mac/Windows		$20
Maximum Developments Inc.	Master Grade	www.maxium.com/	Grading Program	1.5	Mac/Windows		$59.95
RCI Software	RCI Music Library	www.riden.com/	Database for Music Ed.	5	Mac/Windows	Separate versions for each ensemble (band, chorus, etc.)	$49 - $199
Microsoft	Excel	office.microsoft.com	Spreadsheet	2003	Mac/Windows	Part of MS Office Suite	$149
Apple	AppleWorks (Spreadsheet)	www.apple.com/appleworks/	Suite of Productivity Tools	6.2.9	Mac	AppleWorks is a suite of programs, including a spreadsheet.	$79

CLASSROOM AND LAB MANAGEMENT

Manufacturer	Product	Web Site	Type	Version	Platform	Special Features	List Price
Korg	Group Education Controller (GEC 3)	www.soundtree.com/	Lab Controller System	N/A	N/A	16-student version, not including headset/mics and interfaces; expands to 32 students maximum.	$1,999
Roland	RCS-848 Music Conferencing System	www.rolandus.com/products	Lab Controller System	N/A	N/A	8-student with headset/mics and interfaces; expands to 40 students maximum.	$3,495
Roland	MTLC-16 Music Tutor Lab Controller	www.rolandus.com/products	Lab Controller System	N/A	N/A	16-student with headset/mics and interfaces; expands to 32 students maximum.	$3,999
Suzuki	SPL-10 Personal Teaching System	www.suzukimusic.com/education/pages/pianolab.html	Lab Controller System	N/A	N/A	10-student version; expands to 30 students maximum.	$1,190
Yamaha	MLC100 Music Lab Teaching System	www.yamaha.com/yamahavgn/	Lab Controller System	N/A	N/A	16-student version	$1,795
Yamaha	LC2 Music Lab Teaching System	www.yamaha.com/yamahavgn/	Lab Controller System	N/A	N/A	8-student version; expandable to 48 max.	$2,299
Yamaha	Music In Education Curriculum	www.musicineducation.com/	Lab-based Music curriculum	N/A	Mac/Windows	30-student system, 2 per station; one computer necessary for teacher.	$15,775
Apple	Remote Desktop	www.apple.com/remotedesktop/	Network Management & Monitoring	2.2	Mac		$299, 10-client; $499, unlimited client.
MasterSolution	MasterEye	www.mastereye.co.uk/	Network Management & Monitoring	5	Windows		$35 per station
Netopia	Timbuktu Pro Remote Control Software	www.netopia.com/software/products	Network Management & Monitoring	8.5	Mac/Windows		From $94.95 per station

Index